Beyond World Class

Clive Morton

For Doris

First published 1998 by

MACMILLAN PRESS LTD

Houndmills, Basingstoke, Hampshire RG21 6XS

and London

Companies and representatives a
throughout the world

ISBN 0–333–66910–X

A catalogue record for this book is available from the British Library.

This book is printed on paper suitable for recycling and
made from fully managed and sustained forest sources.

10 9 8 7 6 5 4 3 2 1
07 06 05 04 03 02 01 00 99 98

Formatted by *Ascenders*, Basingstoke

Illustrations by David Woodroffe and *Ascenders*

Printed in Great Britain by Creative Print & Design (Wales),
Ebbw Vale

Contents

Acknowledgements

For the full time practitioner the debt to others within the network is huge. My family have been so supportive despite the absentee and this understanding has been extended by my peers at Anglian Water, Peterborough Hospitals Rolls-Royce, Gateshead Hospitals, the Institute of Personnel and Development and Industrial Society.

Quite apart from encouragement along the way I have stretched friendship to the limit by imposing unfinished drafts on mentors and sympathisers who have provided honest critique. Credit for the result is due in large part to their contributions. I would like to thank: Elizabeth Amos, Dr Neville Bain, Dr David Band, Sir Michael Bett, Dr John Bridge, Rhiannon Chapman, Lord Dearing, Philip Hanson, Sir Geoffrey Holland, Professor John Kay, Dr Ronnie Lessem, Richard Maudslay, Alan Meekings, Chris Mellor, Anne Minto, Professor Leo Murray, Sir Bryan Nicholson, Professor Amin Rajan, Sir Bob Reid, John Rivers, Professor Gillian Stamp, Betty Thayer, Professor Dave Ulrich, David Williams.

Lastly my thanks to Jill Swaby and her husband Nigel for giving up so many evenings in ploughing through my difficult drafts and producing a readable result.

Clive Morton

The author and the publishers wish to thank the following who have kindly given permission for the use of copyright material:

Blackwell Publishers for *The Nonaka Middle-up-down Model* and diagram *The Hypertext Organisation*, Figures 10.5 and 10.6 in R. Lessem and S. Palsule, *Managing in Four Worlds* (Blackwell, 1997); British Telecommunications plc for the diagram *The Quality Journey* (British Telecommunications plc, 1997); Butterworth-Heinemann for the table *The Nine Team Roles* from Belbin, *The Coming Shape of Organisation* (Butterworth-Heinemann, 1996); Decision Development and Lynn McGregor for *Levels of Competence, Differences Between Poor and Advanced Boards*, from Lynn McGregor, *Leading Boards. New Realities* (Decision Development, 1994); *Financial Times* Management, Pitman Publishing for *Constellation of Influences on the Stakeholder Corporation and The World's Top Twenty Corporations Ranked by 1995 Sales*, Figure 1.1 and Table 4.1 in D. Wheeler and M. Sillanpää, *The Stakeholder Corporation* (*Financial Times* Management, 1997); HarperCollins Publishers for four diagrams/tables from B. Garrat, *The Fish Rots From the Head* (HarperCollins, 1996); Macmillan Press Ltd for *Comparison of Process Quality Indicators* from Rommel *et al.*, *Quality Pays* (Macmillan, 1997) and four figures from M. Porter, *The Competitive Advantage of Nations* (Macmillan, 1990); McGraw-Hill Publishing Company for the diagram *Learning Problems and Their Solutions 1950-2000*, from M. Pedler, *et al.*, *The Learning Company* (McGraw-Hill, 1996); Nicholas Brealey Publishing Limited for diagrams *Leaning Into the Future* and *Mobilising the Energy for Change* from: *Leaning Into the Future: Changing the Way People Change Organizations*, by George Binney and Colin Williams; published by Nicholas Brealey Publishing Ltd; Random House for *Cumulative Stock Returns of $1 Invested, January 1, 1926 – December 31*, 1990 from J. Collins and J. Porras, *Built to Last* (Century, 1995), and a diagram from C. Handy, *The Empty Raincoat*, (Hutchinson, 1994)

Every effort has been made to trace all the copyright holders, but if any have been inadvertently overlooked the publishers will be pleased to make the necessary arrangement at the first opportunity.

Foreword

As with winter and summer, so with communism and capitalism: each provides an antidote for the other.

But with the collapse of the Berlin Wall, this is no longer the case. On both sides of the Atlantic, there is a growing body of opinion that today's 'shareholder first' capitalism lacks a social expression. However, there is room for more optimism than this would suggest.

As this book shows, companies around the world are implementing new ideas and working methods that are exemplary and practical. Exemplary because they are breaking new ground in pursuit of enlightened self interest. Practical because they rely on an unusual degree of commonsense

So, this book is as timely as it is necessary. A majority of books on change management in this decade have been written by academics. This one is refreshingly different. It comes from a thinker and a doer: one who has had sweat on his brow turning noble ideas into practical reality.

Clive Morton is one of those rare individuals experienced in the art of reshaping today's workplace in terms of the new socio-economic agenda. His previous book, *Becoming World Class*, was widely acclaimed for raising British companies' confidence in their potential to match the best in the world. This one scales new heights. It shows how to achieve business excellence and social progress at the same time. It is about 'what to do' and 'how to do it', if a company is to go beyond world class.

First and foremost, Dr Morton has a number of down-to-earth messages for business leaders who want to make an impact at the workplace and the market place; on shareholders and the wider society.

Amin Rajan
Chief Executive
Centre for Research in Employment and Technology in Europe

Visiting Professor
City University Business School

Visiting Professor
London Guildhall University

Introduction

Beyond World Class? Is this possible? Have we all become world class already? What is world class anyway and isn't it an overused term?

WHAT THIS BOOK IS ABOUT AND WHAT IT DOESN'T ATTEMPT TO DO

This book is designed to equip the world class company to compete well into the 21st century. Perhaps that sounds far fetched but the perspective of longevity is not that unreal. Many studies in the USA and Europe have shown that consistent and enduring policies give long-term profitable results provided that companies show continuity and are sensitive to their customers, employees, suppliers and the communities in which they live.

The key to *Becoming World Class* (Morton, 1994) was to harness the potential of resources inside and outside the organization to reach operational excellence. To achieve the reinvention and renewal necessary to maintain a competitive edge, *Beyond World Class* gives a recipe that takes the intellectual capital of employees, customers, suppliers and communities beyond competing today to making strategic choices for the future.

The fundamental theme is that no organization or company is an island and cannot hope to maintain or go beyond being world class unless it operates in partnership with the world outside the factory gates.

A company can, by operational excellence, become 'world class' but its products are likely to be 'commoditized' and unless it 'reinvents itself' through innovation and a wider perspective, it will cease to be world class and probably will cease to exist.

The scope therefore is very broad. I place the world class company in the setting of a constituent part of a three-legged stool comprising:

- the individual,
- the organization, and
- society

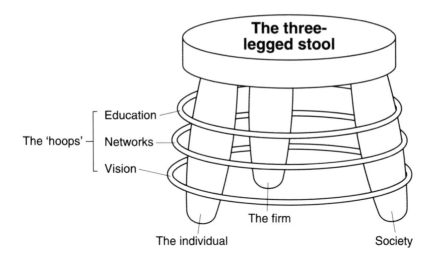

which all need to contribute for the others' viability. Further, for stability and growth, the 'legs' of the 'stool' need support and connection via the 'hoops' of

- education,
- networks, and
- vision.

My aim is to demonstrate the win–win of all three 'legs' being able to grow, develop, and be in control of change affecting them, rather than be unwilling victims of it.

Because of this unusual scope, the treatment is similarly broad. The core is a practitioner's eclectic account of what works, based on personal experience of leading change in large organizations. The framework of change is extended beyond the organization into an economic region to show successful partnerships in practice, and examines the situation of the individual in rapid change.

Apart from the natural role of practitioner, I have adopted 'academic' and 'social philosopher' perspectives because I fundamentally believe we need mapping tools and access to philosophy to navigate a successful path for individuals, organizations and society. Although it contains methods the reader can apply, it is not essentially a 'how to' management book – its purpose is to challenge the prevalent mindset.

WHAT'S WRONG AND WHAT IS POSSIBLE?

My journey started over 35 years ago when I was appalled at the dysfunction in industrial relations at that time. Today the dysfunction that motivates is the helplessness that people experience in the face of change they feel they cannot control and the sad waste of human potential inside and outside our companies which, if used properly, could give a step change in competitive advantage.

We are the most fortunate of industrial age generations. We have no excuses. We now know what works, and what works counts. Evidence is contained in this book that:

- people management practices can give 20 per cent productivity and profit improvement compared to 6 per cent from a combination of R&D, innovation and quality;
- maintaining effective trust relationships and communication (voice) with suppliers and employees flows through to consistently higher productivity and profits;
- agility of organizations is a function of a culture of learning and change within – speed of response going beyond Quality, Cost and Delivery;
- those companies that are 'inclusive' in their relationships inside and with their communities stay the course, are consistently more profitable and more able to make strategic choices for the future;
- those companies that exploit total quality systems to the full, outperform the market place in every sense;
- leading companies are those who live with ambiguity and deal effectively with dilemmas such as short term and long term, control and autonomy, and so on.

We also know what works for individuals. Education, of the right sort, for the right people can give anything up to a 40 per cent return on investment. We know that in terms of life-long learning, business-led education gives the best results for the individual, business itself and society.

In terms of individuals and companies we know that the best crucible for positive chemical reaction is the economic region – the links of education, networks and vision can have a virtuous circle effect (the aim is encapsulated in matrix form in the diagram opposite. If these elements of 'social capital' are not there – 'without a vision the people perish'. Why are these lessons rarely applied?

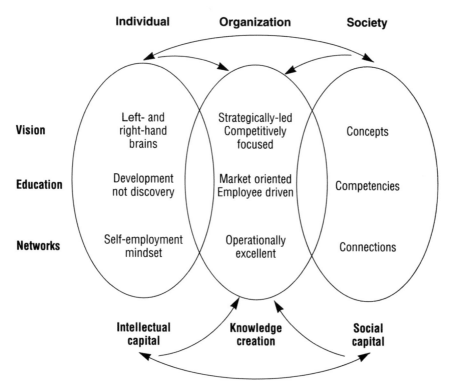

A mission for sustainability

THE JOURNEY TO BE FOLLOWED

The book goes full circle from the individual; through teams, to change in companies (in theory and practice); corporate governance; leadership, growth and strategy; stakeholder capitalism; regional economic development; and back to our starting point: the individual.

The design of this journey is deliberate. We commence by asking in Chapter 1: Based on the changes experienced in the past 50 years and the accelerating pace of change, are we making it different for the next generation?

Is our holistic education and training system geared for their world of tomorrow or too locked into the traditions of the past? Is education run for the state and politicians, not for an industrial society? Why does the West lag behind the Japanese in product development and rejuvenation? Does our infrastructure support the concept of portfolio careers and self-employment?

Chapter 2 takes the issue of learning and change from individuals to groups or teams to knowledge creation to answer the question, 'How do the Japanese reinvent themselves using an innovative workforce when the West relies on innovative leaders – is the challenge again getting the best from both worlds?'

Chapter 3 moves us from learning to change. What is the right formula?

Top down
Bottom up
Start in the middle, or
Leading and learning?

The chapter gives an international perspective on change stories from the USA, Europe and Japan and deals with leadership, ambiguity and panaceas. 'The future belongs to companies that can be the best of East and West and start building a universal model to create new knowledge within their organizations' (p. 54).

The core of eclectic 'practitioner' experience from manufacturing and service sectors is contained in Chapter 4 related to the knowledge-creating cycle defined in Chapter 2 and proven change models applied in an international context.

Chapter 5 asks, 'Which tools and techniques work? What about teams, culture change and emotional intelligence? What leads to competitiveness? How do we know there is value added?'

Change and learning in organizations is a lost cause without change and learning at the top. Chapter 6 examines: Can or should Boards be teams? Is the Learning Board realistic? Have we bottomed governance? How can the whole organization contribute to strategy? Does this give the capability for strategic choices?

Chapter 7 continues the journey outside the organization. Is there real value to the company in a stakeholder approach? Or is it fudge that dilutes the focus? Does it help bring the left and right brains together?

What are the sources for economic revival?

The economic region, the crucible for networking, learning and growth, is examined with contrasts between the USA and UK in Chapter 8.

Lastly we return to the individual in Chapters 9 and 10 dealing with the situation through the eyes of the individual without an assured career, encouraged to have a 'self-employment mindset' but to be at the same time the creative spark for tomorrow's knowledge-based society. Is there a working hypothesis?

First, let's examine where today's generation is in the world of work and education.

1 The Learning Society

INDIVIDUALS AND TEAMS

Under the Paradox of Age,[1] Charles Handy in *The Empty Raincoat* talks of the 'cohort factor' for each generation. He says that it is very unlikely that our children will have the same sort of life cycle as we have had or that ours has resembled that of our parents.

His parents' generation was broadly the same as mine, experiencing a world war, going through a long and deep recession in the thirties and valuing security above all else, and they too expected to work until almost the end of their lives. My father commenced work with his first and only employer, Stewart and Ardern in London, under a mechanical engineering apprenticeship just after the First World War and gravitated into an office job at about the time of the General Strike of 1926. He perceived himself as under-qualified and through the 1920s and 1930s depressions decided, like most of his contemporaries, to sit tight and hold onto what was at least a job even though poorly paid. He retired from the same firm 50 years later but went back part-time after a one-year gap!

My mother, who had started work in the City at a lowly clerical level, followed a night school route towards secretarial skills and thence teaching of business studies in order to supplement the family income. The impediment to advancement for my father was always placed at the door of lack of qualifications and I grew up in an atmosphere steeped in the Protestant work ethic with the key to success being clearly labelled as academic progress.

My sister and I were the first of the brood to go to state grammar schools and to university (courtesy of Rab Butler's 1944 Education Act) and in the heady early 1960s the world seemed our oyster. I received six competing job offers for structured careers in civil engineering companies in 1964 and chose to join John Laing for what promised to be a well-planned career for life.

Experience, achievement, progress was great but the idea of the security of a job for life was boring to me, as I perceived my father's adherence to this as a shackle. This, combined with my personality profile, meant that I opted for a very varied career. Also, a first degree wasn't enough. During my civil engineering studies I had gained an avid interest in industrial relations and this was fed by the chaos I saw on the construction of the Barbican redevelopment in the early 1960s. With re-forming zeal I naively set out to make the world a better place.

My daughters find work a very different world in the late 1990s. My eldest now follows a Charles Handy-type portfolio career, being an artist, sculptor and also an organization development consultant for corporations small and large.

My youngest has almost followed her grandmother's example except that, like most of her contemporaries, she fully participated in tertiary education first but wanted to get into the media and the only route was to obtain keyboard skills, taking a lowly position to gain entry with accelerated progress since. She has no perspective that jobs for life are on offer. And I suspect it will be some while before I become a grandparent!

This transition from one generation to another has happened in an unplanned way. As Charles Handy puts it[2] 'The paradox of ageing is that every generation perceives itself as justifiably different from its pre-decessor but plans as if its successor generation will be the same as them. This time it needs to be different.'

My question is – are we making it different? Are we planning for successor generations relative to the world they will experience? Is our holistic education and training system geared for their world of tomorrow or too locked into the traditions of the past? Is education run for the state and politicians, not for an industrial society? Why does the West lag behind the Japanese in product development and rejuvenation? Does our infrastructure support the concept of portfolio careers and self-employment? My self-employed daughter says not – witness the difficulty the self-employed have gaining financial backing, mortgages and credit compared with those in 'proper' jobs – even though those proper jobs may peter out next week.

It seems to me that our current thinking, stemming from the philosophy of the supremacy of the individual and that of market forces, is visibly making our corporations leaner and more efficient but that for those that fall out of the system – the 'devil take the hindmost', as Charles Handy sees it: 'The market is a mechanism for sorting the efficient from the inefficient, it is not a substitute for responsibility.'[3]

Undoubtedly the impact of market forces has shaken talent out of darkness into light. Small businesses have grown, individuals have discovered the 'doughnut' principle and started to fulfil their potential by filling the empty spaces in the Charles Handy 'personal doughnut'. This is fine if you have a portfolio of skills or competencies that someone wishes to buy. Again from Charles Handy, 'the problem for the unemployed is not so much that they are hungry but that they have no core of the doughnut (and therefore self esteem) to their lives'.[4]

The Royal Institute of International Affairs (RIIA) Chatham House Forum, *Navigating Uncharted Waters*, predicts that the 'artisan' professional has a limited life:[5]

> Portfolio jobs, fashionable a few years ago, were said to be the way professionals could be more like artisans, polishing a corporate culture here and sanding down a research budget there, 'just in time'. Information technology was to make this easy to achieve, both by making markets for these services and by allowing people to work from home. Our assessment is that as firms focus more upon their core, they will indeed look for 'just in time' services, but they will tend to acquire this by pursuing the 'lawyer' model – going to dedicated firms – rather than by hiring mobile talent. There may be exceptions, but issues of continuity, trust and shared tacit knowledge of what is required make it far easier to deal with a firm that you know. Further, the economics for individuals of operating in terms of an 'artisan' model are not encouraging.

I experienced the positive and negative of market forces in the construction industry during the 1970s. It was pre-Thatcherism but very Thatcherite. On the altar of market forces all was to be sacrificed; over the space of a few years all manual work was subcontracted, often to labour only or 'the lump' as it was coined. This was a product of the inability of the industry to manage industrial relations, change and efficiency. Subcontracting certainly reduced costs and gave short-term efficiency gains and as a by-product unearthed some entrepreneurial talent; however, it robbed the industry of longer-term resilience and the ability to reinvent itself in an era of change and depression. It also cascaded the adversarial contract ethos further down into the industry structure – something that many are trying to reverse today following the Latham recommendations on partnership and joint working.

The lessons for other industries are not that outsourcing and subcontracting are necessarily bad but that supply chain relationships as now being adopted from Japanese experience give mutual responsibility and support in bad times as well as good.

What on earth has this to do with Becoming, let alone Beyond, World Class?

My thesis is that no firm or corporation is an island. It cannot put up the shutters and ignore the world outside. The attitudes of those it employs or to whom it subcontracts are influenced by that outside world. When redundancy or outsourcing occurs, those that are left do not often say 'good riddance' but more frequently 'will I be next?'. Also, society for growth depends on the positive interaction between individual, enterprise and the community to make sense of the future (the three-legged stool). The question is – is there enough glue (or hoops) to hold it all together? To answer the questions on education and training we first need to examine how we learn, how our traditions direct our learning and how this contrasts with competition in the Far East.

LEARNING SOCIETY – TEAMS OR GROUPS OF INDIVIDUALS?

The core of *Becoming World Class* was the story of how a subsidiary of a Japanese multinational was set up successfully in the UK, how lessons were learned and applied both in that factory and in other non-Japanese 'brown field' sites in the UK.

I identified various elements of Japanese culture that probably were not transferable but that Western corporations have to compensate for in order to compete.

The first was the Group approach where Japanese see themselves first and foremost as members of a group, or team, and ultimately members of a corporation. The identity with others they work with and work for is enormously strong.

The most enduring import to the West has been Total Quality and Kaizen as demonstrated to great effect in implant companies, their suppliers and competitors.

Enthusiasts for these so-called Japanese management systems in the West in other companies have often ended up frustrated and bemused by the inability of industry to thoroughly embrace and persist with 'total quality' and 'kaizen' or continuous improvement. These approaches are all too often regarded as yet another management fad, the chief executive's bright idea which will be replaced by another next month. This is in part a function of the West's addiction to panaceas or catch-alls only to be easily discarded in the attractive light of the next 'total solution'.

The 'learning organization' coined by Peter Senge in *The Fifth Discipline* (1990) looks like suffering from the same fate when regarded as a solution to a problem rather than something more fundamental. Japanese corporations, in the main, don't label themselves learning organizations but are in fact right down to their roots – capable of adapting to change with extraordinary rapidity. Why is this important?

Because as we shall see, competitive edge for corporations is no longer a function of the Deming absolutes: quality, cost and delivery, these are now the entry points to the market place.

What differentiates from the competition is *'speed of response'* to customer requirements. Speed of response is a function of the ability of the firm to adapt to change and this in turn is a product of culture and whether the organization has agility.

So what is the difference in approach between Japan and the West towards the learning organization and how is this relevant to the individual, the team and the success of the organization?

Professors Ikujiro Nonaka and Hirotaka Takeuchi of Hitotsubashi University in their recent book *The Knowledge Creating Company* argue that Japanese success is not down to the usual list of factors, including manufacturing prowess, lifetime employment and so on but to the Japanese skills and expertise at 'organizational knowledge creation'.

By organizational knowledge creation we mean the capability of a company as a whole to create new knowledge, disseminate it throughout the organization and embody it in products, services and systems. Organizational knowledge creation is the key to the distinctive ways that Japanese companies innovate. They are especially good at bringing about innovation continuously, incrementally, and spirally.[6]

How Japanese companies innovate – the difference between 'Kaizen' and 'Hoshin'

Kaizen is now part of management speak in the West and where it has been rigorously applied it has worked well. Where no Western plant (irrespective of ownership and management) ever reaches Japanese standards is in the production of innovative ideas. Table 1.1 demonstrates the difference.

If this distinction and tool is available to the West, why isn't it applied? Why are Japanese companies generally more innovative?

Both Nonaka and Takeuchi and separately Dr Ronnie Lessem in his highly regarded work on *Total Quality Learning* (1991) trace learning and knowledge back to classical roots. Western approaches to knowledge are seen to be rooted in Greek philosophy – the foundation of Western epistemology (the theory of knowledge): Plato, who thought that human beings aspire toward the eternal unchanging and perfect ideas that are known only through reason, versus Aristotle

Table 1.1   *What the words mean in practice*

	Kaizen	Hoshin
Translates as	'… good change …'	'… navigation/compass …'
Purpose	Continuous improvement	Breakthrough
Operates by	Incremental steps	Start-up/acquisition
Addresses	Existing products and services Existing systems and work processes	New products/markets New/unique systems and work processes
Achieves	Consolidation in existing markets Competitive advantage by product/service improvement or cost reduction	Entry into new markets Competitive advantage by being a new entrant or providing a unique or different offer
Requires	Attention to detail Problem solving Gaining consensus Cross-functional expertise	Innovative thinking Readiness to disrupt markets Risk taking Often speed of action

Source: Colenso, M. (1998) Managing in the 21st Century, *Professional Manager,* January

taking an empiricistic perspective in valuing experience in building knowledge.

The 'Cartesian split' was continued later by René Descartes, a continental rationalist (I think therefore I am), and John Locke, the founder of British empiricism, who compared the human mind to a *tabula rasa* or 'white paper, void of all characters'. (I wonder whether this is the origin of the expression 'a blank sheet of paper'?)

This is not the place to trace the latter philosophical development of the Western concept of knowledge, but suffice to say that Western education is inevitably rooted in these origins which value reason and logic above all else and have an intrinsic aim of fulfilment through the realization of individual potential towards an eternal unchanging summit (while playing down the role of experience building knowledge).

For the British, aspirations of mirroring ancient civilizations have run deep in the past, as beautifully put by Correlli Barnett in *The Lost Victory,* p. 124: 'a belief in the British Empire as a civilizing mission in the Greek and Roman mould; and a high minded "liberal education" inspired by classical literature and philosophy … the public schools and the universities of Oxford and Cambridge with their chapels and their games and their codes of manners constituted not only brewing vats for this heady stuff but also the jugs by which it was slopped out to successive generations of youth emasculating the sons of manufacturers and merchants into "gentlemen".' The Plato/Aristotle divide being perpetuated throughout by the 'practical' man rejecting liberal education.

Japanese intellectual tradition starts, as we would expect, at a totally different point. Whereas Western roots point to the potential and progress of the individual, Japanese traditions, stemming from Buddhism and Confucianism, talk of:

Oneness of humanity and nature
Oneness of body and mind
Oneness of self and other.

Contrasts that this throws up include that the Japanese see time as a continuous flow of updated 'present' in contrast to Westerners' sequential view of time, grasping the present and forecasting the future in a historical retrospection of the past.

The Japanese on the other hand place a high value on being flexible in accordance with the flux and transition of the world in the 'here and now' as the ultimate reality. Samurai education placed a great emphasis on building up character and attached little importance to prudence, intelligence and metaphysics. Being a 'man of action' was considered more important than mastering philosophy and literature. Hence Japanese epistemology values direct personal experience, in contrast to Western epistemology which values abstract theories and hypotheses.

Final contrast:

While a typical western individual 'conceptualizes' things from an objective vantage point, a Japanese person does so by relating her or himself to other things or persons.

For the Japanese to work for others means to work for oneself. The natural tendency for the Japanese is to realize themselves in their relationship to others.[7]

In summary, the ultimate reality for the Japanese lies in the delicate transitional process of permanent flux and in visible and concrete matter rather than that for the Western philosopher in an eternal, unchanging invisible and abstract entity; that is, the thinking self sees the eternal ideal as a detached spectator.

All this may seem a bit deep for an examination of the difference in approach between Japan and the West towards the learning organization and how it is relevant to the individual and the team.

However, the analysis adds another dimension to the contrast in approaches between the West and Japan and may explain why the fundamental aims and aspirations are so different.

In essence, the difference in examining management practice between the West and Japan is between 'discovery' and 'development'.

If your system tells you that knowledge is about discovering what already exists in perfection somewhere, that is, following Plato, then the route to education is through absorbing current knowledge and using reason and logic.

If on the other hand you have no perception of eternal, unchanging and perfect ideas, you can argue that human beings can actively *create knowledge* (that is, develop) to change the world rather than merely discover what is there.

To bring us down to earth, this can provide an explanation of why in the West all learning has to lead to a piece of paper, a qualification, a means of personal entry and security where knowledge is not naturally shared and where education doesn't necessarily lead to competence in employment or working with others and where invention is left to the eccentric Nobel prize winner in the back room.

In contrast, the Japanese salaryman has no system of professional qualifications, sees learning as on-the-job related to employer needs, is enthusiastic about continuous improvement (Kaizen), shares knowledge with his group of fellow workers and innovates in little and big ways every day (Hoshin).

Dr Ronnie Lessem in *Total Quality Learning*[8] distinguishes in terms of Western learning between the Greek, or latterly European traditions, and modern American thought. Even though value is placed on individual progress by both traditions, the source is different. Greek roots are in the belief that man is closest to divinity when he is most completely himself. Individualism through the cult of heroic manhood and the pursuit of honour through action – making the most of his gifts to surpass others in the exercise of them.

American individualism on the other hand stems from an externalized passion for people, competitiveness or shared values that inspire the individual to attain excellence.

Neither tradition would hold with the oriental Confucian idea of obedience which would be seen as an affront to human dignity.

Other obvious traits stem from this analysis. Action has intrinsic value in Greek tradition – the goodness of the action lies in the action itself. A tradition which, I would argue, gives in the mindset of many managers, an over-emphasis if not obsession about decision making and the speed at which decisions are made.

Ronnie Lessem concludes in comparing American and Greek traditions: 'Whereas for Tom Peters product champions and business heroes are symbols of the power and simplicity of individual achievement, for the ancient Greeks their heroic figures symbolized existential depth and complexity. While one scales to the heights of "doing" the other plumbed the depths of "being".'[9]

Small wonder that educational products are different either side of the Atlantic and notable that neither model has anything in common with the Japanese.

The nearest geographically and culturally to oriental thought must be the American model with its emphasis on communally shared values – perhaps a recognition of the essential need for coalition between individuals, born out of adversity.

This may lead us to conclude that shared values, seen to be the quintessence of successful organizations, can be achieved in Japan and the USA more readily than in Europe.[10]

This analysis also tells a lot about successful innovation in the West – because there are companies that are effective at reinventing themselves. Companies such as Virgin and Carlton Communications have continually moved into new markets and shown great agility while making healthy profits. Almost without exception, such companies gain energy from and are driven by charismatic leaders. This is the distinction in comparing with the Japanese whose reliance is not on the 'business hero' but on the harnessing of collective brain power. We will turn to look at Western companies that do achieve this in Chapter 3.

THEORY OF KNOWLEDGE CREATION

In developing their theory of knowledge creation, Nonaka and Takeuchi distinguish between 'epistemology' (the theory of knowledge) which we have been examining up to now and 'ontology' concerning the levels of knowledge-creating entities (individual, group, organizational and inter-organizational).[11] They distinguish under epistemology between 'tacit' and 'explicit' knowledge, arguing that the key to knowledge creation lies in the mobilization and conversion of tacit knowledge (Table 1.2).

Table 1.2 *Two types of knowledge*

Tacit knowledge	Explicit knowledge (objective)
Knowledge of experience (body)	Knowledge of rationality (mind)
Simultaneous knowledge (here and now)	Sequential knowledge (there and then)
Analog knowledge (practice)	Digital knowledge (theory)

Source: Nonaka, I. and Takeuchi, H. (1995) *The Knowledge Creating Company*, p.61

By inspection we can see that Western epistemology will find 'tacit' knowledge of lower value and difficult to measure or test. Since debate in Western education today is all about measurement, standards, qualifications, objectivity and conformity, this gives individuals, teams and corporations an uphill struggle in knowledge creation.

This is not to say progress is impossible, far from it, but we do need to recognize that our heritage puts us at a greater disadvantage than is first apparent – do we need to change the system?

Industry has to motivate individuals in a way the education system has not trained them to operate – to share knowledge, to value tacit knowledge (experience, here and now, practice).

None of this is new, of course – the conflict between the academic and practical man has been there throughout industrial history; however, the speed of necessary change and widespread competition puts a different light on the dichotomy. Traditionally this fight between academic learning and the practical man had the historical framework in common. The academic could point to 'discovering' fundamentals, to historical frameworks, practical man to the harsh world of experience, that is, using history as a guide to the future.

Now the fight between 'tacit' and 'explicit' knowledge is about 'development' and knowledge creation where clearly the Japanese have an advantage.

The challenge then is threefold:

The individual needs to master and balance 'tacit' and 'explicit' knowledge, valuing each as complementary. Then make the leap from individual mastery to knowledge sharing with others, that is, giving up 'knowledge as power'. Thirdly, to focus the first two on developing new worlds, new markets. Unfortunately in the West the framework to protect the individual's vulnerability is often not there. Outside the corporation, in order to gain recognition and potential entry to a job, explicit knowledge is all there is – leading to pieces of paper, qualifications, professional memberships and so on.

Inside the corporation the flavour has been one of competition – for progression, promotion, favour, even jobs. Knowledge became an insurance to be retained in the quest for indispensability. Small wonder shared learning becomes difficult.

The conclusion is that our education system has laid foundations for an employment world that no longer exists. The individual is left to cope as best he or she can (Chapter 10 will explore this in greater depth).

The premise of this book is that we should all have the opportunity of being in control of our destiny. The current approach still only allows the elite to attain a transitory period of control and does not develop the potential for sustainable growth.

The team is a relatively new label and with some, it has stayed as a label only. The foreman or supervisor became the team leader and nothing changed. In other cases it has been the key to empowerment, where the shop floor has been able to escape the shackles of 'control and constrain', releasing potential.

Rarely does the team concept work above this level in Western organizations – this in part is the challenge for this book: How do we achieve teams at Board level and below? How do we help middle managers share knowledge and redefine their role and prevent them becoming the 'corporate concrete' that cannot motivate empowered teams? How do we harness the reinventive capacity in teams to feed into future strategy? Hoshin as distinct from Kaizen – we will return to this in Chapter 6.

Lastly, can we compete with the Japanese in evolving knowledge-creating companies – true learning organizations?

Notes

1. Handy, 1994: 39, 40.
2. Ibid.: 41.
3. Ibid.: 15.
4. Ibid.: 73.
5. RIIA Chatham House Forum, 1997.
6. Nonaka and Takeuchi, 1995: 3.
7. Ibid.: 31.
8. Lessem, 1991: 236.
9. Ibid.: 240.
10. Ibid.: 275.
11. Nonaka and Takeuchi, 1995: 57

2 The Learning Business: Models for Evolving the Knowledge-Creating Company

In the period which we might call the modern industrial technology age – the time from 1920 to 1990, when Ford, General Motors, Du Pont, and many other large corporations were growing up – there were several driving forces behind the success of every winning company. The most important was efficiency of manufacturing; the ability to mass-produce, specialize work, and cut every cost down to the smallest tenth of a percent. Second, the winning companies learned to be effective mass marketers. A third attribute was rapid adoption of technology, and a fourth was financial acumen – the ability to analyze activity in detail, determine how to get the best rates of return, and keep capital moving. The fifth driving force was a set of elementary people skills, which companies developed through sincere efforts to move from Douglas McGregor's 'Theory X' to 'Theory Y'. All these forces gave momentum to the wave of modern industrial technology.

Now, I believe, a new wave is forming: the beginning of a twenty-first-century era which is yet unnamed.

(A CEO's perspective. William O'Brien – US Hanover Insurance)[1]

This is the learning business. In this chapter we will learn how we learn before turning to issues of change.

Peter Senge in *The Fifth Discipline* (1990) is credited with establishing the first framework for the learning business.

Senge coined the term 'systems thinking' – a conceptual framework for the necessary mind shift from seeing the parts to seeing the whole. This is not a new discovery but describes the body of knowledge and tools that has been developed over the past 50 years in the West to help people see learning patterns more clearly.

He argued that the learning organization has the capacity for both generative learning (active) and adoptive learning (passive) as the sustainable sources of competitive advantage. His prescription for managers is:

1. Adopt 'systems thinking' – a way of thinking about, and a language for describing and understanding, the forces and interrelationships that shape the behaviour of systems. This discipline helps us see how to change systems more effectively, and to act more in tune with the larger processes of the natural and economic world.

2. Encourage 'personal mastery' of their own lives – learning to expand our personal capacity to create the results we most desire, and creating an organizational environment which encourages all its members to develop themselves toward the goals and purposes they choose.

3. Bring prevailing 'mental models' to the surface and challenge them – reflecting upon, continually clarifying and improving our internal pictures of the world, and seeing how they shape our actions and decisions.

4. Build a 'shared vision' – building a sense of commitment in a group, by developing shared images of the future we seek to create, and the principles and guiding practices by which we hope to get there.

5. Facilitate 'team learning' – transforming conversational and collective thinking skills, so that groups of people can reliably develop intelligence and ability greater than the sum of individual members' talents.[2]

Above all Senge emphasizes the importance of 'systems thinking' as the 'discipline that integrates the disciplines, fusing them into a coherent body of theory and practice'.[3]

Why a Learning Business?

Mike Pedler, John Burgoyne and Tom Boydell in *The Learning Company* (McGraw-Hill, 1997) argue 'We never actually "get there", for as we solve one problem or issue, another emerges, the seeds of which were sown by our previous solution. We can depict the evolution of the Learning Company in this manner, as a stage in the development of approaches to learning in organizations' (Figure 2.1).

The saga of providing solutions to problems and at the same time producing the seeds of dysfunction is true to life, as is the issue of being on a never-ending journey in terms of development. The authors do not specify Problem Stage 4 although in the context of the Anglian Water Change Programme referred to in Chapter 4 it could be encapsulated as 'initiatives' – rather parallel to Pedler *et al.'s* reference to:

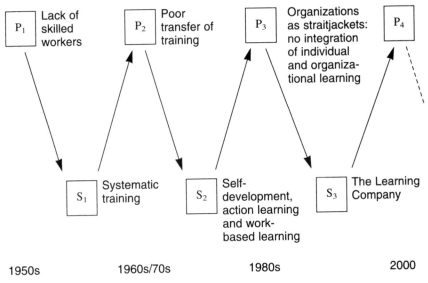

Fig. 2.1 *Learning problems and their solutions 1950–2000*
Source: Pedler *et al.* (1996) *The Learning Company*

There was also a tendency in companies to use top-down organization development and change programmes to try to change or to 'bust the bureaucracy', which ran out of energy and resources long before they achieved their targets (in one major UK utility there were 13 different company-wide change programmes, each championed by a director, each competing for resources, each getting in the way of the other 12).[4]

Nonaka and Takeuchi in *The Knowledge Creating Company*, while acknowledging that Senge does use an integrated approach which promises to convert individual learning into corporate and bring together reason and intuition, nevertheless feel that the Senge model lacks ideas on knowledge creation (p. 45).

The battle, according to Nonaka and Takeuchi, is to gain synergy between tacit and explicit knowledge (see Chapter 1, p. 9) in order to gain knowledge creation in the learning organization. Western thinking emphasizes *explicit* (impersonal or written) knowledge as representative of unchallengeable truth; the Japanese tend to stress *tacit* (personal) knowledge as 'here and now'.

The solution is to pursue 'knowledge conversion' as a social process between individuals gaining interaction between tacit and explicit knowledge. This leads to some rather complicated terminology peculiar to Nonaka and Takeuchi but with patience and application is understandable.

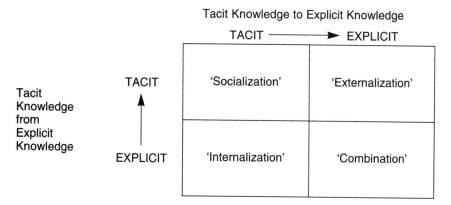

Fig. 2.2 *The modes of knowledge conversion*
Source: Nonaka, I. and Takeuchi, H. (1995) *The Knowledge Creating Company*

The four modes of knowledge conversion are (Figure 2.2):

- **Socialization: from Tacit to Tacit – Sharing of ideas**
  Socialization is a process of sharing experiences, creating tacit knowledge such as shared mental models and technical skills.

  The key to acquiring tacit knowledge is experience. Apprentices have classically acquired craftsmanship through observation, imitation and practice. The collective form of socialization might be, say, brainstorming for detailed discussions to solve difficult problems in development projects. Products of this are often not just sharing experience but enhancing mutual trust among participants.

  This form of interaction can be also outside the firm, between, say, product developers and customers. I remember being very struck by a practice I came across in Komatsu in the early 1990s. After much effort over the space of four years a new model had been developed, for the first time involving design and development activity outside of Japan, using British designers, linking with the team from Japan. With much fanfare regular European customers were given a preview of the new model, seen to be a step change relative to current production. I was amazed to find that these potential customers were asked, 'what would you like to see on the next model?', that is, the model *after* this one being launched.

  Perhaps this is another example of difference between West and East. We have often heard of new products being the ultimate in development terms where perhaps the Japanese with differing education roots (see Chapter 1) understand we are all on a

continuous development curve and nothing is ever the ultimate.
Tacit knowledge can be seen as both individual and organizational
knowledge.

- **Externalization: from Tacit to Explicit – Emergence of new concepts**
  Externalization is often driven by metaphor or analogy where
  analytical methods fail. Nonaka and Takeuchi give the development
  of the Honda City model as an example. The design team used the
  metaphor of 'Automobile evolution', that is, where is it going? How
  do we challenge conventional wisdom? Another Western example
  could be the development by Dr Barnes Wallis and team of the
  famous 'bouncing bomb' concept in World War II, conceptualized
  from the game that small children (and adults) often play on the beach
  with pebbles skimming the water's surface.

- **Combination: from Explicit to Explicit – Testing against what is already known**
  Combination is a process of systemizing concepts into a knowledge
  system. Individuals exchange and combine knowledge through such
  media as documents, meetings, telephone conversations or
  computerized communication networks. Before the information age,
  formal education and training at schools was the common form.
  Today it is epitomized by the Internet as the most comprehensive
  information medium ever known.

- **Internalization: from Explicit to Tacit – Acting on the new ideas**
  This is Learning by Doing. When experiences through socialization,
  externalization and combination are internalized into an
  individual's tacit knowledge in the form of shared mental models or
  technical know-how, they become valuable assets – witness the
  project teams for the Honda City model design or, to take a UK
  example, the Land Rover Discovery development team in the late
  1980s.

Sharing new ideas with others

However, this explicit knowledge will remain with individuals or the team
unless it is 'socialized' to become 'tacit' for the organization as a whole.
In other words, it needs to be shared by verbalizing, written up, put onto
the Internet, whatever, otherwise it becomes an extension of the old adage
'knowledge is power'.

Steve Gatley of EML (1997) encapsulates the Nonaka and Takeuchi
knowledge creation cycle as:

Nonaka's theory focuses on how knowledge is created when groups of people share their ideas (tacit to tacit), and then emerge new concepts (tacit to explicit) which can then be combined with existing know-how (explicit to explicit) and then turned into new products or services thereby building new organizational expertise (explicit to tacit). Nonaka's theory is represented in [Figure 2.3].

Viewed from a western individualist perspective there at first appears nothing remarkable about this theory – people have good ideas in brainstorming sessions and then these get turned into products. There are, however, two important differences between this and the concept of the organizational knowledge creation. First Nonaka is teaching that new organizational knowledge comes from groups getting together – 'group-think'. This is not the same as saying that good ideas come from individuals who happen to be in the room together. Nonaka asserts that it is not individual bright ideas which drive the process of innovation, rather he sees the act of social interaction ('socialization'), as being the real engine of innovation. This has important implications for the ways in which we go about understanding and responding to market opportunities.

The second difference is the separation of individual and organizational knowledge. This aspect of Nonaka's theory creates the opportunity for a company to begin to examine what it collectively

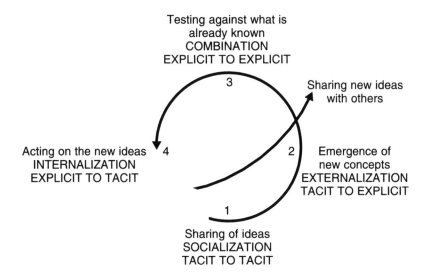

Fig. 2.3 *Knowledge Creation Cycle*
Source: Gatley, S. (1997) *The Journey Goes On … . EML.*

'knows' over and above what the individuals within it 'know'. The unusual and important contribution made by Nonaka is that he teaches us that an organization does not just have a set of values and a culture, but also has a form of know-how or intellectual property, which is created by and exists only as a result of the combination and interaction of the people within it.

Nonaka shows how this organizational learning results from a cyclic process and shows how this not only results in new knowledge for the members of the team, but also results in the sharing of this knowledge with other people in the organization.[5]

On my first week in 1996 with Anglian Water I visited a new 'state of the art' sewage works in Lincolnshire. I met two process operators who had, from the telling, manfully ironed out many teething troubles experienced during and after commissioning of the plant. I asked whether the design engineers had been involved in solving the shortcomings or even knew about them. The response was, 'they wouldn't listen to us anyway; we're just process operators'. When I spoke to the engineers they said they would welcome a written report. I commented that I guessed these two would probably rather walk round the works five times than pen a written report. The outcome was that the two process operators gave a presentation to the designers on their commissioning 'experiences' and are now 'consultants' on the next major project. A shared learning experience of internalization.

The essence of the learning business is the effective translation from individual learning to organizational learning.

We have focused on two causes of inhibition in a Western context: the divide in epistemology between 'tacit' and 'explicit' and the adherence to individual learning in contrast to the Japanese instinct for group-think.

Submerged under both these causes is a deeper issue to which we will return: the difference between 'doing' and 'being' – close to purpose and the 'soul' of individuals and organizations.

If we are convinced that future competitiveness will come from the effective 'learning business' and that we must bridge between:

> tacit and explicit

and

> individual and collective learning

('knowledge is power' to 'shared knowledge is power') then we need a *process* to produce the result.

Such a process to facilitate organizational knowledge creation is expressed by Nonaka and Takeuchi as five enabling conditions:

1. **Organizational intention** – meaning an organization's aspirations to its goals. Typically this will express how vital knowledge creation is to achieving business goals, indicating the commitment and value the organization puts on both the goal and the route. For instance, in Anglian Water, innovation, knowledge creation and the Learning Organization have had a high profile visibly supported by the then Group Managing Director Alan Smith since the early 1990s. All employees (3000 out of 5000 had participated by end 1997) have been encouraged to join in a 'transformation journey' (see Chapter 4) which helps individuals address very fundamental philosophical and practical questions about themselves, their situations in life and work in relation to their teams and the organization.

2. **Autonomy** – or empowerment within acceptable limits to give self-motivation to gain and apply knowledge typically in cross-functional teams. The analogy used is that of comparing this group to a rugby team rather than the typical interaction of individual technical specialists – the relay race. The term *concurrent engineering* has been coined to describe how such engineering teams interact with varying specialist groups.

3. **Creative chaos** is a willingness to question fundamental thinking and perspective. This often represents an interruption of our habitual, comfortable state of being. This doesn't have to be a product of a crisis; it can be provoked by leadership trying to evoke a sense of crisis by proposing challenging goals. However, space must be given to participants to think through to gain the benefits of 'creative chaos'.

4. **Surfeit of information** – this is the opposite of 'the need to know principle' fondly used by many in management in the past. It could be described as information overload: the existence of a level of information that goes beyond the immediate operational requirements. So, for organizational knowledge creation to take place, a concept created by an individual or group needs to be shared by other individuals who may not need the concept at that point. This encourages the two-way sharing of tacit knowledge.
   This principle can be built into an organization by adopting the 'rugby style' product development in which different functional departments work together in a 'fuzzy' division of labour or perhaps to divide the product development team into competing groups.

Another approach is strategically to rotate people between functions for their own development, knowledge creation and understanding.

5. **Variety within** – According to Ashby (in *An Introduction to Cybernetics*, 1956), an organization's internal diversity must match the variety and complexity of the environment outside.

Developing a flat and flexible organizational structure in which the different units are interlinked with an information network is one way to deal with the complexity of the environment.

How do these 'enabling conditions' link with the knowledge cycle? Nonaka and Takeuchi illustrate how tacit knowledge is shared:[6]

A self-organizing team facilitates organizational knowledge creation through the *variety* of the team members who experience a *surfeit* of information and share their understanding of *organizational intention*. Management injects creative chaos by setting challenging goals and endowing team members with a high degree of *autonomy*. An autonomous team starts to set its own task boundaries and as a 'boundary-spanning unit' begins to interact with the external environment accumulating both tacit and explicit knowledge.

These enabling conditions then impinge on each part of the knowledge spiral in turn:

Socialization	(Sharing tacit knowledge and ideas)
Externalization	(Creating concepts/justifying concepts)
Combination	(Building an archetype! Testing against known)
Internalization	(Sharing tacit knowledge again/Acting on the new ideas)

IMPACT OF ORGANIZATIONAL STRUCTURE ON THE KNOWLEDGE CREATION PROCESS

Nonaka and Takeuchi then proceed to tackle what this means for organizational structures, in essence saying that neither of the old alternative 'top down' or 'bottom up' management models is suitable for today's knowledge-creating companies.

Essentially the top down model assumes that only top managers are able and allowed to create knowledge, and the model therefore ignores the potential of the rest of the organization.

Bottom up organizations are typically flat and horizontal. Few orders and instructions are given by top managers who serve as sponsors of entrepreneurially minded front-line employees. Autonomy not interaction is the key operating principle: this means that knowledge created is very difficult to disseminate and share within the organization.

> Put another way, both managerial processes are not very good at knowledge conversion. The top-down model provides only partial conversion focused on combination (explicit to explicit) and internalization (explicit to tacit). Similarly, the bottom-up model carries out only partial conversion focused on socialization (tacit to tacit) and externalization (tacit to explicit).[7]

A new role for middle management

In both these alternative models, middle management is neglected or bypassed. In top-down organizations middle managers have a minimal role in creating knowledge. Given the tendency in the bottom-up model for top managers to act as direct sponsors, middle managers don't seem to have much of a role there either.

Nonaka and Takeuchi suggest a new model strangely called '**middle-up-down management**' to indicate the continuous interactive process by which knowledge can be created (Figure 2.4). For instance, in this model knowledge is created by middle managers, who are often leaders of a team or task force, through the spiral conversion process involving both the top and front-line employees. The process puts middle managers at the very centre of knowledge management – at the intersection of the vertical and horizontal knowledge flow of information with the company.[8]

This theory is diametrically opposed to conventional Western management wisdom which has often failed to find a proper role for middle managers; here Nonaka and Takeuchi argue they are the key to continuous innovation.

> We see middle managers playing a key role in facilitating the process of organizational knowledge creation. They serve as the Strategic 'Knot' that binds top management with the front line. They work as a 'bridge' between the visionary ideals of the top and the often chaotic realities of business confronted by front-line workers, they are the true 'knowledge engineers' of the knowledge creating company.[9]

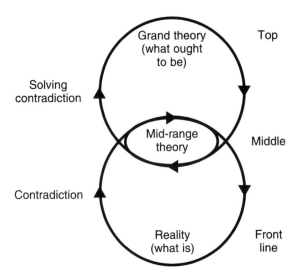

Fig. 2.4 *Middle-up-down knowledge creation process*

Nonaka and Takeuchi identify a useful list of competencies for **middle managers** as 'knowledge engineers'.[10]

1. Project co-ordination and management
2. Ability to create new concepts
3. Ability to integrate methodologies for knowledge creation
4. Communications and facilitation skills
5. Able to employ metaphors to help others articulate imagination
6. Able to engender trust among team members
7. Able to envision way forward based on understanding of the past

All this adds up to a shift of power and leverage to middle management, not away from them, as has been the trend in the West in recent years.

These new knowledge engineers, however, have to work in a supportive context. Their bosses, **top management**, have to display the following competencies in this model:

1. Ability to express a knowledge vision to give a sense of direction
2. Capability to communicate their vision in the context of corporate culture to project team members
3. Ability to measure quality of created knowledge against organizational criteria

4. Uncanny talent for selecting the right project leader
5. Willingness to create chaos within the project team by setting inordinately challenging goals
6. Skill in interacting with team members on a hands-on basis and gaining their commitment
7. Capability of directing the whole process of organizational knowledge creation

Another way of contrasting the comparative management approaches with the Nonaka middle-up-down model is provided by Ronnie Lessem and my colleague at Anglian Water, Sudhanshu Palsule (Table 2.1).

Table 2.1

	Top-down	**Middle-up-down**	**Bottom up**
Agent of knowledge creation	Top management	Self-organizing teams	Intrapreneur
Management processes	Leaders as commanders	Leaders as catalysts	Leaders as sponsors
Accumulated knowledge	Explicit – documented/ computerized	Explicit and Tacit: shared diversely	Tacit: embodied in individuals

Source: Lessem, R. and Palsule, S. (1997) *Managing in Four Worlds*, Blackwell.

Nonaka and Takeuchi argue that creating knowledge management demands a different approach to management structure. Their analysis is supported by the example of the flexible American military structure in World War II when the Americans successfully integrated a task force spanning naval, airforce and army despite the separate bureaucratic structures. Their Japanese foes at the time could not unlock their addiction to separate bureaucratic structures and lost the battle for the Pacific. Japanese industry today has many examples of the integration of knowledge-creating teams with normal structures while increasing the knowledge base for all to access. That doesn't, however, always help the Japanese in overall strategy, as their economy shows.

The reverse – what does this mean for organization structures?

The argument is that knowledge-creating companies need a non-hierarchical, self-organizing structure working in tandem with their hierarchical formal structure. The company will end up with three inter-connecting layers (termed a 'Hypertext' organization) (see Figures 2.5 and 2.6):

> *'business system' layer for normal routine operations in conventional pyramid shape.*

> *'project team' layer where multiple project teams engage in knowledge-creating activities such as new product development. Team members are brought together from a number of different units, assigned to the team for the life of the project.*

> *'knowledge base' layer where organizational knowledge generated by the other two layers is recategorized and marshalled for access.*

An example from my own experience is with Peebles Electric, a transformer manufacturer in Edinburgh UK within the Rolls-Royce Industrial Power Group (see Chapter 4 for a case study). Manufacturing cells were set up which threatened to replace the existing hierarchical structure. A new project team was established with a 'diagonal slice' of membership across the organization to recast the pay and reward structure. This it did, over time and not without trauma, and in the process helped the company adapt to having a structure within a structure giving radical solutions and knowledge creation.

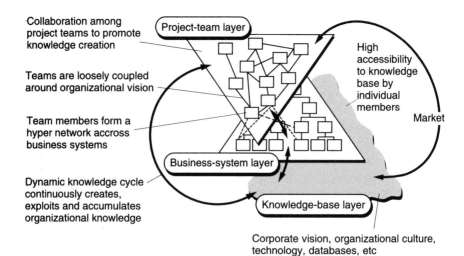

Fig. 2.5 *The hypertext organization*

Source: Nonaka, I. and Takeuchi, H. (1995) *The Knowledge Creating Company*, p. 169.

Knowledge

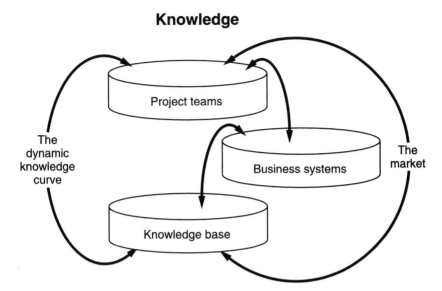

Fig. 2.6 *The hypertext organization, another perspective*
Source: Lessem, R. and Palsule, S. P. (1997) *Managing in Four Worlds*, Blackwell, pp. 185, 186.

This form of overlaid and interacting structure should not be confused with a matrix structure. As Nonaka and Takeuchi explain:[11]

1. In the matrix structure an employee usually belongs to two structures at the same time. In the learning organization model the individual reports to only one structure at one point in time.
2. The learning organization model naturally produces knowledge whereas a matrix organization is not primarily orientated toward knowledge conversion. Also, knowledge is communicated and accessed more effectively; projects have concentrated resources and finite deadlines; top management ownership concentrates the mind. In effect this structure fosters 'middle-up-down' management.

APPLYING KNOWLEDGE CREATION IN A GLOBAL CONTEXT

Much of the context for this encapsulation of Nonaka and Takeuchi's theory of the learning organization comes from Japan and the Western observer has to ask: is this transferable or applicable in the West? In the global context they cite an interesting case study on Shin Caterpillar Mitsubishi which represents the flip side of my own experience with Komatsu.

Shin Caterpillar Mitsubishi (SCM)[12] was the joint company formed between Caterpillar of the USA and Mitsubishi Heavy Industries after Caterpillar's entry into Japan in the early 1960s. This was the event, of course, that prompted Komatsu in Japan to adopt Total Quality Control (TQC),[13] following the teaching of Deming, and also gave the impetus to expansion at home and overseas eventually accelerating Komatsu to be the worldwide rival of Caterpillar. The example concerns the joint development of hydraulic earth-moving shovels by American designers steeped in their own tradition and their Japanese opposite numbers who came from, as we have seen, a tradition poles apart. The fascinating thing to me is that this example from Nonaka and Takeuchi was mirrored in Europe in the early 1990s where Japanese design teams worked alongside their British colleagues at Komatsu UK and their German opposite numbers in the new Komatsu subsidiary of Hanomag – a specialist manufacturer of hydraulic shovels!

Nonaka and Takeuchi highlight a series of clashes in product development and their resolution which create shafts of light on knowledge creation in a global context.

- **Clash No. 1** Relative importance of cost, quality, performance and safety.

  In Japan, cost and quality were the overriding factors due to the vicious price war in the Japanese market.

  In the USA, safety and performance were the overriding factors, due to heightened sensitivity to potential law suits in the USA. The US engineers felt their customers would be prepared to pay a high price for high performance.

- **Clash No. 2** Who should lead the concept creation process?

  In the USA marketing had a strong influence (close to the customer?)

  In Japan a technology-led model was the norm with R&D taking the initiative.

  Mitsubishi's design focused on minimizing production costs. However, Caterpillar, who ran dealerships worldwide, had different priorities – over 50 per cent of the profit came from parts' sales and after-service.

  The two sides were facing a completely different cultural conceptual process.

- **Clash No. 3** How was the development project to be carried out?

  In the USA typically the process was sequential (like a relay race) in four phases: concept, prototyping, pilot running and mass production (typical product development cycle 5–10 years).

  In Japan the process started with concept, but prototyping, pilot running and preparing for mass production would take place in parallel (rugby analogy – concurrent engineering) (typical product development cycle 3–4 years).

- **Clash No. 4** Should the design be standardized throughout the world? This made sense to Caterpillar because of interchangeability of parts and standard production systems throughout worldwide plants. But to Mitsubishi their plants were vastly different from those of Caterpillar. This was resolved when the Japanese invited the two Caterpillar manufacturing vice presidents to see the Akashi plant on the ground – the Americans conceded the point.

In trying to resolve the clashes both sides came to realize that the factor hindering mutual understanding was not merely language but differences in values and in approaches to problems.

The resolution was for SCM to manage the project in Japan using Japanese methods on the conditions that the joint venture (JV) would make no compromise in performance and safety and that progress would be regularly reported to Caterpillar!

The design team in Japan was a joint Japanese/American team who discovered precisely those differences that we found between Japanese, British and German workers in the Komatsu ventures. The nature of communication showed up the different learning styles.

The Japanese didn't see the need to communicate tacit knowledge verbally – this was something they had in common. (This is not unlike the 'tummy speak' of Japanese who instinctively know what their countrymen are thinking.[14]) With their American colleagues they had to 'externalize' the knowledge process to ensure understanding.

To gain as much worldwide standardization as possible the JV set up interplant meetings to gain 'socialization'. Also, new design concepts were tested with dealers round the world for the first time for this team.

They quickly discovered, as we did, at Komatsu UK, that drawing office practice between Japan and the West is totally different – this helped both sides re-examine what was best in an international context. For instance, when a Japanese manager spent time managing the project at Aurora in the USA he started an informal meeting once a week which developed communication channels and contrasted practice between Japan and the USA. This started a new trend of American designers visiting plants and 'touching' the machines they developed. Also, this Japanese manager talked of the cost measurement and cost-cutting scheme currently practised at Akashi. Caterpillar staff turned his verbal account into a powerful piece of computer software and implemented a 'cost monitoring system'[15] enabling Caterpillar to compare parts costs anywhere in the world and to track daily cost fluctuations.

Thus the *tacit* knowledge accumulated in Japan was effectively documented and transformed into an *explicit* system by American computer skills.

This example shows, despite the angst of the process, a synthesis between Japanese and American strengths, that is:

Japanese – **Socialization**
Interplant meetings
Self-organizing teams
American – **Externalization**
Interactive 'why' questions
Specified design drawings
Standardized operations manuals
Combination
The cost monitoring system

Both sides tried to overcome weaknesses in knowledge creating, for example:

- Japanese engineers learned to 'externalize' tacit knowledge into explicit and then 'internalized' it.
- American engineers learned to 'socialize' tacit knowledge from interaction with other people or direct experience on site and 'internalized' it.

'Discovering and remedying weaknesses, both at the individual and organizational levels, holds the key to an effective organizational knowledge creation process on a global scale.'[16]

Finally Nonaka and Takeuchi conclude that for this to happen three conditions are necessary:

1. Top management of participating organizations should show strong commitment to the project.
2. Assigning capable middle managers to the project as 'global knowledge engineers' is critical.
3. Participants should develop sufficient trust among themselves.

I can support this from my own experience in setting up the Komatsu UK plant in 1986. These were the ingredients for success – in common with any joint project anywhere in the world involving diverse cultures.

SUMMARY – CONCLUSIONS FOR THE ASPIRING LEARNING BUSINESS

1. If we accept that Japanese organizations find it easier to create knowledge because of their traditions and learning patterns, the West must recognize the need and compensate for apparent weaknesses.

Hence elements of Senge's model are valid and cross over to Nonaka and Takeuchi, for example building a shared vision and facilitating team learning. We need to recognize that western education points people to *personal* discovery towards individual fulfilment so shared learning and joint knowledge creation with others doesn't come naturally. This throws up innovative leaders but not an innovative workforce.

Hence, as many experience, we have to work hard to gain teamwork and continuous improvement (Kaizen) and even harder to gain ideas and new knowledge creation (Hoshin).

2. Despite the complicated and strange terms Nonaka and Takeuchi use, the theory gives new insight and can be seen to work in practice. Every development team since Adam in East or West has, perhaps without articulating it, to a greater or lesser degree experienced

Socialization (sharing experiences and ideas)
Externalization (metaphor or analogy – gaining new concepts)
Combination (systemizing concepts – and testing against known)
Internalization (acting on the new ideas – learning by doing)

Regarding the last I am fond of that quotation from Confucius:

What I hear I forget
What I see I remember
What I do I understand
    (451 BC)

Doing things together of course gives shared experiences. What Nonaka and Takeuchi's work does is to put it into a challenging framework where we can systemize it to gain best practice.

3. The underlying conditions are important for success:

- Knowledge creation has to rank high and be linked with the organization's goals (organization intention)
- Autonomy for knowledge-creating teams

- Creative chaos (challenge)
- *Too* much information and concurrent working (rugby style)
- Variety

4. Impact on organizational structure:

Top-down or bottom-up or 'middle-up-down'?
A new role for middle management

This is an exciting concept potentially filling a vacuum created by the Goths and Vandals of post-Taylorism when middle managers became the scapegoat for cost and inflexibility in organizations.
Key words are:

Facilitating a bridge
Knowledge engineers
Shift of power?

To be effective they need support. Their bosses, top management, must have:

- Ability to express knowledge vision
- Capability to communicate and inspire
- Ability to measure output of created knowledge
- Ability to select project leaders
- Willingness for chaos creation
- Ability to interact
- Capability to direct whole process of knowledge creation

A new structure? (Hypertext organization) (see Figures 2.5 and 2.6)

'Business system' layer (bureaucratic)
    for normal routine operations
'Project team' layer
    for product development
'Knowledge base' layer
    where knowledge is retained, recategorized, accessible

This sounds fine in concept, but will top management give power away, let go, to the other two layers or will, as ever, the 'right way up' pyramid be seen as the place to be?

5. Applying knowledge creation in a global context:

    Differing cultures force an examination of mindsets (see P. Senge)
    Each has something to learn
    Managing diversity is global
    It is about knowledge creation not compromise

Finally for success, international teams need support:

    Top management of the participating companies
    Capable global 'knowledge engineers'
    Trust

Learning to Change

Now we need to link Learning to Change. My argument is that effective change is a process and change is not possible without learning. The dysfunctions in our education inheritance similarly affect the process of change.

Notes
1. Senge *et al.*, 1996.
2. Ibid.: 6.
3. Senge, 1990: 12.
4. Pedler *et al.*, 1997: 14.
5. Gatley, 1997: 2.
6. Nonaki and Takeuchi, 1995: 85.
7. Ibid.: 126.
8. Ibid.: 127.
9. Ibid.: 128.
10. Ibid.: 156.
11. Ibid.: 170.
12. Ibid.: 212–22.
13. For more detail see Morton (1994): 29–38.
14. Ibid.: 19.
15. Nonaka and Takeuchi, 1995: 220.
16. Ibid.: 222.

3   Change Management

'You change the people or you change the people.'

The mantra of 1990s management either side of the Atlantic. Yesterday's macho manager who forced change by correcting and directing lesser mortals in a top-down fashion is often today an enthusiast for 'empowerment' and self-managed teams. What happened?

In the early 1980s management could blame the government for excessive state ownership and the trade unions for restrictive practices. If only these boundary conditions were removed then worldwide competitiveness could be achieved. In the UK the Thatcher administration changed all that. The new political and fiscal regime led to massive reductions of the labour force in manufacturing and construction, some to do with overmanning, some where protection in relation to world competitiveness had been removed by fiscal policies. In the USA, towards the end of the decade a new management philosophy sprang up – Business Process Re-engineering, where managers were encouraged to ask themselves, returning to fundamentals in process terms: 'what resources do I really need for this process or set of processes?'.

This is not dissimilar to the route taken by production engineers in Japan since the early 1950s[1] and christened 'Lean Production' by Jones, Womack and Roos and in *The Machine that Changed the World* (1990) (for a comparative analysis of the business improvement programmes, TQC: lean production and re-engineering, see *Becoming World Class*, pp. 160–2). However, the route followed in Japan after the 'back to basics' analysis was traditionally different. Workforces surplus to requirements, small or large, would be transferred to other potential growth areas of the company or to subsidiaries, or to suppliers, clients and so on in that incredible mutual obligation network that is Japanese business.

The West has had no such network, often has not had the belief that there are growth possibilities out there somewhere, and has rejected any form of long-term obligation to employees, hence the surplus really are surplus to requirements.

Workforce numbers have fallen dramatically. The City in measuring company performance has looked and still looks for cuts in numbers employed year on year as an indicator of cost reductions and dividend growth. Wall Street gets jittery when unemployment falls and when corporate America seems to loosen its strangulation grip on squeezing out more numbers from the corporate workforce. Far from full employment being the goal, we have become conditioned to the idea that there is a high natural level of unemployment that is desirable. Fine concept if you're in work, receiving dividends from profitable companies and have no children or grandchildren looking for work. This thought process brings us back to Chapter 1 – where is the individual in all this?

So for the complaining macho manager of the early 1980s all obstacles have been removed. Government has sold off as much of the public sector as it can. Privatization has been the most enduring philosophy from this period and undoubtedly the economy has gained. The trade unions are more compliant, even initiators of change; the workforce is convinced of the need for flexibility (usually the flexibility of others and don't forget the entitlement culture). Overmanning is a thing of the past. Middle management is emasculated, downsized, delayed and generally the scapegoat in being pictured as 'corporate concrete' inhibiting or at least not embracing change.

The born again 1990s manager now tells the workforce that they are empowered, released from bondage, recognized for having brains to be employed in the interest of continuous improvement. What is left of middle management is bypassed and self-managed teams are created. This leaves top management to pursue strategy rather than firefight, to network to their hearts' content and pacify the City with their short-term focus.

Unfortunately, either the corporate engine won't start or it runs out of tune; in any event we still can't compete. Quality suffers and top management asks the five 'Ws' and one 'H',[2] only to find that empowerment means

no controls
no system
no support
no ownership
no instruction
no improvement

in other words, no growth in 'tacit' or 'explicit' knowledge. (See Chapter 2.)

The corporate West has done its usual flip from one panacea to another. Top-down command and control doesn't work – just produces a cowed, uncooperative workforce so – 'let's take the brakes off', go 'bottom up', give people their head, go for self management, empowerment and you find motivation.

It is actually two sides of the same coin: distance management and management by desertion. Earl Haig and his generals epitomized 'distance management' in the First World War, living in and directing the war effort from Paris while the lads, run by the NCOs, slugged it out in the trenches. Management by desertion still means you leave them to it, you just don't have any NCOs! Small wonder many Western workforces keep their heads down in initiatives, fully anticipating the next wonder solution to burst on the company when the CEO returns from leave having read up on the latest fashion, or following a Board away-weekend on their version of Mount Sinai, producing the corporate vision in tablets of stone.

So how does the West compete? How can effective change be brought about?

TOP-DOWN CHANGE

All the evidence points to top-down change being the start point and ongoing momentum for change in Western organizations. George Binney and Colin Williams of Ashridge Management College in the UK in *Leaning into the Future* have identified common features[3] of top-down change programmes:

- Leader as hero
- Vision
- Drive
- 'They' are the problem
- Training

Tony Eccles in *Succeeding with Change* (1994) highlights the need, in top-down change, for sheer willpower by management:

> The pressures for change in an organization have to contend with the forces of inertia that will resist any significant displacement of the status quo.

Eccles quotes Lord Shepperd of Grand Metropolitan: 'Self generated strategic change requires the stamina, the endurance and the resilience to just keep coming back to that strategy'.

Resistors may be fearful of change; Lord Weinstock, ex-Chairman of

GEC, has said: 'Almost by definition you have found fault and want to make things better. If you want to change, then there must be some people faults – so they are fearful.'

There are two ways of reacting to this situation. If the macho tendency is there, albeit undercover, then the fear culture is OK – it can be seen to force people to change. If you follow W. Edwards Deming then you could believe that a priority is to 'drive out fear' to gain individual and team contribution.

As Binney and Williams admit: '"Top down" change programmes often do not work. They do not produce the intended effects; instead of transforming organizations, they produce mediocre results. Very often these programmes are short term fixes, achieving necessary changes such as cost reduction, but not shifting corporate cultures in the way that is needed for sustainable success. ... Because (top down) programmes assume that change must be "done to" organizations people often have a sense of being imposed on, of not being valued or respected. They become angry and cynical, less rather than more likely to give of their best for the organization.'[4] (again a distinction between 'doing' and 'being').

Equally, Binney and Williams question the 'zealous application of the view of organizations as "living systems" and the "bottom-up", self organizing approach to change which it has spawned'.

Typical features of the bottom-up approach would be:

- Leader as facilitator
- Awareness
- Release
- 'We' need to change
- Reflection

Managers need not feel under relentless pressure to 'make change happen'; instead their job is to facilitate, to enable others to realize more of their potential. This view argues that change in the nature of organizations cannot be 'managed' at all. In the 'living systems' picture, change in the nature of organizations becomes a process of explanation in which leaders as well as followers are learning.[5]

Hence Binney and Williams argue that just as 'top-down' programmes have not delivered the expected results, so too have 'bottom-up' efforts led to frustration. Their examples include:

- not making progress in dealing with key business issues, unfocused;
- 'stationery cupboard' syndrome or major effort in dealing with minutiae;

- staff frightened off by empowerment. Frozen because they were comfortable being told what to do.

Binney and Williams' prescription for this dilemma is a combination of the strengths of each approach:

> *leading* from the top
> and *learning* from the bottom (see Table 3.1, p. 50)

that is, successful leaders in change combine leading and learning.

This formula has some congruence with that of the knowledge-creating company examined in Chapter 2 and we will return to the debate on which route to follow when we have looked at some examples of change in practice.

MAKING CHANGE HAPPEN: EXAMPLES FROM THE USA AND SWEDEN

Top down – first to last?

A well-documented story of change is that of the revolution led at General Electric (GE) by Jack Welch as CEO since 1981. There is little doubt that the revolution he started was due to his vision of where the company needed to go and the impetus behind the changes came from his energy and sheer determination.

He saw what others couldn't. As Noel Tichy and Stratford Sherman comment in *Control Your Destiny or Someone Else Will* (1992):

> Hardly anyone, inside the company or out, thought GE needed fixing. But where others saw strength, Welch saw weakness. GE's executives, disciplined but submissive, knew how to follow the company's rigid rules. But when the outside world started to change, many of GE's procedures and systems became irrelevant ... the CEO pushed for radical change long before most people recognized it as necessary.[6]

As with the earlier UK examples, the key ingredient was the focus from the CEO on change: 'the process of transformation requires personal commitment and the willingness to persevere'.

Noel Tichy, a professor of organization at the University of Michigan School of Business and a long-time consultant to General Electric, took a two-year sabbatical from the university to run, as a change agent, GE's

Management Development Institute at Crotonville which became the hothouse for organizational renewal and represented a significant change in Welch's style during the first decade of his revolution.

In the first few years Welch was nicknamed 'Neutron Jack' as he divested GE of non-core business and dramatically reduced its worldwide workforce from 420000 in 1981 to eventually 285000 in 1991 even though 150000 were added along the way through acquisitions.

None of this endeared him to the workforce or gave them any feeling of confidence: 'If Welch's vision shocked GE workers; his behaviour terrified them. While he was talking about "liberating" and "empowering" GE's employees, they were worrying, with reason, about their jobs. He challenged lifetime job security with "Companies can't give job security, only customers can" '.[7]

However, over the decade Tichy could see a definite shift in Welch's style: 'Having started out as the man with the bullhorn, in effect yelling at subordinates who couldn't keep pace he evolved into a coach, willing to pause … to help others along.'[8]

Tichy views the development of work-out (where employees are encouraged to think freely of business solutions and criticize top management without fear of retribution) as evidence of a major change in Welch's thinking.[9] He used to argue against incremental change on the theory that only quantum leaps made enough of a difference; work-out represented Welch's personal commitment to the Japanese idea of Kaizen or 'continuous improvement'.

'Another major shift … was from hardware to software' in Welch's phrase. Later Welch worked on the soft issues of corporate culture and behaviour, freeing himself to devote more energy to boosting self-confidence. 'That, in turn, required different behaviour from the CEO: You can't boost people's self confidence by yelling at them. Welch had always been interested in the soft side of management; now he was beginning to appreciate its power.' The old culture was holding GE back. In a quote recognizable in civil service type bureaucracies round the world, a newly arrived manager at GE in the 1980s remarked: 'I noticed that GE Executives entering my office for the first time would invariably tilt their heads back in an automatic, almost sub-conscious way. I couldn't figure out why until somebody told me they were counting the ceiling squares in my office to determine whether they should grovel before me or boss me around!'[10]

By 1988 Welch had found a way to open a real dialogue with GE's whole workforce: 'By then we had taken out the fat. Over 100000 people were gone. For a lean organization, the only route to productivity is to build an energized, involved, participative, turned on workforce, where everyone plays a role, where every idea counts."[11]

Work-out, designed to reach the entire workforce, has a down-to-earth commercial objective. Welch goes on to say: 'Our urge to liberate and empower the GE workforce is not enlightenment – it's a competitive necessity. When you look at the global area, that's what our competitive advantage is. We have got to unleash it.'

CEOs like Welch have opportunities for insights through networking. Tichy highlights an event in 1985 when Olivetti Chairman Carlo Beneditti challenged him on common global issues. He returned with a deepened conviction that the world had changed and the time to globalize was then – he was touching hands with a new generation of business leaders in Europe who thought the same way as he was thinking.[12]

Globalization took a lot of selling: 'The lower you are in the organization, the less clear it is that globalization is a great idea.'[13]

Tichy highlights four focus areas developed for performance on a global basis:

- Products and services: offering the world's best design and technology at the world's best prices.
- Organization: integrating worldwide, purchasing, manufacturing, distribution and marketing networks. Learning and communication to enable the organization to adopt new techniques quickly.
- Human resources: developing a cadre of cosmopolitan executives marked by what GE calls 'global brains': the ability to understand and respect the natural and ethnic biases of others, and to feel comfortable anywhere in the world.
- Alliances: finding ways to cooperate with other companies – sometimes even competitors – who can help you quickly surmount trade barriers and other obstacles.[14]

These ideas were accepted by the immediate circle but on his visits to Crotonville to meet managers under training, Welch still came away frustrated with blockages in the organization, where managers were 'not walking the talk'.

Something had to be done. Work-out was designed to deliver the Crotonville experience to the great mass of GE employees. It began with four major goals:

- Building trust: GE staff at all levels had to discover that they could speak out as candidly as top executives could do without jeopardizing their careers. Only then would GE get the benefit of its employees' best ideas. Welch regarded this goal as so important that he allowed the programme to proceed for years without proof that it was working.

- Empowering employees: The people closest to any given task usually know more about it than their supervisors. To tap workers' knowledge and emotional energy, the CEO wanted to grant them much more power. In return he expected them to take on more responsibility. 'There's both permission and obligation.'
- Elimination of unnecessary work: The quest for higher productivity was only one reason for pushing this goal. Another was the need to provide some relief for GE's over-stressed workers – also to show to them some tangible benefits for the programme.
- A new paradigm for GE: Ultimately the CEO wanted work-out to define and nurture a new boundaryless organization. The process was analogous to the way Crotonville participants defined GE's shared values but the scale was much larger. In effect, Welch wanted the whole organization to participate in redefining itself.[15]

Of course, such a shift in an autocratically run organization can release a lot of pent-up frustration, as Tichy graphically illustrates.

A shop steward on work-out challenged management over the poor quality of screws supplied at his plant. The manager chartered an aircraft to fly the steward and colleague to the suppliers' plant that day and it solved the problem – it sent a powerful message and also converted the complainer from maverick to leader.

This puts me in mind of the visit by the 'frustrated' Welding Section Quality Circle at Komatsu UK to the supplier of profiled plate where shop floor workers met shop floor workers and raised the quality of delivered parts.[16]

Another example for GE was at the Schenectady turbine plant where workers complained about the performance of milling machines. They won authorization to write the specifications for $20m worth of replacement machines, which they tested and approved themselves. The result was that the cycle time for milling dropped by 80 per cent, dramatically lowering inventory cost.

Welch wrote: 'It is embarrassing to reflect that for probably 80–90 years we've been dictating equipment needs and managing people who knew how to do things much better and faster than we did.'[17]

The final quotation from Jack Welch in Tichy and Sherman's book shows how far he had travelled in his thinking:

I think any company that's trying to play in the 1990s has got to find a way to engage the mind of every single employee ... If you're not thinking all the time about making every person more valuable, you don't have a chance. What's the alternative: wasted minds? uninvolved people? a labour force that's angry and bored? That doesn't make sense. If you've got a better way, show me. I'd love to know what it is.[18]

Is this a 'top-down' manager latterly converted to 'bottom-up' thinking? Teams are much more prevalent in GE today but they still do not function in a self-organizing manner,[19] according to Nonaka and Takeuchi.

What is clear is that Welch himself drove the entire process of change – coming up with the concepts (both strategic and operational), refining them, communicating them in an understandable manner through the use of metaphors and analogies and reiterating them repeatedly.[20]

A change agent in top-down mode

My second documented example draws on the experience of Jan Carlzon in *Moments of Truth* (1989).

Jan had been President of Scandinavian Airlines since 1981 and has been credited with creating the stunning turnaround success of SAS in the 1980s. He is acclaimed for giving a new model for management by turning the traditional pyramid of authority upside down in showing managers how to serve as well as to lead. The example of SAS has revolutionized standards in airlines throughout the world.

His is a personal anecdotal account of his philosophy and experience which shows him as a change agent with a feel for people but the element in common with Jack Welch is there – he initiated and pushed change from the top.

As he says on p. 5 of *Moments of Truth*:

In order to become a customer orientated company extensive changes will be required on the part of front line employees. Yet, the initiative for those changes must originate in the executive suite. It is up to the top executive to become a true leader, devoted to creating an environment in which employees can accept and execute their responsibilities with confidence and finesse. He must communicate with his employees, imparting the Company's vision and listening to what they need to make that vision a reality. To succeed he can no longer be an isolated and autocratic decision maker. Instead, he must be a visionary, a strategist, an informer, a teacher, and an inspirer.

Before becoming President of SAS at the tender age of 36 he had been persuaded to become President of Linjeflyg, Sweden's then loss-making domestic airline. On his first day he called all the staff from all over Sweden to the main hangar and said to them:

> This Company is not doing well, it's losing money and suffering from many problems. As the new President I don't know a thing about Linjeflyg. I can't save this Company alone. The only chance for Linjeflyg to survive is if you help me – assume responsibility your-selves, share your ideas and experiences so we have more to work with. I have some ideas of my own and we'll probably use them but most important, *you* are the ones who must help *me*, not the other way around.[21]

The speech apparently went down well as the expectation was for Jan to tell them what to do. It was a good start.

Carlzon puts down his success to developing leadership:

> I succeeded because I reoriented each Company toward the needs of the market it serves. To do this I learned to rely more on the front line people, who deal with the customers, and less on my own edicts. In other words, once I had learned how to be a leader rather than a manager, I was able to open up each company to new market-oriented possibilities and to the creative energy of its employees.[22]

The results are interesting. SAS staggered Boeing by putting passengers first and not technology, unlike other airlines at the time – demanding instead more space for cabin baggage, no middle seats, wider aisles and reduced cabin noise. When the Boeing sales people returned to base and talked to the designers they found the designers had already produced designs that would coincidentally accommodate SAS's basic require-ments but hadn't brought them to light because nobody had asked for them!

Jan Carlzon also discovered that the use of gates at terminal airports such as Copenhagen was a function of convenience to the ground staff, not the passengers who might have to walk up to half a mile in transferring flights. After this, SAS planes were towed between concourses, giving a great deal more passenger comfort.

Having empowered the front line, SAS ran into a common problem – its supervisors had not been educated in the new role they had to play: 'We had let our middle managers down. We had given the front line the right to accept responsibility, yet we hadn't given middle managers viable alternatives to their old role as rule interpreters. We hadn't told middle management how to handle what might, at first glance, look like a demotion.'[23]

In essence he recognized that in the new way things must be handled differently: 'Having done away with the old hierarchical structure, we couldn't order our employees to do things differently. Instead, we had to convey our vision of the company and *convince* them that they could and should take responsibility for carrying out that vision.'

Hence an example of top-down initiative with the expectation of bottom-up momentum taking over. However, the focus is still on one man's leadership and vision.

Job security and commitment

As a postscript, bearing in mind we have been comparing the USA and Sweden, Jan Carlzon's views on job security and commitment are interesting:

> Sweden's 'Aman' laws which guarantee that an employee cannot be fired without good cause, have compelled us to take a hard look at employment security. Perhaps many US businesses executives would take issue with this legislation but I think it is a blessing. It provides a basic platform of security that allows the decentralization of responsibility and encourages some risk-taking.
>
> Surprisingly, in decentralizing SAS, we have met with less success in the United States than anywhere else. We like to think of America as the land of the free and the home of the brave, but Americans are actually reluctant to take risks in their daily jobs. I think this is because most US companies do not offer real job security. Either you keep the boss happy or you don't get paid next week.

(This has implications for the new flexible forms of employment examined in Chapter 9.)

Bottom-up management: 3M

In contrast with the previous two examples, the 3M (Minnesota Mining & Manufacturing Company) example, now famous around the world, represents the antithesis to the top-down management style at GE. There is no external profile for the top executives of 3M, they have no equivalent to Jack Welch or Lee Iacocca. 'Instead, individual inventors and entrepreneurs are more the focus of attention. The stories of how a lab technician named Dick Drew created masking tape and scotch tape or how a sales manager named John Barden created a dispenser with a built-in blade for tape have become legend. More recently the story of how Alf Fry created those ubiquitous little stick-on yellow note pads known as "Post-it Notes" has been heard of over and over again in and out of the company.'[24]

The guiding principles at 3M are autonomy and entrepreneurship leading to the following practices:[25]

- Absence of over-planning
- Brevity of paperwork
- Acceptance of mistakes as normal
- Regular crossing of boundaries
- Encouragement of initiative taking
- Flow of ideas from below
- Minimum interference from above
- Inability of the top to kill an idea
- Maintenance of a small and flat organizational structure

3M's origin may have given rise to its management style. The original investors in a Minnesota mine found that they had made a mistake. The minerals were not valuable as expected, but low grade. This forced them into developing by-products that had high value. A company of practical problem solvers who tolerated mistakes was born as a result. Today 3M researchers can spend up to 15 per cent of their on-the-job time pursuing their own dreams. Output is measured to back this up in that each 3M division is expected to derive 25 per cent of its sales from products that didn't exist five years beforehand.[26] There is also something called the eleventh commandment: 'Thou shalt not kill ideas for new products.'

At 3M senior managers act as mentors, coaches and sponsors. Nonaka and Takeuchi quote the following mainly to describe their role: 'The captain bites his tongue until it bleeds' – a Japanese naval expression illustrating the patience the captain has to endure when watching a junior officer bring a big ship alongside the dock for the first time.[27]

To a certain extent this example of bottom-up management is a product of the market place and an unstable environment, not purely a philosophical or dogmatic choice. It fits the classical analysis of T. Burns and G.M. Stalker in *The Management of Innovation* (1961) where an organic management system with a non-bureaucratic system is appropriate to an uncertain, niche market led environment.

Is there then any self-generating model we can choose that doesn't depend on either the game of Russian roulette, as to whether at the right time, a reforming energetic CEO, in top-down fashion, knee-jerks the stable mechanistic bureaucratic structure into being competitive; or the benign benevolence of the 3M bottom-up model where almost from a detached viewpoint innovation is encouraged but not planned or controlled? Could this be repeated or applicable in companies not in variable niche markets?

Nonaka and Takeuchi pursue their knowledge creation model with the example of Canon in Japan.[28]

'Middle-up-down management'

The start point for the acceleration of Canon creating the mass market in photocopiers was the direction from top management at the end of the 1970s to develop a radically new desktop copier able to be used by anyone and produced at minimum cost. The seemingly impossible target was for a $1000 copier when the cheapest standalone copiers of the time were in the order of twice this price. A 14-member cross-functional feasibility team headed by a middle manager was formed and spent much time on fundamental analysis of how both reliability and cost could be improved simultaneously. They found that 97 to 98 per cent of copier service problems were related to the drum and its surrounding mechanisms. Since on-site servicing is inevitably costly and the new generation of copiers would be spread in even more remote locations, any reduction in periodic maintenance might mean that the copiers could be sold for much less.

After many impromptu, 'camp' away-day type sessions, studying an empty beer can after drinking, somebody had the bright idea of making the drum disposable – just like the beer can. This was the breakthrough; a piece of reverse logic that meant that on-site maintenance could be performed by the user inserting a new cartridge including the drum after so many copies. This is not unlike the classic story of re-engineering mentioned earlier when Taiichi Ohno did the reverse of the car makers in Detroit – instead of pressing out the maximum number of parts between die changes he flipped the logic and reduced the time taken to change dies from 1 day to 3 minutes![29] (over a development period of 10 years!).

The business results, of course, are well known. The mini-copier project generated 470 patents, 340 for the new cartridge system alone. Laser-beam printers were spawned from this development in an area where now Canon has an 80 per cent world market share.

To use Nonaka and Takeuchi language it was not the CEO or front-line specialists who were the 'agents of knowledge creation' in the Canon example but the middle managers who were engaged in running and supporting the project, that is, carrying out the process detailed earlier (see Figure 2.3, p. 17):

- sharing tacit knowledge,
- creating concepts,
- justifying concepts,
- building archetypes, and
- cross levelling knowledge.

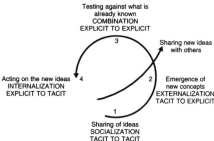

Key features that meant for the success of the Canon taskforce:

- Frank and open discussion within and outside the multi-functional group
- Middle managers supported even though not under their control
- Youth – average age under 30 within the taskforce
- Canon corporate philosophy of self-innovation
  self-knowledge
  self-government
- Top management owned and supported as catalysts but didn't interfere, and also acted as test beds for the prototype mini-copiers.

Nonaka and Takeuchi would argue that the top-down example deals primarily with 'explicit' knowledge, the bottom-up with 'tacit' knowledge, but the middle-up-down covers both types of knowledge.

The quest of bridging the extremes between top-down and bottom-up in terms of change has also, as we saw, been pursued by George Binney and Colin Williams.

They tend to encapsulate the contribution from the top as 'leading' and from the bottom as 'learning' and hence come up with the combination term 'Leaning into the Future'.

In that, they are talking of a process whereby all participants learn by doing. I find myself at one with the concept. My worry is whether it only remains as a concept merely producing a more considerate or sensitive form of top-down change.

Their two extreme models of change[30] relate to the Burns and Stalker (*The Management of Innovation*, 1961) concepts of:

'Organizations as *machines*'

or

'Organizations as *living* systems'

The 'organizations as *machines*' concept leads management to believe:

- Change needs to be driven
- You have to start afresh
  – re-engineering
  – no recognition of past expertise
- Everyone is for change – for others
- Change can be planned and predicted and controlled

The 'organizations as *living* systems' concept leads to:

- Organizations are adaptive, dynamic and self-organizing
- Change is a way of life but adjusting is painful
- Release potential for change
- Work with the natural capacity of people and organizations to develop
- The answer is within
- Reinforce emerging patterns – don't force the pace
- We *all* need to change – leaders admit they have to learn
- Live with uncertainty
- Feelings, emotion and intuition are important

However flexible of thought, many managers will see this as far too laissez-faire to be competitive.

Also, from a philosophical viewpoint the living systems metaphor rests on the assumption of functional unity[31]: each element of the system supporting and aiding the others, as in the human body. In reality this doesn't happen in organizations – conflict naturally occurs.

Also, as Binney and Williams point out (p. 5) these two metaphors do not come ideology free. The mechanical model is linked to the view that control is paramount and that senior managers do the thinking while others implement; the living systems thinking is associated with the assumption that organizations flourish as they allow their people to develop their potential to the full.

Binney and Williams' approach in coining 'Leading and Learning' is not to decide which is right or wrong between the models but to integrate an approach to change which combines the best. However, it is important not to lose the richness of 'being' as opposed to 'doing' implicit in the living systems model.

LEADING AND LEARNING

Successful leaders shape the future and adapt to the world as it is. They are clear about what they want to change and they are responsive to others' views and concerns. They are passionate about the direction in which they want the organization to go and they understand and value the reality of the organization, why it has been successful and what its people are good at. They lead and they learn.[32]

The Binney and Williams formula is based on two sets of paradoxes (Figure 3.1):

- Forthright *and* listening leadership
    Forthright – Dealing with denial
    Listening – Sharing responsive quiet leadership
  The power comes from combining the two.

- Direction and autonomy
    Direction – Providing a framework
                Standards
                Expectations
                Clarity
    Autonomy – Enable people to take initiative
                'Freedom within the framework'
                Take risks
                Challenge and support

This provides realistic boundaries to the dilemmas facing any organization wishing to empower its workforce.

Binney and Williams point out that the nature of leadership has changed irrevocably today – there is no realistic option in today's industrial world of returning to the autocratic leadership we knew yesterday.

Compliant workforces went along with overmanning. Now that there is little 'fat' in lean organizations, commitment is essential for competitiveness.

Also, the analogy of organizations as bureaucratic machines is no

Leading	and	Learning
Top-down programmes		**Bottom-up approach**
LEADER AS HERO Knows the answer; inspirational; wills others to follow.	**FORTHRIGHT *and* LISTENING LEADERSHIP** Combines assertive leadership with responsiveness to others.	**LEADER AS FACILITATOR** Self-aware; enables others to realize their potential.
VISION Clear and inspiring visions, which explain why clean breaks with the past are needed, energize people to change. The answer is 'out there'.	**SEEING CLEARLY** The energy to change – and to develop existing strengths – comes from seeing clearly where the organization is now and what possibilities are open to it.	**AWARENESS** People change as they become more aware of their own needs and their interdependence of the world around them. The answer is 'within'.
DRIVE Change is driven through by determined individuals who plan carefully and minimize uncertainty.	**WORKING WITH THE GRAIN** Individuals shape the future by combining clear intention with respect and understanding for people and organizations. They work with, not across people's hopes and fears.	**RELEASE** Effective leaders release the natural potential of people and organizations to adapt to change and are prepared to live with uncertainty.
'THEY' ARE THE PROBLEM Individuals see the need for change in others.	**ALL CHANGE** Leaders encourage others to change by recognizing that they too need to shift.	**'WE' NEED TO CHANGE** Change starts with me/us.
TRAINING People are taught new ways of working in extensive training programmes.	**LEARNING WHILE DOING** Most learning takes place not in the classroom or training session but as people do, as they interact with others and reflect on their experience.	**REFLECTION** People learn when they step back from day-to-day tasks and reflect deeply on their thoughts and feelings.
Organizations as machines	**Complementary opposites**	**Organizations as living systems**

(Title above table: **Leaning into the future** =)

Figure 3.1
Source: Binney, G. and Williams, C. (1995) *Leaning into the Future: Changing the Way People Change Organizations*, Nicholas Brealey

longer a relevant model since all organizations are in a state of flux to one degree or other.

We can conclude then that the conditions we accepted in the past that dictated a mechanical ethos for managing bureaucratic institutions are no longer appropriate. The priority in leadership is to gain commitment. The organizational ethos has to be akin to the living systems model.

This still leaves the dilemma with which we started in this chapter – how effectively to combine the top-down and bottom-up models.

Binney and Williams' formula for leading and learning is a process:

- *Seeing clearly*: Developing a shared understanding throughout the organization of what is reality and what are the possibilities. Key ideas are openness; dealing with denial; customer focus and benchmarking.
- *Working with the grain*: Mobilizing the energy for change, recognizing that there is *no one way* of implementing change in organizations. A useful spectrum of options is contained in Table 3.1. All these formulae have been tried at one time or another in organizations – often management then despair of gaining a single simple solution. Perhaps there isn't one.
- *All change*: The ability to inject a new mental model or mindset, of 'seeing things with new eyes',[33] so that challenge within is the accepted norm and that the whole team takes responsibility. Individuals take responsibility for their own growth and learning, that is, the Peter Senge 'personal mastery' concept. Managers redefine their role in terms of mentoring and coaching. Upwards appraisal or 360-degree feedback encourages honest two-way flow. Time and transition from ending to beginning is another whole study.[34]
- *Learning while doing*: Classic learning models – the cyclical process identified in Deming's Plan: Do: Check: Action or David Kolb's[35]

  Observing and reflecting
  Conceptualizing
  Experimenting
  Experiencing

  Binney and Williams rightly recognize that while these models have been widely used they tend (particularly with Deming's PDCA) to be pigeonholed into problem-solving tools for junior staff and have little impact on learning styles at the top of organizations. Binney and Williams believe that each organization has to express the logic of the cycle or spiral[36] in its own language for it to come alive – an experiential element.

This focus on 'learning while doing' also has relevance to the debate over methodology in education for the individual (Chapter 2). Qualifications-based learning for the individual tends not to be experiential: it is 'explicit' rather than 'tacit', to use Nonaka and Takeuchi terms, whereas 'learning while doing' or on-the-job training tends to be tacit.

Also, more importantly for teams, 'There is no problem of "transfer-ability of learning" or of "reinsertion" if everyone has been involved in a

Table 3.1 *Mobilizing the energy for change*

	Approach	Major strength	Major weakness/ issue
	OPEN INVITATION Encourage contributions and suggestions from everyone, particularly those who do the work/ have direct customer contact	• Can readily tap ideas and energy at all levels • Can signal that people in operations are valued	• Need for prompt response to ideas or mechanism for people to take ideas forward themselves • How to promote adequate recognition? • Need for clear boundaries
	ORGANIC GROWTH Bring together teams from across functions and across hierarchy to address key business issues	• Opportunity to break down hierarchical and functional barriers and learn other perspectives • Learning about corporate perspective • Enthusiasm often generated by working in new way	• How to overcome initial apprehensions so that all can contribute fully? • How to sustain enthusiasm and make links with rest of organization? • How to retain and spread learning once *ad hoc* team dissolved?
	WHOLE TEAM Work team as a whole involved in improvement/development	• Teams are tackling real-life issues and context • Learning takes place where it is needed – in the work team	• How to provide enough safety so that underlying assumptions and problems are addressed? • How to spread learning beyond initial teams?
	PROCESS Key individuals responsible for business process set about transforming that process	• Reflects how work is actually done • If done well, can identify key improvement opportunities	• Need to ensure 'big picture' issues are considered and underlying assumptions tackled • How to stay focused on value to customers? • How to involve key actors so that they do not feel imposed on?

Source: Binney, G. and Williams, C. (1995) *Leaning into the Future: Changing the Way People Change Organizations*, Nicholas Brealey, 15.

particular experience.'[37] This is where facilitation can be so powerful in aiding shared experience. However, many Western managements have had hang-ups about the use of facilitators – regarding them as outsiders, potential sources of leaks of confidential information or fundamentally a potential loss of control or manipulative power.

DEALING WITH DILEMMAS

In pulling all this together Binney and Williams argue that far from needing to choose between 'top-down' or 'bottom-up' change, living with dilemmas is part of life's rich pattern and is something that the successful leader of change doesn't just live with but uses to good effect.

Charles Hampden-Turner in *Charting the Corporate Mind* (1990) describes the 'practical dilemmas' that managers have to deal with. Releasing individuals and teams for training is laudable for development. Maintaining the needs for production is often an opposite tension.

Hampden-Turner shows that the more successful companies were in combining the qualities of coherence and individual excellence, the more profitable their factories.[38]

LIVING WITH AMBIGUITY

This is difficult for Western managers brought up on a diet of clarity, tidiness and the removal of contradictions and paradoxes. It is, however, the real world. When we discuss what makes a successful company in Chapter 6, one key issue will be the ability to live with paradox. The same is true for individuals (see Chapter 9). It puts me in mind of the dilemma that the first Japanese managing director of Komatsu UK, Torio Komiya, had when a Japanese adviser and a British manager couldn't get on with each other.[39] To Torio Komiya, the individuals should resolve their own differences.

ABANDONING THE SEARCH FOR THE PANACEA

As Binney and Williams recognize: 'While many people are very cynical about "business process re-engineering", "total quality management" or any other latest fad, many managers continue to look for "the answer", a company to copy, a programme or technique to apply.'[40]

This is the basic problem in the West. The philosophy of education from the Greek; the Judaeo-Christian ethos of only one God: therefore only one solution to life, makes it hard to manage diversity, to live with ambiguity.

To follow Binney and Williams' polemic is to bring the study of change in organizations back to the Orient. 'Taoist philosophy, which originated in ancient China [and subsequently travelled to Japan: my note], has long emphasized how nature is characterized by the continuous flux and wholeness shaped by the dynamic interplay between opposites (symbolized by yin and yang meaning originally the dark and light sides of a hill).'[41]

Small wonder then that the locus of Japanese education, that is:

> Oneness of humanity and nature
> Oneness of body and mind
> Oneness of self and other

(see Chapter 1, p. 7) provides a basis of synergy for Japanese companies collectively to embrace change without resisting and clinging on to what the old order meant to me as an individual. It also has the beauty of integrating 'doing' with 'being', in contrast with the separate compartments of 'action man' and 'academic' in the West.

CONCLUSIONS ON CHANGE MANAGEMENT

1. Neither the top-down nor bottom-up models are complete solutions for change management.

> Top-down tends to gain compliance but not commitment.
> Bottom-up can produce ideas but these are not necessarily focused on real business issues unless directed and then it is not truly bottom-up.

Middle managers are encapsulated in both models. Neither model gives complete learning, that is, combining 'tacit' with 'explicit'.

2. Western business prefers top-down as a model and change often depends on 'leader as hero' perceiving that change is necessary and driving the process through (for example, the models of Jack Welch or Jan Carlzon). However, organizations recognize the crucial role of gaining willing commitment – engaging the minds.

3. The only naturally occurring models that appear to be self-generating in terms of ongoing competitive change are those that embrace a Taoist philosophy of 'continuous flux' and wholeness shaped by the dynamic interplay of opposites. With their roots it is easy to see why Japanese companies can find that both knowledge creation and evolutionary change comes naturally.

4. What workable formulae are available for Western companies wishing to adopt sustainable, self generating change?

-   *Binney and Williams' prescription, 'Leading and Learning'* (*Leaning into the future*)

    -   Forthright and listening leadership
    -   Seeing clearly – shared understanding
    -   Working with the grain
    -   Recognize the need for *all* change
    -   Learn while doing.

In essence: sensitive, listening, considerate leadership with good communication; a pragmatic attitude based approach rather than philosophical solution.

-   *Nonaka and Takeuchi prescription, 'Middle-up-down management' and the 'Hypertext' organization*
    Redefinition of roles:

    -   Top management as catalysts, vision articulators, and setters of challenging goals
    -   Middle managers as champions of change, facilitators and leaders of change groups, centre of knowledge management at the intersection of vertical and horizontal flow of information, key to continuous innovation and knowledge engineers
    -   Task forces – multi-functional, open and given legitimate status within the structure
    -   Knowledge-creation is the goal rather than change per se. Knowledge from each task force to be captured and added to the knowledge base layer of the organization as a whole.

These new roles and different emphasis must be legitimized and supported by a radically different structure within a structure, 'a non-hierarchical; self-organizing structure working in tandem with its hierarchical formal structure' (see Chapter 2, Figures 2.5 and 2.6).

This alternative approach has the advantage of:

- retaining a hierarchical structure for day-to-day running of the organization;
- creating and legitimizing project teams that fundamentally contribute to knowledge creation and change, giving a crucial role to middle management;
- adding knowledge and flexibility to the corporate capability by linking the two systems – adding to knowledge base.

In essence the Binney and Williams formula is about individual approaches and processes initiated by top management – and this is key to brokering successful change.

Nonaka and Takeuchi propose a process which is embedded in new structural approaches which promise to give self-generating change and knowledge creation not requiring 'leader as hero' for sustaining power.

The truth is there are no panaceas and for success organizations need both approaches. *'The future belongs to companies that can be the best of the East and West and start building a universal model to create new knowledge within their organizations.'*[42]

It is no good trying to produce change unless this is led by learning and the end objective is sustainable development.

Notes
1. See the account of Taiichi Ohno of Toyota in Morton (1994): 153/4.
2. Originally Rudyard Kipling's six trusty friends in journalism – Why, Who, Where, When, What and How.
3. Binney and Williams, 1995: 3.
4. Ibid.: 3, 4.
5. Ibid.: 4, 5.
6. Tichy and Sherman, 1992: 5.
7. Ibid.: 8.
8. Ibid.: 209/210.
9. Ibid.: 211.
10. Ibid.: 33.
11. Ibid.: 65, 66.
12. This process is a fine example of double loop learning. For how this works in practice see Chapter 6.
13. Tichy and Sherman, 1992: 187.
14. Ibid.: 188.

15. Ibid.: 200, 201.
16. Morton (1994): 90.
17. Tichy and Sherman, 1992: 204.
18. Ibid.: 251.
19. Nonaka and Takeuchi, 1995: 159.
20. Ibid.: 133.
21. Carlzon, 1989: 11.
22. Ibid.: 19.
23. Ibid.: 66.
24. Nonaka and Takeuchi, 1995: 135.
25. Ibid.: 135.
26. Ibid.: 140.
27. Ibid.: 139.
28. Ibid.: 140–50.
29. Morton (1994): 153.
30. Nonaka and Takeuchi, 1995: 32–50.
31. Morgan, 1986.
32. Binney and Williams, 1995: 52.
33. Marcel Proust: 'The real art of discovery consists not in finding new lands but in seeing with new eyes.'
34. See Bridges, 1991.
35. Kolb, 1974. Also Lessem, 1991: 284.
36. See development of Deming into Juran's cycle of improvement, Morton, 1994: 137.
37. Binney and Williams, 1995: 147
38. Hampden-Turner, 1990.
39. Morton, 1994: 23.
40. Binney and Williams, 1995: 163.
41. Ibid.: 161.
42. Nonaka and Takeuchi, 1995: 255.

4   Strategic Change in Practice

1   MANUFACTURING

Rolls-Royce Industrial Power Group

In April 1994 I joined Rolls-Royce Industrial Power Group as Board member for personnel – an opportunity to return to manufacturing after my spell with Northern Electric Plc (the change programme was detailed in *Becoming World Class* pp. 93, 94, 103–13). I was now becoming a peripatetic change agent!

Richard Maudslay, then Managing Director of Rolls-Royce IPG, wanted to change the ethos of personnel from reactive to proactive. He was conscious that within this large group of companies the people function had got stuck with the 1970s and 1980s syndrome of staff number accounting. Recruitment had been at a low ebb and survival via cost cutting had been the dominant theme – necessarily in the past decade when much of what was Northern Engineering Industries (merged with Rolls-Royce in 1989) had been in retrenchment in the face of fierce international competition, changes in technology and market consolidation by the main players GE, ABB, Mitsubishi Heavy Industries, GEC Alsthom, Westinghouse and so on.

First define the commercial needs. Change should not be for its own sake, nor for self-gratification of the human resources (HR) function. In consultation with other members of the IPG Board we saw the commercial needs of Rolls-Royce IPG as to:

- improve the competitive position;
- integrate technologies;
- create synergy throughout the Group;
- release potential and reduce costs;
- create partnerships.

The IPG Board was in reality a holdings board, bringing together a great range of diverse businesses operating in disparate markets world-wide. It was flippantly described as everything in Rolls-Royce that didn't fly! (Rolls-Royce Motors had long since been part of the Vickers Group,

56

not Aerospace). IPG was made up of the old NEI Group of companies predominantly in power generation, boilers, electricity transmission and distribution, and materials handling, together with the aero-engine derivative business (that is, aero engines on the ground or at sea) of Rolls-Royce aerospace and nuclear engineering, civil and military. It was a big conglomerate, employing 19 000 people worldwide with a turnover exceeding £1.5 billion, representing some 40 per cent of Rolls-Royce business in total.

Competition was intense, the market worldwide was huge but Rolls-Royce IPG generally had very small market shares, with the exception of Industrial and Marine Gas Turbines (IMGT) where because of the aero-engine derivative base the market shares tended to reflect the tripartite competition between GE, Pratt and Whitney and Rolls-Royce which had dominated the aero-engine business for past decades. Market consolidation by competitors of Rolls-Royce IPG together with its own small market shares, plus shortage of capital for major infrastructure projects worldwide, meant that margins were particularly tight and international contracting had become a very hazardous business. IPG therefore needed every ounce of contribution from its workforce.

The Group had been driven by the need to generate profit and cash for short-term survival for some years. The philosophy propounded by Sir Terence Harrison, who brought NEI through the 1980s and later provided the focus of profit and cash for Rolls-Royce Plc as its Chief Executive, was cascaded down the organization so that the most lowly levels of management in IPG knew what their priorities and responsibilities were.

Like most issues of focus, it had its downsides. It meant that transferring good practice, knowledge and cooperation across separate company boundaries was difficult to say the least.

Hence the priorities in 1994 were to integrate technologies between IPG companies and with Rolls-Royce Aerospace. There was some success. Fan blade technologies from aerospace were successfully used in the power generation business but too often a myopic view was taken that did not allow for synergy between companies and groups.

Transfer of learning could be seen in retrospect as Tacit to Tacit Stage 1 – dependant on chance interaction. This was to change.

The years of focus on survival, consolidation and cost cutting had limited the vision of much of the people resource and there was a need, as Richard Maudslay saw it, for employees to keep one eye on the horizon while training the other on today's task. We believed there was much potential in the workforce that could be realized by encouragement and that in turn could lead to new ideas, growth *and* reduction in cost.

Lastly with the inward focus on the performance of discrete IPG business units, insufficient opportunity had been taken to gain advantage from partnership – partnership both within IPG and with suppliers, customers, and even the competition.

Agenda for change

My first task was to set the agenda and concept for the personnel function in each constituent IPG company. My first Board meeting in May 1994 was an opportunity to launch the embryonic scheme to my colleagues. I was conscious that despite Richard's desire to raise the sights and to enhance the personnel function many of my fellow Board members would be sceptical of any high-flown initiative that could be seen to lose touch with reality. Also, up to that time it was not a Board that discussed or decided on policies that would determine handling of people issues within each business – that was very much left to local determination. Hence the new proactive role at the centre had to be as catalyst or even *agent provocateur*.

The programme of change started with the need to do the 'day' job well.

1. Personnel in each company should first *excel in basic business disciplines* – create the right environment by, for instance, getting the administration right. (There is often an inherent problem here – people who are attracted to careers in HR are often not natural administrators. If they are, they may not be good negotiators, change agents or strategists.)

   However, the essential point was they could not be excused the efficient running of the HR function to go off into flights of fancy over change management.

   Having established this performance focus, it was time to move on to change.

2. *Reactive to proactive (1st stage)*
   The task was to:
   - be the organization's communications champion;
   - find and develop the 'right stuff' in line managers and other employees;
   - link training and learning to business objectives;
   - encourage employee involvement and promote freedom to act (this last was coined to avoid the dreaded E word, empowerment) – at that time seen to be 'soft' and impractical;
   - essentially to obtain a positive response from people.

3. *Reactive to proactive (2nd stage)*
    Eventually to:
    - find a role for the trade unions (partnership);
    - challenge the leadership;
    - be creative – learn to say 'let's do it' – essentially integrating personnel with business needs.

I was pleased, the Board bought into the concept and the words, and probably wondered whether that was the last they would hear.

Using the Nonaka and Takeuchi cycle we had got to externalization: Tacit to Explicit – emergence of new concepts Stage 2.

People strategy evolution

The next stage was to gain the acceptance and support of the 20 or so personnel directors of IPG companies around the globe. In part this was easy – they were looking for a lead from the centre, encouragement and acknowledgement that the function may have a strategic, change management role. On the other hand they were fiercely independent and they did not take kindly to a 'big brother' IPG telling them how to run their business.

There had been a tradition of half-yearly personnel conferences – mainly to review where the business was heading and to report back on progress against quasi-definitive targets. I seized the first opportunity to put the ball back into the individual personnel director's court. Kelvin Cox, my external facilitator and mentor, and I reasoned that we could from the centre (on the basis of the nod from the Board) put together a personnel strategy within which the constituent companies could work. Instinctively we felt this was the wrong route. We needed ownership from these personnel directors, not a lot of effort at the centre that gathered dust on someone's shelf.

We then used the opportunity in autumn 1994 to brainstorm with them what the key elements of the people strategy should be, to shift the people ethos from reactive to proactive. The final result took many iterations and much work by 'pairs' of personnel directors working between companies, often for the first time, to hammer out the following template:

Guiding Principles – People Strategy
- Personal development
- Communications
- Continuous improvement

- Recognition and reward
- Involvement and consultation
- Leadership and relationships

(The full policy is included as Appendix B.)

This at last gave a common currency between disparate groups that accorded with what the Board wanted – synergy, sharing of best practice, effective management development and realization of potential.

It was a process of testing the model against what was already known, that is, combination: Explicit to Explicit, Stage 3.

Alignment: the template – buy-in by management

Fine words so far, destined to wither on the vine unless they became integrated with *each* trading company's business plan.

The term 'template' was used in the 'Way Ahead' plan (see Figure 4.1) to appeal to the engineering ethos, as was the model of 'Specification' through 'Design', 'Build', 'Operate and maintain' to 'Review performance'.

It was then the individual personnel director's role to see that the Guiding Principles devised collectively translated themselves into an Implementation plan within each trading company together with definitive targets against which measurements could be taken. (There the

Personnel strategy	Developed by	The model
Guiding principles	IPG personnel group/MDs	Specification
Operating template	IPG personnel group	Design
Implementation plan	Trading company	Build
Putting in place	Trading company	Operate and maintain
Measuring achievements (against operating template and plan)	Trading company (to Rolls-Royce IPG standards)	Review performance

Fig. 4.1 *The Way Ahead*

technology of 'balanced scorecard' was borrowed from the *Harvard Business Review* article by Kaplan and Norton and used effectively.)

This was internalization Stage 4 Explicit to Tacit: Acting on the new ideas.

The limiting factor, frankly, was the degree to which personnel was integrated with each separate trading company. With many, if the personnel director had not got a good relationship of influence with his or her trading company managing director, then progress was impossible.

The pincer movement

Some happy coincidences came together to make the task easier. The IPG Board came to recognize that the conventional wisdom in 1994 of business process re-engineering reducing manpower and therefore cost, plus the myopic focus on profit and cash, was not holistic enough to produce tomorrow's viability.

The opportunity to learn across the wider group came when Sir Terence Harrison decided to bring together both the Rolls-Royce Aerospace and IPG Boards for the first time to brainstorm priorities and where the business was going (Stage 5 – sharing new ideas with others). Following this watershed, smaller groups of MDs of trading companies below IPG Board level were formed to take the thinking on to encompass business strategy from a trading company level. Fortunately Kelvin Cox was also chosen to facilitate these groups which then concentrated on *business strategy* and *performance* measures, again using the balanced scorecard technique. It wasn't then difficult to inject the thinking on Guiding Principles (People Strategy) to make it a three-cornered approach.

A framework for the world class company

At about the same time I was introduced to a hierarchy of needs for a world class company devised by James Maxmin, ex-CEO of Laura Ashley (see Figure 4.2).

He has argued that many companies get stuck at the first rung of this ladder, concentrating on **operational excellence**. This is the stuff of business process re-engineering (BPR) but ends up as a qualification for market entry, not a differentiation with the competition. It can be seen as convergent philosophy because all competitors will emulate. Like the stuff of TQ – Quality, Cost and Delivery – it can only give advantage over the competition for the time it takes for the others to catch up. IPG perceived itself to be in this position in 1994, concentrating on operational

---

What does 'world class' demand?

The company that is:

- Strategically led
- Competitively focused
- Market orientated
- Employee driven
- Operationally excellent

What is 'world class'? – Figure 4.2 explained

- Re-engineering not end in itself
- Five attributes
- You know when you are dealing with a World Class Company
  - *Strategically led* – about *not* doing things as well as doing what we are good at – issues of strategic choice. Core competencies. Adapts to changes in market place. Sensitivity. Thinks globally and acts locally.
  - *Competitively focused.* Looks outward, benchmarks against competition. Boundaryless/teams/anti-hierarchical. Looks at other World Class Companies. Concept of strength.
  - *Market oriented.* Seeing Business through eyes of customer. Does it create value to customer? Way of life. Way of thinking: actions never punished if designed to add value for customer.
  - *Employee driven.* Senses and embraces change. Own momentum. Training – Education. Reward system. Learning based. Access to information and authority to act. Exciting, fun, challenge, enjoys no complacency.
  - *Operationally excellent* – usual start (and end) point. Stuff of re-engineering = fallacy. Rarely adds value – without and inside business. Qualification not differentiation.

Fig. 4.2 *James Maxmin's hierarchy of needs for a world class company*

excellence via BPR and a focus on profit and cash (see Figure 4.3). This can be seen as Tacit to Tacit, Stage 1.

The four rungs above, according to Maxmin, can potentially add value for the aspiring world class company (this is coincident with Professor Michael Porter's thesis that companies need to go beyond operational excellence to make strategic choices; see Chapter 6).

By 1995 Rolls-Royce IPG had spread its mental wings and had embryonic policies in place two or maybe three rungs up into the value added area.

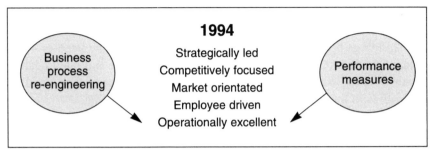

Fig. 4.3 *The changes in Rolls-Royce IPG*

Guiding Principles for people strategy were in place; business strategy was very much on the agenda and the perspective on performance measures was widening. Added to which, customer care programmes were being added in various IPG trading companies (not easy in one-off capital programmes where repeat orders are unlikely) (see Figure 4.4) – again progression through Stages 2 to 4 of the Knowledge Creation Cycle.

Progress in Rolls-Royce from 1996 onwards has been in the area of making hard decisions on strategic choices, for example withdrawing from markets where there is no future despite past investment and commitment. I would argue that the mindset is not free to progress to strategic choice unless it achieves in stages the fifth rung – strategically led.

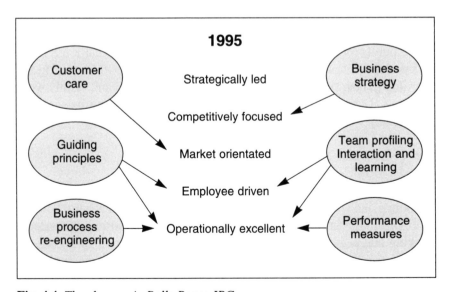

Fig. 4.4 *The changes in Rolls-Royce IPG*

Do we work as a team?

The 'holdings board' model of the IPG Board in 1994 saw itself more as a coalition of interests than a team. Distance and time militated against closer working – after all you don't bring the President of the Canadian companies to the UK too many times a year unless it's vital.

However, I had two problems in this context. First, we had agreed that to avoid mistakes in high-level recruitment, a range of psychometric and assessment tests would be used to aid management decision. Hence the users should understand personally what they meant. Second, it was my view that the biggest problem a board that wishes to develop has to deal with is denial – denial that prevents people facing reality, that gets encumbered by position, rank, speciality, history and in particular poor interaction between its members. I didn't have consensus on the last point but Richard Maudslay was certainly convinced on the former.

Hence I launched into a career-limiting (personal) initiative of encouraging the whole Board to go through team profiling in a similar fashion to any prospective candidate. Fortunately it went down well with the individual Board members who agreed to a collective feedback at the next Board away-day. This was a major breakthrough; it put team profiling on the map for the Board and it encouraged its use in trading companies. Myers Briggs personality preferences and Action Profile[1] became part of the language and those with a different profile from the majority were encouraged to contribute where before they may well have 'kept their heads down'. Various layers of management started to appreciate the value of different profiles aiding decision making in a world that tended to be purely dominated by measurement of historical hard facts and undervalued intuition, feeling and perception. By 1996 it was heart-warming to hear the IPG Board describe itself as a team and visibly work as a team. (Again in Knowledge Creation Cycle terms this was accelerated learning from Stages 2 to 4 with new converts off to Stage 5!)

Getting from here to there

The necessary measures were in place potentially to scale James Maxmin's ladder by adding some prescriptions from Richard Senge's Fifth Discipline in terms of shared vision, strategic positioning, systems thinking and personal mastery (see Figure 4.5), the former springing out of the experiential work within IPG on business strategy – a compilation of the trading companies' work with judgement on potential synergies between elements of the group, and the latter being linked to the Personal

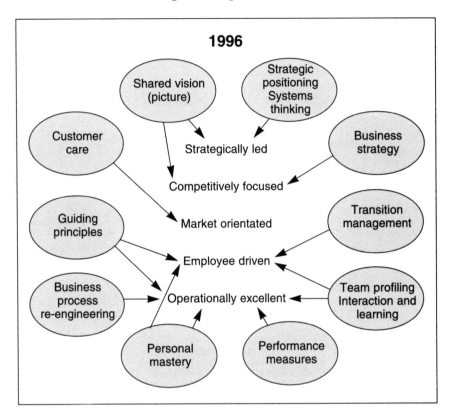

Fig. 4.5 *The changes in Rolls-Royce IPG*

development, Leadership and Relationships modules of the Guiding Principles.

Some brilliant work resulted in the evolution of the IPG 'stick of rock' model for competency development, linking continuous professional development for engineers and specialists through to experiential competencies required for top management, giving a perspective of competency development for the individual with a constant relevance throughout his or her career of those personality factors both inherent and capable of development (see Figure 4.6). Such progress would not have been conceivable without the freedom of expression achieved through the iterative learning process (see Figure 4.7).

The last vehicle for accelerated development was that of *'transition management'*, a term borrowed from William Bridges' book *Managing Transitions*. Bridges' work was distributed widely because it has some powerful messages for managing change.

Bridges reinforces the vital issue of 'process' in bringing about effective

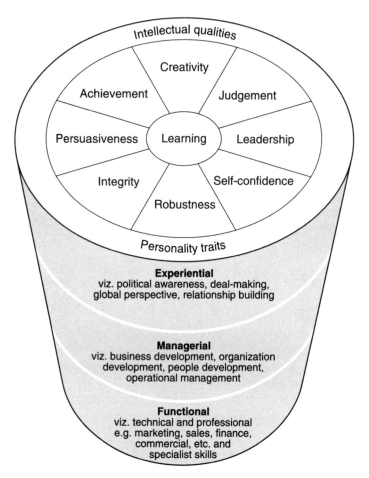

Fig. 4.6 *The 'stick of rock' model for competency development*

change. He postulates that there are three phases in transition within companies: *Ending*, *Neutral Zone* and *Beginning*. All these phases have to be managed effectively. Decision-makers often skip these phases in their mind and therefore do not enable their employees, who are forced through this change process, either to catch up or to be properly supported.

The analogies used in the book are valuable and memorable. Bridges uses the illustration of the 'marathon effect' to make the point about the phases of change. 'The frontrunners take off like rabbits ... about the time the Sunday runners (at the rear) have speeded up, some of the frontrunners are finished and thinking of the next race!' Company executives have gone through transition long ago – they forget that their followers are still struggling.

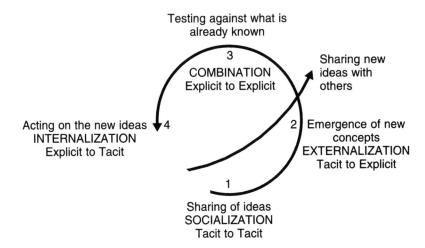

Testing against what is
already known

3
COMBINATION
Explicit to Explicit

Sharing new
ideas with
others

Acting on the new ideas 4
INTERNALIZATION
Explicit to Tacit

2 Emergence of new
concepts
EXTERNALIZATION
Tacit to Explicit

1

Sharing of ideas
SOCIALIZATION
Tacit to Tacit

Fig. 4.7 *Knowledge Creation Cycle applied to change in Rolls-Royce IPG*

Another image that rang true concerned the issue of letting go and leaving the old routes behind. Bridges uses the powerful story of the Spanish conquistador Cortez: 'When he came ashore with his men at Veracruz, he knew that they had great ambivalence about the task ahead of them. Some called it hopeless. Faced with a continent full of adversaries, everyone must have wished they had never come. Cortez burned the ships.'

The high point of the book is Bridges' description of the 'neutral zone' – the area given the least attention by management, and one that can be the most fruitful. The process described in this zone reminded me of the Lewin framework of *unfreezing*, *moving* and *refreezing*, and the opportunities for using this middle period of change creatively.

Bridges provides some useful frameworks for energizing employees in their transition through the neutral zone and for management to launch the 'beginnings' in a simple context to ensure understanding, motivation and involvement. Significantly, he avoids the populist term 'vision' for the way forward, preferring 'picture' to distance himself from 'mystical powers and fantasies'. He says many managers need a quantifiable plan, not an undefinable vision.

Finally, in dealing with non-stop change, Bridges produces a cascade of challenges and responses related to descending levels of management. These aim to break 'the strategic hold of passivity'; to produce a creative response and to restore a sense of control and purpose.

Levels of change	What is meant	Unfreezing	Movement	Refreezing
Individuals	Skills, values and attitudes	Reductions in numbers Training focus	Demonstrate new skills New super-vision/ leadership Personal mastery	Make behaviour patterns secure against change Commitment in line with new values
Structure and systems	Pay systems Reporting relationships Work design	BPR Business training Business strategy (BS) Performance measures (PM) Experiential training	Transition management Changes in reward systems Reporting relationships Systems thinking	Ensure delivery supports rhetoric Performance appraisal
Climate or culture	Openness Conflict management Decision-making	Guiding principles (GP) Communication Customer care	More trust and openness Top management commitment Shared vision Integration of: GP:BS:PM	Committed to use databased feed-back on climate and management practices

Fig. 4.8 *Lewin's change model, Rolls-Royce IPG 1995/6*

The Lewin framework

Readers of *Becoming World Class* will be familiar with my fondness for the Lewin framework as a matrix and mapping tool for creating understandable perspective on the stages of change and how it affects individuals, systems and culture. The Rolls-Royce IPG version is shown in Figure 4.8.

Peebles Electric: a case study in transformation

The overall story of change in IPG of course masks what was happening in detail in each of the companies. The story of trust and transformation at Peebles Electric in Edinburgh spans both conventional re-engineering and radical people change as Ingersoll Engineers described at the end of 1995: 'Imagine a traditional British engineering company in an unglamorous capital goods sector. Weak margins, a competitive, declining home market and traditional practices together equal a running battle for survival.'

Now consider another: its predominantly export-based business includes a recent flagship £9m Chinese order (attributed directly to its competitiveness). Turnover and margins are increasing rapidly.

Twenty-four months apart, these snapshots of Peebles Electric – once of NEI, now part of Rolls-Royce IPG – sit either side of a fast-moving, intensive and people-orientated change programme.

Challenge

The transformation began in August 1993. Arriving at the 90-year-old East Pilton, Edinburgh site (today employing around 600), new managing director Campbell Barr found a gloomy prospect.

Orders for Peebles' transformers (accounting for two-thirds of annual turnover – today around £45m) from the UK's electricity supply industry, power generators and major industrial companies had reduced to a trickle. Export, meanwhile, was minimal and, at best, on a break-even basis.

Survival and success, Barr and his team concluded, required a major switch to export. Achieving this goal – and overseas sales today account for a fast-rising 55 per cent of turnover against 20 per cent two years ago – demanded major cost reductions to boost competitiveness and margins.

As a critical preliminary, external business pressures indicated a need for a final 'downsizing' to remove 36 per cent of costs. Communicated openly and in detail, this move, says Barr, 'set a benchmark. Everyone understood from the outset that we had to find ways of doing the same with less.' (REALITY) – this can be seen as similar to the seemingly impossible challenge by Canon executives for a new-generation copier at half the price of the old one (see Chapter 3, p. 44).

Breaking the mould

The next step was to set about revolutionizing the business – working to a plan developed and co-managed by Ingersoll Engineers under the banner of 'Project Transform'.

'The key,' explains Ingersoll Engineers' Alv Hill, 'was a commitment to overturn traditional department-based organization and hierarchy both on the shopfloor and, crucially, throughout the company.' (new concepts – Tacit to Explicit)

Fundamental to this approach was detailed analysis of Peebles 'contract unique' business and its market–sell–engineer–make process. This required the business re-design to begin at the point of lead identification rather than, as conventionally, working from order-to-delivery.

'If every design is unique and only completed after order, then tendering becomes particularly critical', says Hill. The solution: at the new organization's sharp end sits a multi-functional 'tendering' cell with a team ranging from sales and marketing to design and purchasing.

Behind it lie three customer service cells – again multi-functional.

Behind again lies a fully cellular manufacturing operation – backed by one service cell and one core-cutting cell – not recognized then but effectively a 'hypertext' organization à la Nonaka and Takeuchi![2]

Gaining commitment

In parallel, and fuelling the reorganization's effectiveness, accountability was transferred downwards to project management level – treating each cell as a fully functioning mini-business.

'Previously,' notes Barr, 'from tendering onwards the implications of estimating (with direct and overhead time often accounting for 40 per cent plus of a job) were poorly understood while relevant performance measures were lacking throughout.'

'Today, the reverse applies. Every cell has published targets for both materials and hours on each job so everyone knows exactly what is required: meeting, or beating, these goals makes for healthy competition.'

Embedding this new philosophy, as personnel director Bill Wyper confirms, required 'winning the commitment of the people'.

From the outset, Wyper and the Ingersoll team found them supportive, concerned with job retention but willing to change. However, pulling this through required a large-scale programme of open communications and training (today averaging around six days per employee per annum) designed to shift the focus from individuals to teams. (combination: Explicit to Explicit)

This was complemented by regular benchmark activities exposing multi-skilled, multi-level teams to other successful change programmes (as at Edinburgh neighbours, Blue Circle).

For his part, Wyper measures progress by noting that changes which would once have taken months to negotiate 'today take hours'. On the other side, the real key is suggested perhaps by the union works convenor, Alan Middlemiss: 'There must be TRUST between both parties. This trust must come first from management who hold most of the aces.' (acting on the new ideas internalization Explicit to Tacit)

Technology

Other parallels with Nonaka and Takeuchi enabling conditions (see Chapter 2, p. 19) can be seen in the Peebles case study:

> *Organizational intention*: Campbell Barr made clear what the goal was.
> *Autonomy*: The cells were encouraged to have sufficient autonomy for self-motivation and learning across multi-functional teams.
> *Creative chaos*: It felt very chaotic to those comfortable with the traditional hierarchical approach but at the same time creative and exciting.
> *Surfeit of information*: Over-communication was the target – rotation between groups lubricated knowledge.
> *Variety within*: Peebles gained an external perspective by benchmarking and understanding a complex external world.

The second 'fuel' for Peebles' increased competitiveness lay in a focused effort to improve individual processes.

By 1996, new estimating programmes in the tendering and customer service cells collapsed lead times on specific projects. 'More important,' added Campbell Barr, 'they laid the basis of an embedded archive of knowledge' (now we can see the process).

Barr, too, was looking for further major gains. 'At present, the typical Peebles transformer contains only 5 per cent of standard parts: building on our new knowledge and using enhanced CAD techniques we expect to reach 50 per cent by mid-1996.'

This, he believed, should stimulate a virtuous circle. 'As modular design extends and the design lead time is collapsed from twelve to a target four weeks, so we should be able to run more business through.'

Futures

Looking ahead, the Peebles team saw speed of response matching competitive price as critical factors in its turnaround. There is also what Barr calls the 'morale effect': 'the ability to show Peebles as a living, progressive company is definitely part of our success. This, and the open culture, have impressed visitors from all over the world.'

I would argue that speed of response is a function of culture change. Professor David Ulrich of Michigan University believes that culture change is the only true source of competitive advantage (Figure 4.9).

> **'Culture Change creates a unique competitive advantage that competitors cannot replicate'**
>
> David Ulrich
> Professor, University of Michigan

Fig. 4.9

Intelligence

Two years on from his August arrival, Barr had much with which to be pleased. On key measures such as cost reduction, adjusted to a like-for-like basis, materials costs were down by 6 per cent and labour hours down by 9 per cent – both, he believed, with considerably more to come.

Meanwhile on the critical measure of tendering successes, Peebles had 'transformed' a below 5 per cent hit-rate to over 10 per cent. The real 'driver', Barr concluded, is the 'replacement of endless cabinets of information with a proactive multi-functional team'.

A new pay structure

In the wake of new Guiding Principles and at the end of the re-engineering exercise described above, Bill Wyper decided to tackle the difficult problem of restructuring pay to suit the new cellular structure at Peebles.

A multi-disciplinary 'diagonal slice' team was formed to find a way forward. Benchmark exercises were undertaken with Blue Circle, Scottish Power and BP Grangemouth all of whom had restructured pay systems for different reasons.

The criteria they established for the new reward system were:

- Transparent
- Applies to all categories of employee
- The grades to reflect business structure
- Encourages continuous improvement
- Relates reward to contribution
- Durable and adaptable
- Removes existing anomalies
- Recognizes success

The striking element about this work was the nature of the team. It was self-managed, did not include any personnel professionals, and was representative of all sections in the factory. It drew on benchmarking and external expertise to come up with workable solutions potentially acceptable to management and unions. The important lesson to me is not the result but the manner of arriving at the result – the process. As Angela Bowey, doyenne of pay systems, would have put it, 'the durability of a new pay structure is a function of the *process in design* not the end result'.

International parallels

My experience at Rolls-Royce with responsibility for operations and factories in overseas locations such as Canada and South Africa taught me that these change issues and processes are totally universal. Rolls-Royce Canada, a vibrant company that services and overhauls aero-engines for all major world airlines, had gone through a fundamental transformation, adopting total quality and encouraging potential throughout its workforce. The then Vice President – Personnel, Jean Guillbault, led a team that united with the trade unions to make the plant one of the foremost in terms of productivity and change in the whole of Canada.

The Ferranti-Packard plant at Trois Rivières in Quebec was led by an enigmatic French Canadian, Gilbert D'Amour – a total enthusiast for Deming teaching, and self-directed teams that from what was a small plant with narrow product lines (pole top transformers for the Eastern Canada market) produced unequalled quality at competitive prices with good margins.

Similar processes were adopted elsewhere in Canada and South Africa – the Guiding Principles (Appendix B) were designed with a worldwide audience in mind and Jean among others contributed greatly to their evolution and implementation.

Conclusions

We have shown that with the ultimate advantage of hindsight the change examples at IPG and Peebles Electric in particular bear out the knowledge-creating theories of Nonaka and Takeuchi. Also, that knowledge creation and change are inextricably linked. The middle-up-down model for knowledge-creating managers evolved at Peebles in a really formative way, with proactive middle managers forming exactly the 'strategic knot' that binds top management with the front line – working as a bridge between the visionary ideals of the top and the often chaotic realities of the shop floor.

The overall mental picture I have of the Rolls-Royce experience of change is that of breaking up the ice cap. In that sense it was easy to see results quite quickly – previously constrained talent welcomed the fresh air. What was common to other change experiences was the need to see the wood for the trees. That is where I believe the various models help.

II   SERVICE SECTOR: PUBLIC TO PRIVATIZED HEALTH AND UTILITIES

The health service

In 1992 I was invited to help form the Board for Gateshead Hospitals as part-time non-executive chairman in addition to my role at Northern Electric. Gateshead Hospitals was to be a 'third wave' trust under the 1989 NHS reforms following the White Paper 'Working for Patients' (DoH, 1989).

The operation of the NHS in the UK has been a matter of deep concern to politicians, the population at large, and in particular to those employed in the NHS, since its inception in 1948. Despite the rhetoric often used, the consensus is in favour of the fairly unique UK solution to the universal problem of health provision and the nation has taken the NHS to its heart. The biggest problem for government over the decades has been the escalating cost in relation to insatiable demand for health services. Other related problems which can reverberate loudly in the corridors of power are issues of governance.

Aneurin Bevan, the original Labour minister who acted as midwife at the birth of the NHS, said, 'When a bed pan is dropped on the hospital floor, its noise should resound in the Palace of Westminster'.[3]

Because the nation has taken the NHS to its heart, reforms based on logic and rationale tend to create heated debate and vehement defence, particularly from differing sectional interests.

An overwhelming characteristic of the NHS has been the acceptance from the outset that the service rests on certain separate pillars:

- Medical autonomy
- Nursing autonomy
- Administrative hierarchy
- Lay membership for governance

Some pillars were distinctly more important than others. The principle of medical or clinical autonomy has been respected by government and managers alike as giving doctors the right to define individual patient care and overall patterns of health policy right up to the 1989 reforms. It is this change that probably marks the 1989 reforms as substantially different from any of the earlier attempts by government to reform the NHS in tackling both resource and governance issues.

Self-governing trusts as the provider agencies within an internal market were the major structural innovation contained in 'Working for Patients'.

This potentially gave the opportunity for radical change in the power relationship between doctors and managers in the NHS. Also, the influence of lay members of hospital boards prior to 1989 has been seen by commentators as ineffectual. Rather the administrators or officers have been seen as the dominant element in the governance of the NHS prior to 1989, whether the lay members were from the voluntary sector or local government.

The practice of clinical autonomy goes back far beyond the creation of the NHS. S. Harrison in *Managing the National Health Services – Shifting the Frontier* (1988) defines this as: 'Choice of specialty and practice location; control over earnings; control over the nature and volume of tasks; control over acceptance of patients; control over diagnosis and treatment; control over the evaluation of care; and control over other professionals.'

Prior to the NHS there was little evidence of separate administration in hospitals. Most of these tasks were carried out by the matron responsible to a board of governors. Nursing autonomy as a separate pillar in hospitals was already crumbling in 1948.

> The clinical activities of nurses were circumscribed by doctors and carried out under the overall direction of doctors. It is significant that in the numerous accounts of the creation of the NHS, nurses and their representatives are conspicuous by their absence or marginality and the introduction of the new national health service did nothing, in itself, to enhance their status or role.[4]

By 1989 nurses were subject to the managerial authority of managers within each hospital and indeed are today broadly absorbed in the management cadre – many managers in the NHS having come the nursing route.

The Griffiths Report in 1984 addressed the need for a clear management hierarchy with general managers at each level of the NHS being accountable for the performance at that level. Hence the radical reforms in 1989 rightly focused, following the Griffiths Report, on enhancing the local management of patient care. These reforms then gave the opportunity to resolve on a sensible basis, locally, the competing claims for dominance between medical autonomy, administrative hierarchy and an enhanced lay membership. The driver behind all this was the need to contain costs which were spiralling out of control – to an extent due to a lack of resolution of conflict between these power groups.

The logic that underpinned the reforms was identified by the Social Services Committee findings in 1994[5] as

- a considerably enhanced independent role for authority chairmen
- doctors must accept the management responsibility that goes with clinical freedom
- engagement of doctors more intimately in the management process
- new general managers working in tandem with an increasingly influential chairman seen by the DHSS as the champion of central policy.[6]

The views of commentators vary enormously as to whether the 1989 reforms have been successful and met their objectives. This is not the place to come to a judgement on that issue. My interest in including the subject matter is to set the context for the changes achieved in Gateshead Hospitals between 1992 and 1996, reinforcing the argument that 'Working for Patients' provided the *opportunity* for change – inevitably some trusts and authorities took the opportunity and others didn't. A key issue has been whether doctors have been engaged more intimately in the management process.

Harrison[7] reports on the conclusions of structured interviews with doctors, nurses and managers conducted in 1989. Three anecdotal quotations capture the spirit of the views of consultants on the impact of general management at that time. 'Management stops at the consulting room door'; 'Management has nothing to do with what I do'; 'Power to act against the few clinicians who don't give two hoots.'

On the other hand there are now, since 1989, many examples of doctors who have become fully engaged in the management process and have, for instance, even been actively marketing clinical services on behalf of hospitals, as expressed by a GP (non-fundholder) who summed up the positive changes as 'now I get Christmas cards from Consultants instead of the other way around!'.

Operating NHS Trusts in practice: Acute Trust No. 1

In 1992, as a newly designated chairman of Gateshead Hospitals, I found the NHS language confusing. The environment created by the 1989 reforms was one of the internal market – of purchasers and providers, the logic being that health professionals on behalf of patients (purchasers) specified what services would be required from hospitals (providers) based on health needs assessment for what is termed secondary and tertiary care, and primary care being largely community based via GPs, clinics, district nurses, mental health support and so on.

Gateshead Hospitals, which comprised two hospitals south of the

Tyne (one a 487-bed acute hospital and a 150-bed rehabilitation unit for respite and long-term patient care), were to be the 'provider', following the District General Hospital model of pre-1989 reforms, for the 250 000 population of Gateshead. It had done a workmanlike if unexciting job for the District for many years with some areas of clinical excellence marred by poor performance in others and a lack of corporate feel and zest.

The new Board, fitting the formula of 'Self Governing Hospitals' (DoH (1989) Cmmd 555, HMSO), comprised a non-executive chairman, five further non-executives from the locality and five executives from hospital management (officers in pre-1989 jargon) including Chief Executive, Finance Director, Medical Director, Director of Nursing and Director of HR.

Officers were for the first time in the history of the NHS to join the governing body as members. Also, the non-executive members tended to be drawn from industry and the professions rather than elected councillors from previous models. Non-executive directors were to be 'chosen for the contribution they personally can make to the effective management of the hospital'.[8] 'The NHS needs business-minded men and women with the skills, drive and determination to help it meet the increasing demands for high quality health care.'[9] This emphasis was to change yet again with the Labour administration's changes in 1997.

WHAT WAS TO BE DIFFERENT?

The role of trust directors was specified by the NHS Management Executive in 1990 as:

- to share corporate responsibility for policy and decision making within the trust;
- to monitor progress towards agreed targets (NHSME, 1990, p.1).

The NHS guidance also led non-executive members into the internal management of the trust:[10]

Non-Executive Directors of NHS Trusts may be involved in the work of Committees or Sub-Committees in particular:
(a) to hear appeals by detained patients
(b) to hear staff appeals on terms and conditions of service and disciplinary matters
(c) to monitor procedures for dealing with complaints
(d) to appoint executive directors and consultant medical staff

New powers were to be given to trusts to govern their own affairs:[11]

- Trusts should be free to employ whatever and however many staff they consider necessary.
- Trusts should settle the pay and conditions of staff
- Trusts would be able to own their own assets
- Trust would be free to borrow, either from Government or from the private sector.

There were exceptions, of course. Junior doctors were exempted from the personnel freedoms. The Secretary of State maintained a reserve power to intervene in disposal of assets. The borrowing power was to be constrained by an overall limit.

However, many of the personnel freedoms represented, in concept at least, a significant shift. Prior to 1989, consultants' contracts were held by the NHS region but their services deployed by the District and so-called management of the resources within each hospital with, of course, from 1948 significant freedom for consultants to operate in the private sector alongside their NHS contracts. Merit awards had been determined by the peers of consultants, awarded by Royal Colleges and, often without prior warning, expected to be funded by the hospital(s) concerned. Dealing with performance issues whether personal or professional was a nightmare, often involving tortuous legal proceedings where the split managerial responsibilities outlined above inevitably undermined the strongest of cases.

The 1989 reforms gave the platform for change in consultant management in that:

- Consultant contracts were to be held by the provider (hospital) unit.
- Managers to agree job descriptions and workload issues with consultants ... take part directly in the appointment of consultants, in disciplinary proceedings and play a role in bestowing merit awards.
- Management should be responsible for ensuring that an effective system of medical audit is in place ... the general results of medical audit should be available to management ... management should be able to initiate an independent professional audit.

Commenting on the changes, R. Klein[12] said that 'decisions about what counts for good performance in the NHS could not be delegated exclusively to the medical profession ... the bargain offered *was more influence in managerial decision making in return for less autonomy in medical decision making.*'

IS THE JURY STILL OUT ON NHS TRUST PERFORMANCE?

The structural changes encapsulated by 'Working for Patients' gave the platform for change which was taken up to a greater or lesser extent by all trusts. The effectiveness of trust boards has varied and the performance results of trusts have also been variable. My own view is that there has been an overall improvement in performance as trusts have taken the opportunity of self-management, involving professionals in operation and direction and establishing partnership with purchasers, GPs and external bodies.

Edward Peck in his unpublished PhD thesis for Newcastle University entitled 'Power and Decision-making in the National Health Service' (1996) studied the performance of a Mental Health Trust Board from 1991 through to 1992 and has produced comparative data on other similar trusts elsewhere in the UK. He concludes from an analysis of board meeting content that 'the contribution of the board on the major issues facing the Trust had been marginal rather than useful' (p.188) and that 'the introduction of non-executive directors into the Trust Board has failed to change the balance of power between managers (now executive directors) and members (non-executive directors) that has been common to the NHS for over 40 years' (p. 219).

However, Edward Peck does conclude that the relationship between managers and doctors has changed: 'there is convincing evidence that a shift in the balance of power had started between managers and doctors in the NHS as a consequence of both the content of the White Paper and the manner in which the DoH and the NHSME chose to promote and implement the reforms' (p. 221).

The struggle he identifies for non-executives is due to alienation on the part of non-executives and the history of managers holding all the cards. 'The NHS Management Executive set out to try to recruit business people as non-executive directors who did not have product knowledge. Secondly, the NHS has a long tradition of senior officers judging their success with the members of their authorities on the extent to which they could achieve quiet acquiescence' (p. 226).

The latter comment rings true for any board with public service antecedents – including privatized industries such as utilities to which we will come later in the chapter.

WHERE DOES THIS LEAVE GATESHEAD HOSPITALS NHS TRUST?

The inclusion as a third wave trust in 1993 gave Gateshead Hospitals an opportunity for change, which was seized by the executives and non-executives alike.

The management team was new – the Chief Executive Chris Reed had been responsible for business planning for Northern Region and was keen to cut his teeth as a chief executive in a new trust where results would matter. The enthusiasm for tackling problems was shared by the Board as a whole and these were seen in the following broad areas:

- New freedoms and opportunities provided by the White Paper, such as corporate responsibility for policy and decision making; developing aims and objectives; monitoring performance
- Influencing personnel policies, key appointments, local negotiation
- Tackling the poor perception of Gateshead as a hospital in some areas of clinical service and administrative efficiency
- Understanding and gaining advantage of the complicated internal market framework for the benefit of the trust.

FIRST STEPS – DEVELOPING THE LEARNING BOARD

The Board realized it needed to understand the world it (now jointly) existed in and much more about itself. It needed to go through the classic, forming, storming, norming process if it was to be a team.

In the Gateshead case, because of the personalities involved, the concept of the Board as a team was not difficult. This, as I have since discovered, is a rarity – as discussed earlier in the chapter, gaining understanding from the outset that a combination of executives and non-executives can be a team is the exception, not the rule.

One of our first sessions in 1993 consisted of two full days away using the Belbin personality inventory, gaining understanding of what each member brought to the Board, including the clinical directors who were in post. This was understanding strengths and weaknesses, how to form decision-making teams and how to use the new-found knowledge in a dynamic fashion. At the same time, both to determine forward strategies and to practise in our new groupings, we clustered the issues facing the trust to determine priorities and how we were going to tackle them (see Figure 4.10).

Each member of the Board, both executive and non-executive, and each clinical director was encouraged to specify his or her self-perceived role (see Appendix C) and then to cross-match to the analysed result from the Belbin inventory.

Finally the two days away focused on how we were to work as a team (see Figure 4.11). This I suppose was Stage 2 of the Knowledge Creation Cycle, Tacit to Explicit (see p. 16). The 'forming' of the team carried over

- Surgical service developments
  - Risk analysis of service development and recruitment of new resources in general surgery and urology. Negotiation with purchasers.

- Benchmarking. What are other similar trusts doing in these areas?
  - Development of clinical directorates
  - Management information systems
  - Quality initiatives

- Management structure
  - Analysing resistors and drivers (force field analysis)
  - Interim management arrangements for clinical directorates
  - Membership and frequency
  - Strategy for areas of hospital not covered by clinical directorates

- Improving internal communications
  - Establish diagonal slice group
  - Plans – implementation

- Quality of discharge information
  - Tuning to what GPs require
  - How quickly and method of delivery

- Links with voluntary organizations

Fig. 4.10 First team tasks: How we saw it in April 1993

into practice when Barrie Watson (CERT), our Belbin facilitator, joined several Board meetings as an observer to analyse how we did and help us improve the use of time. Figure 4.12 gives a sample analysis of part of this exercise in terms of the value of the contribution to the debate. It shows a Board in its tentative early stages gaining understanding and not yet being mature enough to be formative or challenging – Stage 3 Explicit to Explicit.

Looking back, it is significant that the priorities indicated by Appendix C shows a concentration, albeit necessarily, on internal issues – the question of relationships with purchasers is hardly considered. However, comparing it with the theoretical model of the Learning Board (see Chapter 6), it was a start.

This was the perception of priorities for the trust in those early days. We knew we had things to improve within our own walls and that was where the concentration was to be.

- Role to have clear and clearly stated objectives.

- Behave with openness and trust providing support and review.

- When opportunities arise or created, spread the (Belbin) gospel of team roles and teamworking.

- Trained facilitators in the hospital to be used to set up awareness sessions.

- Team working principles to be used in the spheres of influence by each member.

- Team roles to be used and developed widely to complement and integrate with functional roles.

- Review team roles and dynamics at the end of each meeting.
  - How did we work as a team?
  - Were there things we could have organized better?
  - Were there individual issues that arose that we should address?

Fig. 4.11 Gateshead Hospitals: Principles for teamworking

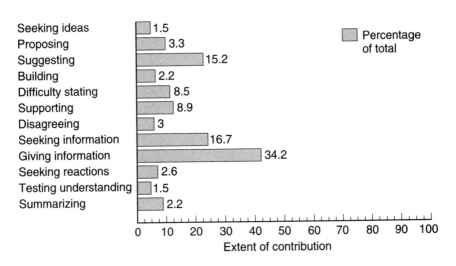

Fig. 4.12 *Gateshead Hospitals Board meeting 9/3/93. Nature of contribution*

This was, of course, the created environment in which we were launched: an artificial environment, based on market theory, to help focus on the separate issues of assessment of health needs, priorities and where money was to be spent (purchasers) and delivery of health solutions for patients and the population at large (providers).

The logic in the early days was taken even further to create definite separation, 'Chinese Walls' of information, between purchasers and providers. This fed the natural NHS tendency to play Machiavellian games and undermine trust.

Coming from the immediate background of Komatsu (for detail see *Becoming World Class*) I knew that for progress of the whole – the provision of health care – divide and rule would only inhibit progress. If manufacturing needed close working relationships with suppliers/customers then so did health care. The promotion of adversarial stances seemed an absolute nonsense.[14]

CONCENTRATION ON CREATING THE CORPORATE VIEW (TACIT TO EXPLICIT)

For the moment, in 1993, we had to get the base right, to ensure we were functioning properly, integrating resources within the hospital and gaining synergy. We believed we needed a corporate focus. At that time, for clinicians, it was immaterial where they operated – it could be at the base in Gateshead or any number of other hospitals.

Many of them saw the task of running the hospital as purely providing the environment for them to operate, in the way they had been trained over the years, to standards of excellence. I heard clinicians express a total detachment from any other responsibility:

'Budgets? That's not my affair, when I run out of money I come and ask for more – I have total clinical freedom – it is your task to run the hospital!'

'Management, you want me to participate in management? Who is going to make up for the time I would lose in clinical practice by sitting around in meetings?'

The comments, taking a historical view of clinical autonomy, are part and parcel of the same logic and in that context defensible – it appeared to the clinician that his or her time and concentration was to be watered down with the stuff of no-added value, administration.

We had to show that it was in the long-term interest for the professionals to identify with the hospital and its goals, and that their investment in time would pay off. At the outset Chris Reed had done a good selling job to a number of clinical specialists and in deciding on the 'clinical director' route had gained agreement for four out of a subsequent nine specialities to join the overall management team (see Figure 4.13 for the eventual GHT management structure, showing how complex health operations are).

The four new clinical directors participated from the start in the new approach (see Figure 4.10 for the self-perceived roles dating from April 1993). The next task was to persuade the rest to come on board. At a local level it was exactly as R. Klein (1989) analysed for the whole of the NHS in terms of the unspoken bargain in 1989 (see p. 76): 'The bargain offered was more influence in managerial decision making in return for less autonomy in medical decision making.'

This was not always straightforward. The benefits of such an arrangement were not immediately obvious and some clinicians were still vehemently in opposition to the NHS reforms and the potential change in the balance of power between doctors and managers.

OPPORTUNISM AND TIMING!

Persuasion and building of trust progressively brought more on board. However, on one famous occasion confrontational negotiation skills were called for. One particular head of a clinical speciality even refused to meet me to discuss the issue of clinical directorates. I tried the softer approach of an invitation to dinner but that was rebuffed. I then heard from Chris Reed that this particular clinician was due to come to the office to discuss workload issues with Chris. I deliberately interrupted the meeting to introduce myself. I referred to the issue of clinical directorates and the policy we had in Gateshead of positively involving clinicians in the management of the hospital. With scarce resources and with what I knew of his ambitious shopping list of service improvements, how could we prioritize and allocate to his advantage without his voice at the table? Having lit the blue touch paper I retired to a safe distance. I was then the bad guy and Chris with his usual aplomb was able to build bridges and bring the next clinical directorate on board.

Clinicians were not the only sectarian group to integrate. Nurses were historically more absorbed in day-to-day hospital management and broadly there was no divide in the thinking on this inside or outside the hospital. The post of Director of Nursing was widened in scope at

	Designation	Scope
Clinical Directorates	CD Medicine	Medicine, Elderly Care, Rheumatology, Cardiology, A&E, Chest Medicine, Diabetes
	CD AICUTE	Anaesthetics, ITU, Theatres, Endoscopy
	CD Breast Screening	Breast Screening
	CD Obstetrics & Gynaecology	Maternity (including community), Gynaecology, SCBU
	CD Children's Services	Paediatrics, Child & Family Psychiatry
	CD Pathology	including Clinical Laboratory services
	CD Diagnostic Imaging	X-ray, CT, Ultrasound, Interventional Radiology
	CD Surgery & Urology	General Surgery (including Breast Surgery), Urology
	CD Trauma & Orthopaedics	Trauma, Orthopaedics
	Head of Gynaecological Oncology	Specialist Women's Cancer Surgery
* Chief Executive		
	* Director of Nursing, Midwifery, Rehabilitation & Business Planning	Nursing, Outpatients, Pharmacy, Midwifery, Physio, Business Planning/Contracting, ENT Link, R&D, League of Friends Link, Clinical Audit, Dietetics, Occ. Therapy
	* Director of Human Resources & Contracting	Personnel, Organizational Development, Contracting/Business Planning, Occ. Health, Chaplaincy, PR & Marketing, Training/ Development, Management Services.
	* Director of Finance	Finance, Information & IT, Legal Services VFM Studies, Trust Fund Co-ordination, Red Cross Link
	* Medical Director	Quality, R&D, Clinical Audit, Medical Links
	Director of Estates	Estates, Capital Programme, Probity, Risk Management/ Insurance, WRVS Link
	Director of Operations	Catering, Portering & Transport, Domestic, Laundry, CSSD, Market Testing, Medical Records, Printing & Stationery, Educ'n Centre, Furniture/ Fittings, Accommo–dation, Car Parks, Security, Telephones, Supplies, Inter Unit Contracts, CHC Link

Notes:
1. CD = Clinical Director
2. R&D is shared between Medical Director and Director of Nursing
3. Contracting is nominally led by Director of HR, and Business Planning by Director of Nursing. In practice, both are part of the same management and planning processes and are therefore shared between the two Directors.
4. * Denotes Executive voting member of Board.

Fig. 4.13 *Gateshead Hospitals Trust management structure*

Gateshead to include critical management issues of business planning and negotiation with purchasers. Nurses have to be pragmatists to survive and that strength can be usefully tapped in other fields.

Non-executive members were a new and potentially wild card. We will deal in Chapter 6 with the dichotomy of thought over the role of the non-executive on boards but in 1993 my perception was that here was a new and rich vein of resource that could help with the corporate view inside and outside the hospital.

We deliberately avoided a cadre approach for non-executives, integrating them in discussions with executives, clinicians, nurse managers and other staff. Their ward visits were not purely designed to 'press the flesh' but to aid the active management and inter-group working. Bed reconfiguration was a hot topic as we approached further financial pressures where ward 'territories' for clinicians needed to be much more flexible to avoid the dramatic headline ward closures that we believed would be the product of a rigid 'what I have I hold' attitude among clinical specialities.

This process of change and learning brought us through Nonaka's four stages. Having put our own house in order we were ready for Stage 5 – sharing new ideas with others.

The next role for non-executives was to promote relationships in the community outside the hospital. Gateshead had become a trust in a very hostile local climate. The North East is traditionally Labour and at the time local politicians were vehemently against Government reforms and forbade councillors from participating in either purchaser or provider activity. The local CHC (Community Health Council – a statutory watch-dog on health care) mainly comprised local Labour councillors who therefore influenced the CHC to, at minimum, keep their distance from the trust and to make negative comments to the press given the opportunity.

Bridge building towards understanding and trust was required and here I found the positive relationships forged with Gateshead Metropolitan Borough Council from my Komatsu days of great benefit. A public relations offensive was also launched. Trust reforms apart, local people did identify with their local hospital in Gateshead even though many local GPs referred some patients across the river to the teaching hospitals in Newcastle upon Tyne. I have the view that the NHS generally too often leaves the press to find the negative, to scoop on stories of bed closures, inability to cope, perceived rationing of care and so on. We mounted a campaign to invite the local press into the hospital periodically to an 'editor's lunch', using the connections non-executives had in the media world. Out of this, using brainstorming, sprang a 'day in the life of' series in the *Gateshead Post* featuring clinicians, nurses and patients.

The time then came to extend an olive branch and invite the CHC to join as partners, not as adversarial observers. Subsequently both CHC and press became such fierce defenders of the Trust that when we were faced with a potential £2m funding gap in 1995/96 they lobbied purchasers and region on our behalf!

The variety of challenges thrown at the Gateshead Trust and the way they were handled showed the benefit of a stable learning board keeping the balance between conformance and performance issues (see also Chapter 6).

Operating NHS Trusts in practice: Acute Trust No. 2

In early 1996 I left Rolls-Royce Industrial Power Group to join Anglian Water as Human Resources Director some 200 miles south of the Rolls-Royce base. Anglian was keen that I retained my non-executive role in the NHS as a contribution to the wider community. I was extremely fortunate to have the support from both Anglian and the NHS to continue for some months completing my work at Gateshead from a distance and later being appointed as chairman of Peterborough Hospitals NHS Trust from November 1996.

In inheriting the chair at Peterborough I found a well-run trust but one that had some mounting challenges not least because of the worsening shortage of revenue to run the hospital and an overdue scheme to consolidate two hospitals onto one site which had excited a lot of local opposition. Peterborough was of the same ilk as Gateshead but larger – over 600 beds with an annual revenue budget of £77m, serving a scattered population of 300 000 split roughly half between urban and rural communities.

The Board was 'Country Club' with a 'distance management' style between non-executive, executive and general management with clinicians and medical staff being poorly represented. The relationships within the 'internal market' varied between adversarial and paternal with little evidence of the partnership style achieved in the North East. Partly this was a product of geography and the personalities involved. This was to change. However, the trust under Chief Executive Malcolm Lowe Lauri had been very innovative in starting a 'transformation project' with the support of 'purchasers' (Health Authority, Primary Care Trust, GPs and the CHC) designed to 're-engineer' processes for the benefit of patients and to improve efficiency.

Cross-functional 'diagonal slice' teams were set up within the hospital with strong links to doctors and health professionals outside the hospital to focus on three key areas:

- Patient visits
- Medical admissions
- Emergency care

WHY WERE THESE THE FOCII?

Essentially because demands in volume and quality terms were increasing year on year and money to fund the provision was falling.

WHAT WAS THE AMBITION?

Patient visit

From	To
Wasted appointments	GP-arranged appointments
Avoidable attendances	Direct access to theatre
Duplication of effort	Multi-skilled clinic staff
Communication	IT-based diagnostic results reporting
Scheduling	Clinic co-ordinator
	GP-managed aftercare
	Single-problem clinics

Medical/Emergency admissions

From	To
Admissions increasing 10% p.a.	Rapid response team
GP having no alternatives to admission	Assessment and observation unit
Hospital staff overloaded – delays in treatment	Specialists in front line
Patients moved within hospital	Direct access to clinics and investigations
Inability to discharge to convalescence	Nursing-home provision
Poor coordination between providers and purchasers	Partnership approach

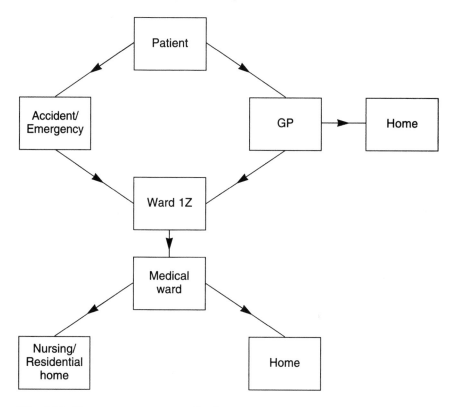

Fig. 4.14 *Current emergency medical care process*

WHAT WOULD THESE CHANGES LOOK LIKE?

The new emergency medical care process allows many more appropriate alternatives to the knee-jerk admission to hospital that gave the 10% increase in admission rate per annum. See Figures 4.14 and 4.15.

The new systems are being brought forward as I write this – a product of partnership involving professionals both inside and outside the hospital. To a manufacturing process engineer it would be perfectly logical, and perhaps inexplicable as to why this hasn't happened before. However, in health care where professionals have jealously guarded their particular special issues and roles for generations and where the internal market health care brought new divisions and functions, such progress is noteworthy if not remarkable. Also, governance within the trust is more like the learning board model with external partnership-style relationships becoming the pattern.

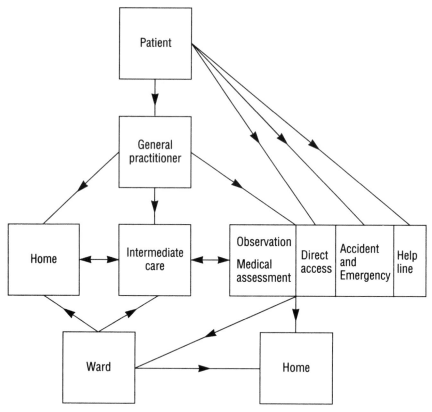

Fig. 4.15 *New emergency medical care process*

Utilities – Anglian Water

The water industry in England and Wales was privatized in 1989 and in parallel with the earlier utility privatizations of telecoms, gas and electricity, each new PLC was suddenly in the business of being commercial, of making a profit, of being responsible to shareholders as well their traditional stakeholders. (For detail on change in the electricity supply industry see *Becoming World Class*, p. 103 ff.)

Since privatization in 1989 Anglian has undergone three fundamental structural changes: the company reduced its workforce by 20 per cent (over 1000 people), became a profit-orientated business and began expanding services beyond the UK – it has now over 1000 people in its International businesses. At the same time it has vastly improved its customer focus, service and delivery while gaining the reputation of a benchmark utility worldwide in terms of performance for its wide range of stakeholders.

Other utilities have gone through similar changes with a prime focus on reduction in the workforce and short-term shareholder gains, and the end result has often been a decline in levels of service both to customers and other stakeholders. Anglian's then Group Managing Director, Alan Smith, was determined that the experience was going to be different.

The start point was that to continue the traditional command and control ethos would not work. Autocratic control was, up to privatization, the insurance against failure. Mistakes in the supply of water can be disastrous (contaminated water cannot be recalled), hence the evolution of a multi-layered hierarchy. The culture was action-based, discouraging development of creativity that could be seen as a deflection from 'the day job'. Employees played by the rules and didn't have the focus to reduce costs and better serve customers.

Between 1993 and 1995 the company undertook a substantial reorganization (Strategic Systems Review (SSR)), designed to reduce the layers of management from 11 to a maximum of five and, in the process, to focus the workforce outwards on the creation of a more customer-orientated business. All of this had to be done without losing water quality and without losing the core public health ethos which had historically underpinned the organization.

In the process of the restructuring 33 per cent of white collar jobs were eliminated, with a saving of £40m. At this level at least, the restructuring had been a success, but employee opinion surveys, while having improved from pre- to post-SSR polling, showed that the company had still some work to do to empower its workforce to respond to the challenges of working in the newly delayered environment. Anxious not to join the 60 to 80 per cent of 're-engineers' which fail at this point in the process, the executive Board spent some time examining how it could improve its leadership of the reorganized business.

Through their own learning 'journey', notably their participation in a specially designed process called 'Executive Stretch', designed by Dr Ronnie Lessem of City University, the Board came to the decision that the most important missing element in the restructuring programme was a process to support the growth and development of the individuals who were most affected – the workforce at large. This resulted in a decision to design and run an 'Exec Stretch for all' programme – later to become known as the '**Transformation Journey**'.

The process has four inputs which are designed to deliver benefits (outputs) in four key areas of the business:

1. Relationships development – self-awareness and communications skills

2. Teamwork – ability to work within and contribute to the growth and development of the work team
3. Operational effectiveness – ability to improve short- to mid-term business/process performance
4. Sustainability – long-term business and environmental improvements.

The Team Learning Cycle

The team learning is divided into a creativity component (Inputs: Parts 1 & 2 – Generating new thinking) and an innovation component (Outputs: Parts 3 & 4 – Acting on new ideas) as shown Figure 4.16.

Readers will quickly recognize that the roots of the Team Learning Cycle are from Nonaka and Takeuchi's work on the Knowledge Creation Cycle (see Chapter 2).

Parts 1 & 2 of each cycle are undertaken during two-day workshops (the 'Travellers Briefs' – abbreviated to TBs) during which teams come together in the company of a facilitator (a 'Journey Guide') to:

- share experiences;
- pass on new knowledge to the organization;
- learn about the next phase of the process;
- decide on a way forward for the team.

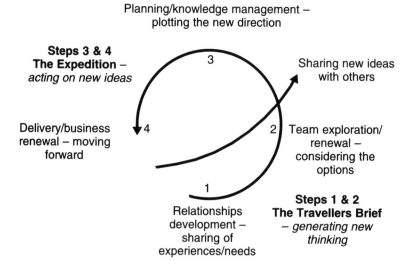

Fig. 4.16 *Team Learning Cycle*

Parts 3 & 4 of the cycle are completed after the workshop, during which (a period of around six months) the team maps and enacts the self-managed learning exercise (the 'Expedition'), when they explore the practical relevance of the issues covered during the workshop.

The Journey begins

In keeping with a key objective of the Journey – that it should be an empowering process supporting a period of substantial organizational change – Journey groups emerge through a completely voluntary process of enrolment. Groups of normally eight to ten people, who may be existing work teams or who may be vertical or horizontal slices of the business, simply request the allocation of a Guide facilitator, set up a date and venue for the first Travellers Brief and then meet on the date agreed. Furthermore, the decisions about the Expeditions they undertake are entirely self-governed – there is no routemap set by management for them to follow.

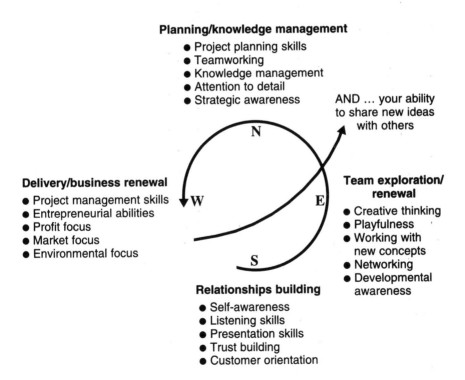

Fig. 4.17 *Team Learning Competencies*

The role of the Guide is to facilitate the process of exploration and learning, recognizing that each of the cycle components has an associated set of competencies (see Figure 4.17), which need to be discussed and developed as the Journey progresses.

In 'journey speak', the travellers pass through the points of the compass equivalent to the four stages of the Knowledge Cycle.

Results

From 1995 to 1997, 3000 Anglian Water employees enrolled voluntarily on the Journey (the number of groups stood at 300 of which to date more than 60 have completed TB III).

The outputs of the Journey have been plotted using a mix of instruments including employee opinion surveys, facilitated self-assessment (team competencies) and data from a two-day review and data collection event known as The Journey Forum (self, team and organizational value) (see Figure 4.18).

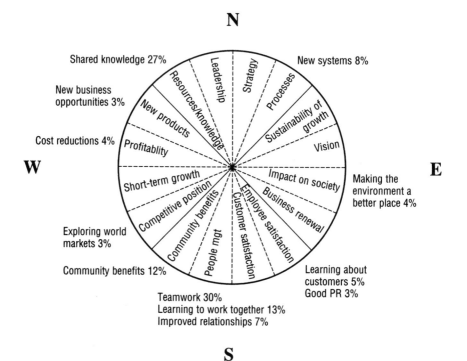

Fig. 4.18 *The corporate compass – Journey outputs*

Solid business benefit is hard to prove since the measurement is part subjective; however, some strong indicators are shown in the following areas:

- Self and team development
  30 per cent of Journey groups reported benefits in this area
- Organizational development
  Areas such as innovation, flexible working practices and operational efficiency
- Skills development
  All groups reported an improvement in their learning competencies. It is significant that those reporting high scores on relationship abilities also performed better than average on other team learning skills.

This would appear to support Nonaka's 'Socialization as an engine for change' thesis (see Chapter 2).

For further details of typical Journey team outputs, see samples in Appendix D all of which show how individuals and teams discovered their potential.

As good as the benefits are for many who participated, it must be acknowledged that the Journey has not touched everyone and business results were not often quantifiable in hard cash terms, as is often the case with change programmes – this is the next challenge.

Expansion of the unregulated business: Anglian Water in international change agent mode

Ian Plover, employee relations manager for Anglian Water, a graduate of both the Transformation Journey and part-time MMBA student at City University Business School, provides solid evidence of the commercial benefits of learning change management.

In 1997 an opportunity arose for Anglian Water International to bid for a water supply concession serving over 1 million further customers in Buffalo USA. Ian takes up the story in his MBA project describing how proactive use of change management lessons from the UK clinched the contract in contrast to the general perception that price would be the deciding factor in winning the contract:

> The unions in America are viewed as all powerful and it was anticipated that we would hit an immovable object that would effectively stifle our relationship with the workforce. Our American colleagues had planned that we would say little, just go through the motions, and get the first

meeting out of the way. They were at the least surprised, when I suggested that we share with the unions our plans, what we intended to do, tell them our concerns and ask them theirs, and they immediately told me that I didn't understand American culture, and that what worked in England would not work here. We had a meaningful debate in which I explained that I was not intending to introduce English culture to America but that through my dealings with unions and employees in partnership I believed that I understood some of the key motivators in circumstances such as this, and that people responded to respect and involvement whatever the culture.

The American management were still opposed to involvement of the unions at this stage, but I referred earlier to a 'leap of faith' sometimes being needed to move away from the expected norm. This was the point where my MBA colleague Dale Evans who was heading the team took the leap of faith in me and said that we would do it my way. Amid mutters of 'you'll regret it' we met the 'Mafia' in a dark windowless room on the site, and as they walked in together having previously met outside, we heard the names Scardino, Panarro, Boticello, and suddenly the rumours seemed more sinister. We broke the ice, we told them our plans and our concerns and the 'man from England' spoke of working together, respect, and partnership. After two hours we parted and agreed to meet again three days later for them to openly share their concerns with us.

After the meeting, one of the American managers so opposed previously to my suggestion of openness came to me and said 'I thought that they would resent a foreigner talking to them in that way, but you said it with such conviction that they believed you – we would never have been able to do it, because it's not the way we do things around here.'

We met again with the unions three days later, when they openly shared their concerns with us, and we agreed that all future meetings would continue in the same spirit. As I left the meeting one of the key union players Larry Panarro spoke to me in the yard and said, 'I think we can do business with you guys'.

The next example involves communication, and I prepared a Newsletter to be sent to every employee on the day that the contract between Buffalo City and American Anglian was signed, explaining who American Anglian was, their key principles and inviting them to share their views with us. This was to be the start of the communication campaign that would keep everyone involved whilst in the *Neutral Zone* [William Bridges' model]. I asked the unions if they wanted to make a statement in the first Newsletter and they agreed saying they would let us know what, in a few days. Unfortunately I returned to England before the official signing so the Newsletter did not go out. We signed a few days later and I received a phone call from the team in Buffalo saying that the Newsletter was delayed because the unions could not agree on a statement.

Understanding their reluctance, as has been demonstrated by the unions in England, I did what I would do in the UK and drafted a statement for them saying how pleased they were to have been involved in negotiations since the beginning etc., and faxed it back to Buffalo. Within two hours I had a call back saying the unions were happy with the statement and had not changed any of it. The Newsletter went out the next day.

We may be 3000 miles apart but people are people the world over – but that's another story.

A demonstration that change management can be a competitive edge!

Knowledge management

In parallel with the Journey, an ambition for Anglian to become a learning organization was realized in the form of the 'University of Water'. Knowledge was to be Anglian's strategic business link and the University aimed to promote the exchange of knowledge between different parts of the organization through best practice networks to provide better customer service, enhance commercial success and deliver quality products and services.

The philosophy was parallel to the Journey and a direct result of the teaching of David Garvin[15] and Nonaka (see Figure 4.19).

David Garvin's definition of a learning organization is 'an organization which is skilled at creating, acquiring and transferring knowledge and modifying its behaviour to reflect new knowledge and insights'.

This concept is represented in structural form in Figure 4.20 on p. 99. Every employee is given this detail together with:

THE OBJECTIVES

Growth – *achieved by linking individual learning to business objectives*
Sharing – *spreading knowledge and learning in teams and across the company. Creating alliances*
Mastery – *taking personal and business capabilities to the highest level*

THE ANGLIAN BRAND OF LEARNING

a　We ensure that learning and business success are linked.

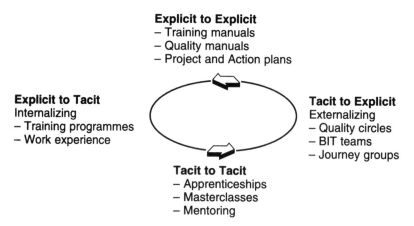

Fig. 4.19 *Working the Knowledge Cycle*

b   We recognize that individuals learn in teams.

c   We work to ensure that the organization learns and that its core capabilities are nurtured.

d   We all commit to sharing knowledge.

e   We believe in the integration of all learning.

f   We encourage learning through local communities.

g   We recognize that every individual's learning will contribute to customer service, total quality management, and efficiency.

h   Company goals will be achieved by an appropriate mix of people and technology.

i   We will ensure that individuals understand what is expected of them in the immediate work environment and in the wider group. We will include a clear definition of the required competencies and skills and our people will share in developing the learning programmes which will meet these expectations.

j   We will use the organizational structure and some of the terminology of the established Universities to guide us and give shape to our ideas.

k   Finally, progress and contributions of individuals, groups and the whole organization to the University, in terms of learning and knowledge creation, will be recognized formally.

The combination of the Journey and the University of Water with its universal access has created the conditions for a learning business, helping to assure the future for Anglian Water and its stakeholders.

The overall mental picture I have of the Anglian experience of change

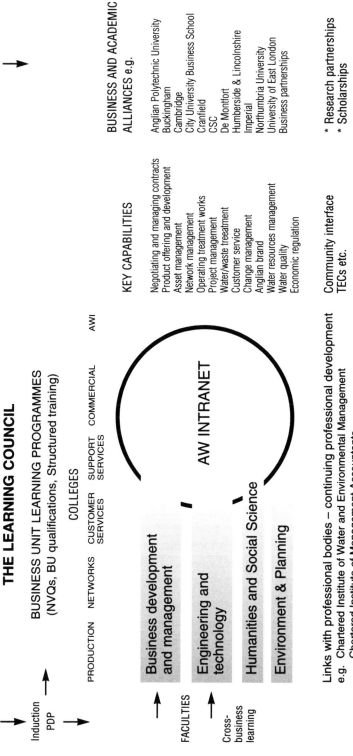

THE LEARNING COUNCIL

BUSINESS UNIT LEARNING PROGRAMMES
(NVQs, BU qualifications, Structured training)

COLLEGES

PRODUCTION   NETWORKS   CUSTOMER   SUPPORT   COMMERCIAL   AWI
                        SERVICES   SERVICES

Induction
PDP

AW INTRANET

FACULTIES

Cross-
business
learning

Business development and management

Engineering and technology

Humanities and Social Science

Environment & Planning

Links with professional bodies – continuing professional development
e.g. Chartered Institute of Water and Environmental Management
      Chartered Institute of Management Accountants
      Institute of Personnel and Development

KEY CAPABILITIES

Negotiating and managing contracts
Product offering and development
Asset management
Network management
Operating treatment works
Project management
Water/waste treeatment
Customer service
Change management
Anglian brand
Water resources management
Water quality
Economic regulation

Community interface
TECs etc.

BUSINESS AND ACADEMIC
ALLIANCES e.g.

Anglian Polytechnic University
Buckingham
Cambridge
City University Business School
Cranfield
CSC
De Montfort
Humberside & Lincolnshire
Imperial
Northumbria University
University of East London
Business partnerships

* Research partnerships
* Scholarships

Fig. 4.20 *Creating and spreading knowledge for sustainable water management*

and learning is one of transition. The 'ice cap' had been broken before I arrived by Alan Smith and colleagues. Many complained of too many change initiatives and the picture emerged of many 'ice floes' on a turbulent seascape. As I write this, the task is to form the ice floes into 'flotillas' to consolidate change into future business benefit. (See Lewin's model applied to Anglian Water, Figure 4.21.)

INTEGRATING CHANGE MODELS

Being an 'NT' type in Myers Briggs terms (for more detail see Chapter 5), the use of models comes naturally. However, I appreciate that for the reader, as useful as models are, confusion quickly sets in with models in apparent conflict for attention. I have deliberately collated the key models referred to so far in Figure 4.22.

This summary is designed hopefully to assist the reader in relating the potential use of the models to other change and learning situations.

Figure 4.22 explained:

Managing transitions. The William Bridges and Kurt Lewin models are essentially navigational maps – vital for being in control of change and for giving an overview of where you are in the change process and where you need to go next.

The Knowledge Creation Cycle. Firstly lays bare the distinction (long seen as unbridgeable) between tacit and explicit knowledge. It does not solve the West's problem between 'doing' and 'being' but challenges us to bridge the gap. Secondly it makes sense of deliberately pursuing a process of knowledge creation, not just to problem solve, but as a development tool for individuals and as a catalyst for group learning and sharing: 'From knowledge is power to sharing the power of knowledge'.

Middle-up-down knowledge creation. Places middle managers as the 'key strategic knot' between the aspirations of the executives for the business and the harsh realities of the front line – not having change done to them but making them into change agents and knowledge engineers.

Lastly, the Hypertext Organization. Puts the problem-solving project teams right at the centre of knowledge creation and development of tomorrow's agile organization. It supports a conventional hierarchical structure for operating the daily business of the firm while legitimizing the market-oriented project team in creating new business systems *and*

Level of change	1994–6 'Unfreezing'	1996–? 'Movement'	? 'Embedding'
INDIVIDUALS (SKILLS, VALUES AND ATTITUDES)	Reductions in numbers SSR changes Development, TJ, TQ Empowerment, PDP, MBA, NVQs	Restructure – further business unit led reductions Competency development TJ and the business	Value and develop employees Operate in safe and sustainable way
STRUCTURE AND SYSTEMS (Pay systems, reporting relationships, work design)	Single table bargaining Experiential training programmes Flattened structures JPA, FLM, EFQM	Partnership with TUs Competency and performance-based pay Workforce 2000 Towards 2000 etc. LIA, IOD, Succession planning, ABC	Flexibility Change through alignment and commitment Agility SPEED OF RESPONSE to customers Focus on efficiency and quality
CLIMATE OR CULTURE (Openness, conflict management, decision making)	Greater openness EOS; Counselling, EAP; Facilitator training (TQ, TJ) Learning Organization	More openness, Upward appraisal, Less conflict Employee feedback Empowerment mirror EOS, EOP Team build University of Water	VALUES: effective competitive responsible responsive friendly
'IMAGE'	ICECAP	ICE FLOES	FLOTILLA

Business results: Market penetration, Market share, Profitability, Shareholder value

Fig. 4.21 *Lewin's Change Model – Anglian Water*

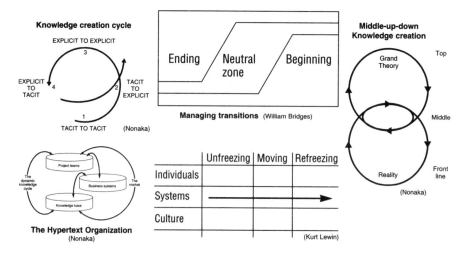

Fig. 4.22 *A medley of models*

enhancing the knowledge base. Figure 4.23 applies the Nonaka Hypertext model to Anglian Water.

Notes

1. Decision-making analysis and interaction tool operated by Anita Hall of Professional People Development UK – for more detail on the approach see Chapter 5, pp. 131–2.
2   See Chapter 2, Figures 2.5 and 2.6.
3. Rayner, 1994: 29. NHS Management Inquiry Report, HMSO.
4. Peck, E. (1996) Power and Decision-making in the NHS, unpublished PhD thesis, Newcastle University.
5. Griffiths, 1994: Social Services Committee Findings, HMSO.
6. DHSS, 1983: 18.
7. Harrison, 1994: 106–22.
8. DoH, 1989a: 23.
9. DoH, 1989b.
10. NHSME, 1990: 2–3
11. DoH, 1989b.
12. Klein, 1989: 240.
13. The internal market concept was to be short lived. The new Labour Government introduced a White Paper in late 1997 abolishing the internal market.
14. In retrospect it is nice to see this confirmed by history with the wholesale rejection of the internal market adversarial approach.
15. Garvin, 1991: 119.

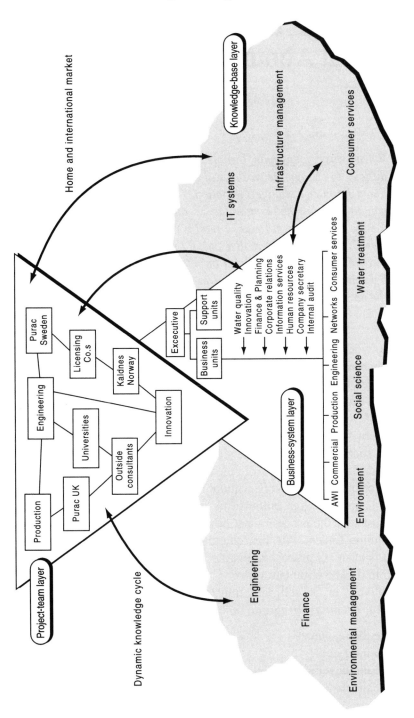

Fig. 4.23 *The Hypertext Organization applied to Anglian Water (courtesy of Steve Kaye)*

5 Change Tools and Techniques – What About Competitiveness?

When I was a young man, I wanted to change the world. I found it was difficult to change the world, so I tried to change my nation. When I found I couldn't change the nation, I began to focus on my town. I couldn't change the town and as an older man, I tried to change my family. Now as an old man, I realize the only thing I can change is myself, and suddenly I realize that if long ago I had changed myself, I could have made an impact on my family. My family and I could have made an impact on our town. Their impact could have changed the nation and I could indeed have changed the world.

(Written by an unknown monk, AD 1100)

Managers worldwide seek the solution to change in practice. Is it top down or bottom up? Or middle-up-down as Nonaka and Takeuchi have coined it (see Chapter 2)? Does it come via top management 'push' or empowered employees? Professor Tony Eccles of Cranfield University, UK, talks of the *Spartacus Challenge* – the task of attempting to name one large modern firm that has implemented a major strategic change 'as a result of a successful revolt of the slaves'[1] – the implication that change needs leadership, momentum from the top. As true as this might be, we all know that change doesn't work without willing acceptance and renewal – it doesn't happen without enthusiastic ownership. We can establish that leaders must start the process – but how to accelerate?

The solution finders will then quickly turn to a systems approach. All you need is business process re-engineering to ensure you focus on what you need to do and eliminate waste.

Alternatively, or as well, let's translate the original Toyota lessons of creating *lean manufacturing* into other sectors as the Lean Enterprise:

    halve the resources
    halve the assets
    halve the development time
    halve the inventory

to achieve twice the output.

And then there is the Quality revolution – or is it now history? The pursuit of quality gave the Japanese their leading edge in the 1970s and 1980s, has led them into the knowledge-creating organizations of the 1990s (see Chapters 2 and 3) and is now regarded as a foundation stone – which, please note, is not rejected by those who follow.

Faddism in Western corporations accepts that quality has its place but now we have surpassed that and are into structural and strategic issues, globalization. Forget manufacturing and everyday service sectors, nurture knowledge workers instead (all true of course) and therefore the 'Janet and John' stuff of quality is passé (not true).

Then there is the school of thought that says that *the issue of change is within*. All we need to do is to get our people to discover their potential for growth and change within themselves or within their teams. Manage by neuro-linguistic programming so that each person exploits their abilities, known and unknown, via a cacophony of new age techniques starting with simple personality profiling, interaction with others, transactional analysis through to no-holds-barred workshops which delve deep into the psyche, emotional and psychological roots. The compelling argument being to deal with the barriers, walls and 'hot buttons' that stop change and get in the way of effective teams.

The confusing morass is a problem for today's managers seeking to be world class. All these solutions are true. They all produce results. They all need each other to a greater or lesser extent. They are all found wanting over time if they are implemented as panaceas without adequate balance. Even their architects recant their own gospel when they see what managers (often well meaning) do with their brain children. James Champy, the guru of business process re-engineering (BPR), has latterly confessed that the original formula has discounted people and can't be sustained. James Champy and his fellow advocate of BPR, Michael Hammer, have estimated that between 50 and 70 per cent of all such initiatives are unsuccessful.[2]

The people ingredient has been closely examined in practice by Mike Oram and Richard Wellins (1995) in *Re-engineering's Missing Ingredient*: 'The rise in scepticism is not due to re-engineering's strong potential impact and the process movement, but rather the degree to which its advocates have been unable to grasp that successful re-engineering depends essentially on building total workforce commitment to unprecedented change.'

They go on to identify the 'missing ingredient': 'More often than not, re-engineers pay exclusive attention to information technology (IT) and process design break throughs. These may be fundamental but, in reality, these constitute only part of the *recipe* for success. The human factor is the vital missing ingredient.'

In my experience 'recipe' is the key word. This is confirmed by Paul Raymer of Stanford University who talks of change being a function of 'better recipes'. The essence of this to me is that there is *no one single ingredient* which produces successful change.

Western management experience is a negative double-whammy in this area. First, as I discussed in *Becoming World Class*, Western executives adhere to panaceas, single solutions, single focus. It is cultural, often has Judaeo–Christian roots, appealing to the 'there is no alternative' school of management to shut our minds to complementary solutions to complex problems.

Even when a change programme is agreed and has begun, the rearguard action continues. 'Change for change's sake' is often heard, which is like the valid but ill-quantified 'insufficient communication' – it can always be levelled because there almost can never be enough communication. 'Too many initiatives' is a more sophisticated and often valid criticism. The motives vary. Confusion because of overlapping or ill-directed initiatives is a reasonable target. The historical sum of initiatives is not necessarily bad – they are often stepping stones to a new order. They can represent reasonable stages in changing mindsets. One initiative on its own is unlikely to shift the culture of an organization.

TOO MANY INITIATIVES?

In a recent study by the Business Process Resource Centre of Warwick University and the Department of Trade and Industry, UK Government, into US best practice in Learning Education and Communications[3] the example of 3 COM was cited:

> 3 COM's recent merger with US Robotics has been very carefully planned to guarantee a swift and effective response to the threat posed by alliances between Cisco, Intel and IBM.
>
> US Robotics is a Mid-West Company, with longer traditions than 3 COM, and has a strong market position for modern products. 3 COM recognize the need to ensure that its planning must focus on rapidly integrating the very different cultures of the two companies if the acquisition is to deliver its planned benefits.
>
> [Figure 5.1] illustrates a planning tool used by 3 COM. The model describes an organization as three interacting systems; namely human,

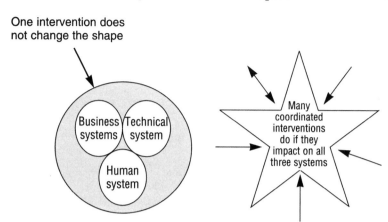

Fig. 5.1 *3 COM Multi-intervention balloon model*

technical and business systems. A single intervention will not change its shape. Addressing complex cultural issues requires multiple planned interventions designed to address the needs of all three systems. 3 COM's organizational development function had 37 simultaneous interventions addressing the one issue of improving customer service in one subsidiary company.

This example rings true for Anglian Water. As I described in Chapter 4, when I arrived in 1996 a whole host of initiatives had been started, some still in place, others moribund or abandoned. The value of many was being questioned. What was the cost benefit of the Transformation Journey? Why spend so much on training? Is TQ still alive? What does empowerment mean?

To try to make sense of this I tried to relate the initiatives current and past to a model I had been familiar with – that of the features of a world class organization put together by James Maxmin (see Chapter 4 – Rolls-Royce experience, and Figure 5.2). This was not much more than a mapping tool. To gain a concept of cohesion I developed the 'umbrella'model (Figure 5.3) hopefully to demonstrate that the various initiatives contributed to vision, values and business results.

Others' experience of living with confusion

In demonstrating to the recipients of 'initiative-itis' in Anglian Water it was helpful to discover that others were beset by the same problems.

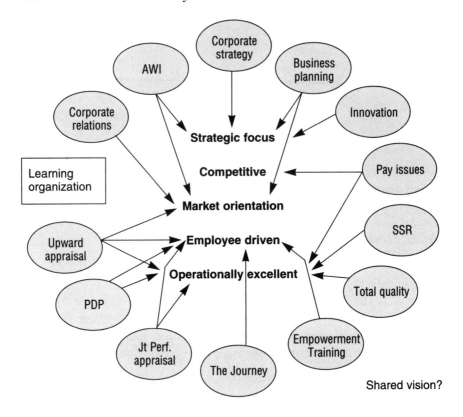

Fig. 5.2

Unipart, the highly successful automotive supplier and logistics company led by John Neill, sees its initiatives as part of a 'yellow brick road' (see Figure 5.4) where each initiative is not seen as a passing fad or flavour of the month but a stepping stone to improved productivity in true 'Kaizen' logic. British Telecom, now the most notable example world-wide of a sucessful privatized utility, sees its succession of initiatives as a 'ladder' of success over the years since privatization from a high cost parochial domestic public service to the world class telecoms giant.

A consortium of institutions in the UK partnered by the DTI and the Department for Education and Employment has published the results of a

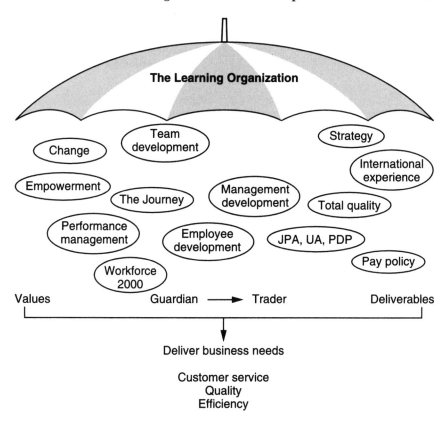

Fig. 5.3 *The 'umbrella' model in Anglian Water*

nation-wide study into effective initiatives for change.[4] They identify five paths to sustained success from studying 67 successful companies:

- Shared goals   –   understanding the business we are in
- Shared culture   –   agreed values binding us together
- Shared learning   –   continuously improving ourselves
- Shared effort   –   one business driven by flexible teams
- Shared information   –   effective communication throughout the company

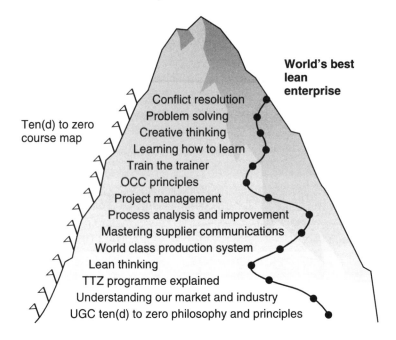

Fig. 5.4 *The 'yellow brick road' (Unipart)*

1986	*Launch of TQM programme*
1987/90	*Quality Councils established*
1990/1	*Project Sovereign (customer focus)*
1992	*Training in leadership and total quality*
1993/4	*Project breakout (process re-engineering)*
1994	*Group-wide ISO 9001*
1994/5	*Development of BT Scorecards*
1996	*Applied for a European Quality Award*

Fig. 5.5 *The quality journey (reproduced by permission of British Telecommunications plc)*

These five paths are then developed into matrix form (Table 5.1).

Table 5.1

	Stage 1 Starting out	Stage 2 Moving forward	Stage 3 New horizons
Shared Goals Understanding the business we are in	• Plan developed from the MD's vision • The plan explained to all staff • Performance against plan is shared	• The vision developed by top team • The vision shared with all the people • Jobs related to the longer-term goals	• Participative planning enabled • Unit planning facilitated • Agile planning operated
Shared Culture Agreed values that bind us together	• Managers are fair and involved • Commitment to your customers • Start to tackle the fear of change	• Build collective confidence • Demonstrate you value everyone • Face problems – be tough	• Lessons are learned, blame is removed • Shape a competitive culture • Change is embraced
Shared Learning Continuously improving ourselves	• Performance measures are defined • Employees are trained for job competence • Recruit and select with care	• People enrolled in their own development • Managers are developed to achieve stretching targets • High performance is expected	• Develop the person • Train managers as coaches • Build tomorrow's capability
Shared Effort One business driven by flexible teams	• Managers developed as team leaders • Team performance measured • Team problem- solving encouraged	• Teams trained as effective working units • Discretion given to teams • Teams made internal customers	• Inter-team working required • Ad hoc teams used • Build the firm as 'the team'
Shared Information Effective communication throughout the enterprise	• Communications effectiveness is checked • Process for reporting decisions is used • Communicate through behaviour	• Be open, good and bad news is relayed • Process in place to allow ideas to be taken into account • Information is shared between teams	• Information is available to allow decisions to be delegated • Everyone is respons- ible for seeking the passing information

The five strands show firstly that differing initiatives are needed to deal with change in the various areas of transition and secondly that they all require some degree of coherence to make sense of it all. (The Lewin Model or William Bridges' Managing Transitions neatly fit this process.) In Anglian Water in 1998 under the new Group Managing Director, Chris Mellor, the change initiatives are being helpfully focused under Vision and Values (see Figure 4.21).

HOW TO PRODUCE CHANGE IN OUR ORGANIZATIONS

I am a firm believer that change is a function of **structure** and **process**. The structural aspect of change is relatively easy for Western management. In fact, rapid structural change appeals to the macho in management. A new managing director is appointed and he needs to make a real difference in his first 100 days. He almost doesn't need the help of a management consultant. He's read the latest *Harvard Business Review* and knows he must have a business that is focused. Divestment of 'non core' elements or businesses is the order of the day . He will produce a structure that is market focused, outward looking, and accountable. Implementation will be swift because speed of decision making and follow-up is everything to the Western manager.

He may rest easy the following weekend as he, with a little help, has changed the company. The truth is nothing has changed, in all probability. Not one behaviour, attitude or belief may have been touched. It is akin to rearranging the deck chairs on the *Titanic* – it does nothing for a hole below the waterline. Or as Professor Amin Rajan of CREATE would say, 'it is like a jelly – as soon as pressure is released the organization returns to its original shape'.

Process, then can be everything; everything that structure is not.

WHAT PROCESSES THEN SHOULD BE FOLLOWED? WHAT IS THE ECLECTIC RECIPE?

Management should be convinced that change is necessary. As we have seen, change is not merely dictated from outside. Those with the levers of power need to start off with 'there must be a better way'. The stimulus may be benchmarking – seeing that others succeed, or perhaps loss of contracts to competitors, loss of market share, a shock to the system rather akin to the famous Sears Roebuck versus Wal-Mart story when Sears explained away loss of market share for years, not noticing that Wal-Mart was advancing. It was only when Wal-Mart was a competitor in terms of level of turnover that Sears took the situation seriously and radical internal change followed.

Diagrammatically this process can be represented by Charles Handy's sigmoid curve (see Figure 5.6). Handy argues that management need to see the necessity of creating a new business 'curve' almost at the point of success – where things are going well, when margins and market share are high, otherwise the company could proceed to slide down the profitability

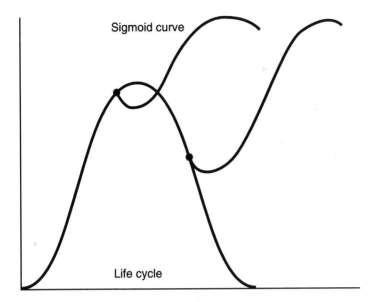

Sigmoid curve

Life cycle

Fig. 5.6
Source: Handy, C. (1994) *The Empty Raincoat*

and viability curve to 'Davy's Bar'. Apart from the Sears example, many other recent notable examples exist of companies not reacting fast enough: IBM and the emergence of the PC; Rank Xerox versus Canon in the development of desktop copiers. It's easy to conclude that these are just the oft-quoted classic examples of latter-day David and Goliath episodes of modern industrial history. The truth is that, of course, history repeats itself and opportunities for change are lost probably more times than they are seized. There is an inherent dysfunction in our development of leaders that prevents those with intuitive thinking (the most likely to see and seize opportunities for change) from reaching the top. Managers are promoted on their ability to control, finitely measure and produce results in micro situations before they are allowed to spread their wings in higher positions. Typically they will be sensors, risk averse – valuing facts and figures above intuition or hunch. It is rare for corporations to produce leaders who can build tomorrow's businesses – there are plenty who can downsize yesterday's companies.

Hopefully, having got through the hurdle of determining that the company must change and rejuvenate itself, the next stage is where to go and how to get there.

A map of change is needed to gain a perception of direction and route. My prescription is the Lewin Model (Figure 5.7), giving a matrix of the

Level of change	Unfreezing	Movement
Individuals (skills, values and attitudes)	Reductions in numbers Development	Demonstrate new skills New supervision
Structure and systems (pay systems, reporting relationships, work design)	New agreements Experiential training programmes	Changes in reward systems Reporting relationships
Climate or culture (openness, conflict management, decision making)	Providing feedback on employees' views	More trust and openness

Fig. 5.7 *Lewin's Change Model: Unfreezing the organization*

overall process of change from Unfreezing through Movement to Refreezing against the parallel changes needed for individuals, systems and culture or climate change. This has been incredibly useful in all the change processes I have managed in the past five years within British companies. This simple model, devised by Kurt Lewin in the 1950s, can achieve a number of key things:

- A recognition that rejuvenation or creating of new business takes time.
- A map that can be shared rather than a perception in the Chief Executive's mind.
- Understanding that individuals' skills, values, attitudes have to change in parallel to new system introduction, and that underpinning all is the need to change culture at the *same time* (not catch up after, since we haven't time, as some would argue).
- A method of plotting and valuing where you are. Too often those affected complain of too much change, too many initiatives without being able to see how each may iteratively help in building towards the desired end result. This resistance to initiatives is compounded by our wonderful addiction to faddism or the latest panacea which somehow means we must discredit the last effort (throwing out baby with the bath water) rather than perceiving how we can use them to build.

Having drawn the map using Lewin's Model we return to the need for **process** as a route for change. Here in my mind the issue is one of

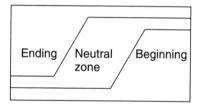

Fig. 5.8 *Managing transitions*
Source: Bridges, W. (1991)

transition. Transition from where we were to where we want to go. The guru who has produced the most helpful model is William Bridges (referred to earlier) in his book *Managing Transitions* (Figure 5.8). He talks of

Endings (where you are leaving the old organization behind)
Beginnings (the new business)

but in between is a no-man's-land of the Neutral Zone where nobody is sure what is happening (for more detail see Chapter 4, pp. 72, 73).

The weakness in the Bridges' Model can be the lack of definition of what to do and roles to play in the neutral zone. It can appear like diversionary activities or not necessarily in line with the direction of change. This is where unaligned initiatives can be unhelpful. The architect of change must have influence to gain the necessary synergy.

WHAT ELSE IS IN THE RECIPE?

Two more ingredients to the eclectic recipe can add structure and learning. The first is the vexed issue of 'top down' or 'bottom up' in terms of change and the second is the learning business. In this application they can end up complementing each other.

The conflict with top down or bottom up is usually related to instinctive belief – how to produce change by top-down edict and 'push', or stimulating uncontrolled change by giving scope to those at the bottom of the organization.

Classic examples of each method are GE (USA) in terms of top-down change and 3M with famous examples of innovative product development on a bottom-up basis (see Chapter 3).

Neither of these prescriptions gives an adequate role for middle management so that instead of giving momentum to change they can be cast in the role of 'corporate concrete'. Motivation of middle managers as change agents is a major challenge to organizations today (see Chapter 3, middle-up-down).

Change in organizations can lead to some very fundamental rethinking on the part of individuals and teams. Some have life choices forced upon them as they face the prospect of 'early retirement' or redundancy. Others have to leave the comfort of a hierarchical organization where status and structure gave security. The middle manager's job was clear – it was to correct and direct. The 'directed' employee didn't have to think – his or her brains could be left in the car park. Many literally, as we have seen, have grieved over the demise of the old organization.

I am reminded of the story of the ex-foreman from Kaiser Steel in the USA who could not bring himself to leave on the day the plant closed and stayed there, for six hours, sitting in his car in the employees' car park. He went on to be a successful stockbroker!

The Learning Business

Recognizing this need of employees to rethink their situations, roles and relationships, Anglian Water introduced the Transformation Journey (see Chapter 4, p. 91) for all staff, back in 1994, to coincide with a major delayering exercise that affected staff grades. So far over 3000 of Anglian's 5000 employees have participated in 'The Journey', discovering and developing themselves as individuals and as teams, and latterly many groups have been demonstrating the pay-back to the business in terms of a new approach of involving the whole person.

Beyond world class – how can organizations capitalize on the tools and techniques available?

General Electric provides a good illustration of three dimensions of major change. Jack Welch and his top management have initiated a number of top-down culture-shaping changes including:

- Establishing a clear, performance-driven vision that commits GE to become either number one or number two in each of its chosen industries by building a culture based on 'speed, simplicity, self-confidence, and boundarylessness'.

- Emphasizing organizational simplification through delayering, a process called 'work-out' (see Chapter 3) aimed at eliminating waste, and another process called 'Best Practices' that seeks to spread success stories.
- Providing corporate resources and attention to support people at all levels – especially the front lines – with essential problem-solving, decision-making and interactive skills.

This environment from the top has also made possible a range of improvements via bottom-up activities and cross-functional redesign and integration.

Of those GE measures:

> The first is a function of top management's determination to commit to a vision.

> The second involves well-documented techniques of process re-engineering, lean production and TQ (see *Becoming World Class*, pp. 160–2, for an evaluation of these measures).

> However, the third requires much more *proactive input from employees* as well as provision of corporate resources to make it work.

Of all the confusing array of tools and techniques and guru advice for change it is this third measure, in my view, which makes or breaks successful change and is the stuff of Beyond World Class. (This is providing the first two measures already have top management commitment and are implemented with re-engineering's missing ingredient – people – at the forefront.)

Teams

GE's output from third-measure ingredients is high performing teams. Why is this so critical? Katzenbach and Smith (1994) pinpoint this:

> We do think there is more urgency to team performance today because of the link between teams, individual behavioural change, and high performance. A 'high-performance organization' consistently out-performs its competition over an extended period of time, for example, ten years or more. It also outperforms the expectations of its key

constituents: customers, shareholders, and employees. Few people today question that a new era has dawned in which such high levels of performance depend on being 'customer driven,' delivering 'total quality,' 'continuously improving and innovating,' 'empowering the workforce,' and 'partnering with suppliers and customers.' Yet these require specific behavioural changes in the entire organization that are difficult and unpredictable for any single person, let alone an entire company, to accomplish. By contrast, we have observed that the same team dynamics that promote performance, also support learning and behavioural change, and do so more effectively than larger organizational units or individuals left to their own devices. Consequently, we believe teams will play an increasingly essential part in first creating and then sustaining high-performance organizations.

How can teams perform better than groups of individuals?

Katzenbach and Smith[5] point out that:

- First, they bring together complementary skills and experiences that exceed those of any individual on the team.
- Second, teams can jointly develop clear goals and approaches and be flexible and responsive to changing demands.
- Third, teams provide a unique social dimension that enhances the economic and administrative aspects of work. By overcoming obstacles, trust and confidence is built.
- Lastly, teams have more fun that both sustains and is sustained by team performance.

So what is a team? 'A team is a small number of people with complementary skills who are committed to a common purpose, performance goals, and approach for which they hold themselves mutually accountable.'[6]

Developing complementary skills
- Technical or functional expertise – this usually requires bringing together a mix of technical or skilled expertise.
- Problem-solving and decision-making skills. Teams must be able to identify the problems and opportunities they face, evaluate the options they have for moving forward, and then make necessary trade-offs and decisions on how to proceed.

- Interpersonal skills. Common understanding and purpose cannot arise without effective communication and constructive conflict that, in turn, depend on interpersonal skills.[7]

This is different from yesterday. A measure of the necessary shift in behaviour is given by Katzenbach and Smith (Table 5.2).

Table 5.2 *Behavioural changes demanded by performance in the 1990s and Beyond*

From	To
Individual accountability	Mutual support, joint accountability, and trust-based relationships *in addition to* individual accountability
Dividing those who think and decide from those who work and do	Expecting everyone to think, work, and do
Building functional excellence through each person executing a narrow set of tasks ever more efficiently	Encouraging people to play multiple roles and work together inter-changeably on continuous improvement
Relying on managerial control	Getting people to buy into meaningful purpose, to help shape direction, and to learn
A fair day's pay for a fair day's work	Aspiring to personal growth that expands as well as exploits each person's capabilities

Source: Katzenbach, J. and Smith, D. (1994) *The Wisdom of Teams: Creating the High Performance Organization* McGraw Hill, p. 211

Before we pursue this last area further it is as well to take a devil's advocate view.

Teams – a critique

Michael West and Rebecca Lawthom of the Institute of Work Psychology at the Centre of Economic Performance at the University of Sheffield have challenged the perceived effectiveness of teamwork.

One of the earliest studies to compare the effectiveness of people working alone and in teams dates back to the beginning of this century, and a French agricultural engineer, Ringelman.

In 1913, he published the results of a study in which agricultural students had been instructed to pull against a rope attached to a dynamometer, which Ringelman used to measure the amount of pull. He found that teams were pulling only 75% as hard as the aggregated work of seven individuals.

At its worst, therefore, teamwork can sometimes be less effective than the sum total of individual efforts. Yet according to a survey of more than 400 British managers conducted under the auspices of the Centre for Economic Performance, more than two thirds of the small and medium sized companies involved intend to make some investment in implementing team based working; nearly half of those on a major scale. 82% of companies have already introduced team based working to some extent – and 91% plan to extend this in the future.'[8]

So where do teams fall down?

West and Lawthorn point to evidence that while teams make decisions better than the average quality of decisions made by individual members, work teams consistently fall short of the quality of decisions made by their most capable individual members (a function of a lowest common denominator?).

Why is this?

The root cause is analysed as personality factors such as the *introverted* nature of some members being overwhelmed by the *extrovert* tendencies of others. Going with the majority is another trait. Poor communications skills inhibit, as do status, gender and hierarchy, causing some member contributions to be valued and attended to disproportionately.

Social loafing has been perceived. Individuals may put less effort into achieving high quality decisions in meetings because they may believe their contribution will be hidden in overall team performance. Diffusion of responsibility occurs when assumptions are made about others shouldering necessary actions.

Another interesting area concerns the production of ideas in brainstorming sessions. Research since 1958 has regularly confirmed that individuals generate ideas at a faster rate alone rather than in teams. In one study five individuals working alone for five minutes produced 68 ideas against a 'real team' equivalent producing 37. (I have witnessed this dysfunction effectively dealt with by the 'post-it-note' technique of splitting the team on initial brainstorming and then bringing the individual brainstorm back into the team for processing.)

Satisfying is another criticism – making decisions immediately acceptable to the team rather than the best possible decisions – eliminating options early.

Finally Janis in his studies of government policy decisions identified *group-think* where the priority is seen as achieving agreement rather than quality of decision making.

There are other practical inhibitors to effective teamworking. With the competitive focus on Japan and the evidence of the effectiveness of teamworking in a Japanese context (my first volume *Becoming World Class* partly contributed to this!), Western management have rushed into the rhetoric of teamworking and have given little time and resource to getting it right. Teamworking on the shop floor is widely regarded as the major factor in a dramatic turnaround in both the US and the UK car industry fortunes in the 1990s.

In retrospect researchers from the Warwick Business School,[9] Harry Scarbrough and Mike Terry, point out that plant investment, logistics improvement, new products and better capacity utilization have led to higher productivity in areas where teamworking was absent.

To me, this doesn't negate teamworking. It is one more piece of evidence that being world class means benefiting from a whole range of improvements – not single panaceas.

Bruce Warman, Personnel Director of Vauxhall (General Motors in the UK), agreed that introducing teamworking consistently into an established factory can be problematic. 'There is a time pressure problem – you have to create time for team meetings and team training', he said. 'The workforce teams and managers will also have a history and preconceptions about how things are done.'

The experience at Rover in the UK of teamworking combined with the firm's promise to guarantee jobs has significantly increased input from the shop floor. 'You even get people coming forward and saying we can do this with nine instead of ten people, they would never have done this before because they would do themselves out of a job.' (Tony Howard, Industrial Relations Manager at Rover)[10]

Bruce Warman believes teamworking is vital for efficient production. 'If you are to have a lean manufacturing system you have got to have teamworking.'

Teams – essential, so how do we make them work?

Let us return to the Katzenbach and Smith analysis of developing complementary skills, that is

- Technical or functional expertise
- Problem solving and decision making
- Interpersonal skills

The first element has been the primary selection criteria for team membership, since teams were invented, and is not usually a problem area – except when the members are told by convention to confine their contribution to their specific areas of expertise!

From the critique above, it's easy to see that the difference between high performing teams and low performers lies in the effectiveness of the last two elements for developing complementary skills.

Here I return to my favourite theme of 'knowing yourself and others'. Experience of high performing teams reinforces this. Tom Nicholson, Managing Director Operations for British Aerospace, challenged orthodox approaches in 1993 in the Corporate Jets business. The change programme he instigated, known as 'Performance through People',[11] was to tackle:

- relocation of manufacturing;
- radical changes in working practices;
- world class process for suppliers;
- leaner, customer focused business.

The vehicle was to be high performing teams. The route taken was:

- to open up selection process to all;
- a nomination process for the new integrated production teams;
- selection based on assessment centres, competency-based interviews, psychometric testing and performance management records (that is, what you knew instead of who you knew or length of service).

The teams were not left alone but given necessary HR support (see Table 5.3 for the HR migration to 'world class') and continuous communications on key messages and outcomes of the project. A clear communication strategy was developed, identifying all stakeholders within the business, their respective information needs and the means by

Table 5.3 *Human resource migration path to 'world class' – British Aerospace*

Class 5	Class 4	Class 3	Class 2	Class 1	World class
Menu of courses		Skill matrices	Competency-based training	Open learning	Learning company
				NVQs	Personal development plans
	Ad hoc communication		Single status	Investors in People	Team-based reward
					Upward appraisal
TU-focused communication	Cascade briefing		Team briefing	Multi-directional communications	
					Multi-discipline teams
Management control		Delegated responsibility	Devolved responsibility	Multi-functional teams	Empowered teams
					Competency-based grading
	Objective setting	Performance appraisal	Performance-related pay	Profit-related pay	Benefits menu
				Career counselling	Shared values
	Functional development routes	Secondments	Lateral development routes		

which these would be met and effectively ensuring that the teams were integrated back into the business and given facilitation help to accelerate their own learning. The pattern is similar to the experience of Peebles Electric in Rolls-Royce and the Transformation Project at Peterborough Hospitals (see Chapter 4).

So it is possible to have high performing teams that produce a sum of the whole greater than the sum of the parts. But they do need help and connections. In Chapter 8 we will be looking at the vital linkage between world class companies and economic regional revival. Rosabeth Moss Kanter in *World Class* (1995) refers to the three 'C's of world class players:

Concepts
Competencies
Connections

I believe these three 'C's apply to individuals and teams as much as companies.

Concepts   Teams need to know where their work is in the overall scheme of things, where the work will lead and how it will it be supported.

Competencies   For teams these are the 'complementary skills' of Katzenbach and Smith.

Connections   Here the examples from British Aerospace, Peebles and Peterborough Hospitals are relevant. The success was as much about keeping communications going as a two-way street between the teams and the rest of the business.

By a process of elimination we therefore arrive at the issues of key competence for teams in the areas of 'knowing yourself and others'. The eclectic experience from this volume and elsewhere is that teams need to know what they bring, what shape that gives to the team and how those ingredients can be capitalized upon.

This is not new of course. Dr Meredith Belbin developed his nine team roles in the 1970s, described in *Team Roles at Work*[12] (see Table 5.4 and also Chapter 4 for a description of its use in Gateshead Hospitals).

The **Myers Briggs Type Indicator** (MBTI)™ is the most respected and used team analysis instrument worldwide, based on Jung's theories and evolved in the 1940s (see Table 5.5). MBTI™ is not a selection tool, but it is extremely powerful in identifying personality preferences, giving the platform for more productive interaction between individuals and overcoming some of the perceived weaknesses in teams.

The weakness of all tools available is how people apply them. MBTI™ among others suffers from the 'observatorial' syndrome. An individual will readily recognize and identify with the analysis about himself or herself, assume that there is nothing that can change, and say 'OK next question?' I have encouraged the use of MBTI™ in many teams over years of change and if linked in a developing fashion with progress of the team it can be very powerful. Problem solving can be enhanced by use of the Z model which ensures that differing personality traits within the teams are used effectively to improve the quality of decision making. This means that

Table 5.4 *The nine team roles originally described in* Team Roles at Work.

Roles and descriptions – team-role contribution	Allowable weaknesses
Plant: Creative, imaginative, unorthodox. Solves difficult problems.	Ignores details. Too preoccupied to communicate effectively.
Resource investigator: Extrovert, enthusiastic, communicative. Explores opportunities. Develops contacts.	Overoptimistic. Loses interest once initial enthusiasm has passed.
Coordinator: Mature, confident, a good chairperson. Clarifies goals, promotes decision-making, delegates well.	Can be seen as manipulative. Delegates personal work.
Shaper: Challenging, dynamic, thrives on pressure. Has the drive and courage to overcome obstacles.	Can provoke others. Hurts people's feelings.
Monitor evaluator: Sober, strategic and discerning. Sees all options. Judges accurately.	Lacks drive and ability to inspire others. Overly critical.
Teamworker: Cooperative, mild, perceptive and diplomatic. Listens, builds, averts friction, calms the waters.	Indecisive in crunch situations. Can be easily influenced.
Implementer: Disciplined, reliable, conservative and efficient. Turns ideas into practical actions.	Somewhat inflexible. Slow to respond to new possibilities.
Completer: Painstaking, conscientious, anxious. Searches out errors and omissions. Delivers on time.	Inclined to worry unduly. Reluctant to delegate. Can be a nit-picker.
Specialist: Single-minded, self-starting, dedicated. Provides knowledge and skills in rare supply.	Contributes on only a narrow front. Dwells on technicalities. Overlooks the 'big picture'.

Strength of contribution in any one of the roles is commonly associated with particular weaknesses. These are called allowable weaknesses. Executives are seldom strong in all nine team roles.

Source: Belbin, R. M. (1996) *The Coming Shape of Organisation*, Butterworth–Heinemann

Table 5.5 *Myers Briggs Typology* ™: characteristics frequently associated with each type

ISTJ	ISFJ
Serious, quiet, earn success by concentration and thoroughness. Practical, orderly, matter-of-fact, logical, realistic, and dependable. See to it that everything is well organized. Take responsibility. Make up their own minds as to what should be accomplished and work towards it steadily, regardless of protests or distractions.	Quiet, friendly, responsible, and conscientious. Work devotedly to meet their obligations. Lend stability to any project or group. Thorough, painstaking, accurate. Their interests are usually not technical. Can be patient with necessary details. Loyal, considerate, perceptive, concerned with how other people feel.
ISTP	ISFP
Cool onlookers – quiet, reserved, observing and analysing life with detached curiosity and unexpected flashes of original humour. Usually interested in cause and effect, how and why mechanical things work, and in organizing facts using logical principles. Excel at getting to the core of a practical problem and finding the solution.	Retiring, quietly friendly, sensitive, kind, modest about their abilities. Shun disagreements, do not force their opinions or values on others. Usually do not care to lead but are often loyal followers. Often relaxed about getting things done because they enjoy the present moment and do not want to spoil it by undue haste or exertion.
ESTP	ESFP
Good at on-the-spot problem solving. Like action, enjoy whatever comes along. Tend to like mechanical things and sports. Adaptable, tolerant, pragmatic; focused on getting results. Dislike long explanations. Are best with real things that can be worked, handled, taken apart, or put together.	Outgoing, accepting, friendly, enjoy everything and make things more fun for others by their enjoyment. Like action and making things happen. Know what's going on and join in eagerly. Find remembering facts easier than mastering theories. Are best in situations that need sound common sense and practical ability with people.
ESTJ	ESFJ
Practical, realistic, matter-of-fact, with a natural head for business or mechanics. Not interested in abstract theories; want learning to have direct and immediate application. Like to organize and run activities. Often make good administrators; are decisive, quickly move to implement decisions; take care of routine details.	Warm-hearted, talkative, popular, conscientious, born cooperators, active committee members. Need harmony and may be good at creating it. Always doing something nice for someone. Work best with encouragement and praise. Main interest is in things that directly and visibly affect people's lives.
INFJ	INTJ
Succeed by perseverance, originality, and desire to do whatever is needed or wanted. Put their best efforts into their work. Quietly forceful, conscientious, concerned for others. Respected for their firm principles. Likely to be honoured and followed for their clear visions as to how best to serve the common good.	Have original minds and great drive for their own ideas and purposes. Have long-range vision and quickly find meaningful patterns in external events. In fields that appeal to them, they have a fine power to organize a job and carry it through. Sceptical, critical, independent, determined, have high standards of competence and performance.

Table 5.5 *cont'd*

INFP	INTP
Quiet observers, idealistic, loyal. Important that outer life be congruent with inner values. Curious, quick to see possibilities, often serve as catalysts to implement ideas. Adaptable, flexible, and accepting unless a value is threatened. Want to understand people and ways of fulfilling human potential. Little concern with possessions or surroundings.	Quiet and reserved. Especially enjoy theoretical or scientific pursuits. Like solving problems with logic and analysis. Interested mainly in ideas, with little like for parties or small talk. Tend to have sharply defined interests. Need careers where some strong interest can be used and useful.

ENFP	ENTP
Warmly enthusiastic, high-spirited, ingenious, imaginative. Able to do almost anything that interests them. Quick with a solution for any difficulty and ready to help anyone with a problem. Often rely on their ability to improvise instead of preparing in advance. Can usually find compelling reasons for whatever they want.	Quick, ingenious, good at many things. Stimulating company, alert and outspoken. May argue for fun on either side of a question. Resourceful in solving new and challenging problems, but may neglect routine assignments. Apt to turn to one new interest after another. Skillful in finding logical reasons for what they want.

ENFJ	ENTJ
Feel real concern for what others think or want, and try to handle things with due regard for the other's feelings. Can present a proposal or lead a group discussion with ease and tact. Sociable, popular, sympathetic. Responsive to praise and criticism. Like to facilitate others and enable people to achieve their potential.	Frank, decisive, leaders in activities. Develop and implement comprehensive systems to solve organizational problems. Good in anything that requires reasoning and intelligent talk, such as public speaking. Are usually well informed and enjoy adding to their fund of knowledge.

Source: Myers Briggs, I. (1993) *Introduction to Type*, 5th edn, Palo Alto, CA: Consulting Pschologists Press

extroverts (E) don't dominate, introverts (I) are encouraged to contribute; the balancing between sensors (S) (those only happy with facts and figures) and intuitives (N) (big picture types) is effective; and logic and rationale (T) (thinking types) don't squeeze out the vital contribution of feeling (F) types or vice versa. In addition, judging (J) types are not so ordered that perceivers (P) types flexibility is stifled. In essence that viable *options are not eliminated early* and that the *sum total of contributions from team members is used effectively*.

Interpersonal skills can be greatly enhanced when first, the individual members understand their own type; second, how it relates to others in the team and lastly how knowledge and necessary adaptation can enhance their individual contribution.

Managers are naturally suspicious of such 'psycho babble' until they can see what such elementary application of widely accepted and well-founded psychology can unlock. I have heard previously cynical colleagues say 'I have worked with X for over 20 years and only now [after using personality profiling and interaction] do I understand what makes him tick.' This unlocks the door. The important next stage is changing behaviour. The field of knowledge here is of course enormous and daunting to the hard pressed manager. There is a justifiable fear of delving too deep and being deflected from the 'day job'. I believe it should be taken in pragmatic stages, ensuring results are there to be seen – not giving rise to some areas leaving the rest of the organization behind – and rooted in the overall management of change.

Emotional intelligence

We will return to examples of what this means in leadership terms in Chapter 6. For industry generally there is a growing recognition that what is termed '*emotional intelligence*' has been neglected, inhibiting progress. Daniel Goleman surprised himself when his book of that name (1996) became the number one best seller tapping into a wide range of markets. He argues that our view of human intelligence (IQ) is far too narrow, and that our emotions play a far greater role in thought, decision making and individual success than is commonly acknowledged. Emotional intelligence includes self-awareness and impulse control, persistence, zeal and motivation, empathy and social deftness. These are qualities that mark people who excel, whose relationships flourish, who are stars in the workplace.

High performing organizations, according to Goleman, tend to have high levels of emotional intelligence among their members and strong links between their emotional capabilities and skills – this process has to start with teams, and tools, such as the MBTI™, are keys to unlock the understanding and dynamics.

The critical thing is to link tools to other processes such as the following.

1. Transition management

This is designed to help people through and to give meaning to the tools of self-analysis. Nancy Barger and Linda Kirby (1996) have done this in a helpful volume which links MBTI™ to William Bridges' 'Transition Management' thinking referred to earlier in this chapter.

Their model is helping employees thrive in the 'New Frontier' using the vivid metaphor to Americans of the Oregon trail, starting with what has to be left behind (remembering the analogy of Cortez landing in South America and burning the ships). 'You can look back at the wide, dry sea of America strewn with the discards: food, bedding, clothes, trunks full of ball dresses, books, furniture, ... everything in fact.' ('Pioneer Woman' in Susan Butrille 'Women's Voices from the Oregon Trail' quoted in *The Challenge of Change in Organizations*[13])

The Barger and Kirby formula is the constructive use of differences:[14]

E (open and communicative)	*and*	I (calm and reflective)
S (pragmatic and structured)	*and*	N (visionary and innovative)
T (logical and detached)	*and*	F (concerned for people and persuasive)
J (planful and decisive)	*and*	P (flexible and resourceful)

and the necessary steps:

1. Becoming aware of the differences.
2. Seeing and acknowledging the value of other viewpoints.
3. Learning, in a deep way, about the other preferences and perspectives.
4. Seeking out other preferences and perspectives.
5. Incorporating different perspectives into one's own regular processes.

The way to do this is to identify others in the organization who have perspectives, abilities, and skills different from one's own; ask about and listen in an effort to understand their perspectives; and give them weight when making decisions and taking actions. Sharing the leadership role can bring in the strengths of different types ... .

Many top executives may want to develop a 'kitchen cabinet' – a group of people to offer amendments and critiques to their natural perspectives. Most top managers have a group of trusted associates whom they use as a sounding board, but, typically, this group comprises people who share the leaders' perspectives. They may not intentionally be 'yes' people; it's just that their perspectives are so similar that they share the same blind spots [group think]. It's crucial to find and forge trusting relationships with at least a few people who have quite different perspectives. Then make it a positive experience for them to expand your perspective with their insights and knowledge.[15]

This is moving from *observational* to the *dynamic* use of the MBTI™.

2. The new organization as a process

I find that Nancy Barger shares my enthusiasm for making the future through *process*. It is experiential rather than precisely predicted, it is about starting with the values and attitudes *now* rather than seeing them as a product of the new organization. 'Most of the books written on organizational change in recent years are, in psychological type terms, "NT books." They focus on long-term patterns, devise complex systems for understanding, and recommend complicated global restructuring of organizations.' Exceptions in my view are led by such thinkers as Charles Handy. 'Accepting that change is required for survival and that the final goals are not yet clear, we think the basic question for organizations is, How can we survive the chaotic transitions of the present and position ourselves to be ready for whatever future directions develop?'

> Organizational success – present and future – depends upon a committed, energetic, creative workforce. People will be committed, energetic, and creative when the organization includes them in the process of dealing with the present and in creating the organization's future. This will make it possible for the organization and its people to survive current transitions. It will also position the organization and its people to move with maximum flexibility and effectiveness into whatever new structures eventually emerge.[16]

Amen to that.

The Barger/Kirby prescription is short and simple. The new ways that will create the new organization are:

- Honour, encourage, make use of, and develop the particular gifts of everyone in the organization.
- Act and interact with honesty and integrity.
- Share the challenges and the rewards.

3. Revolutionising the decision-making process

The differing approach to decision making between Japan and the West was discussed at some length in *Becoming World Class* (pp. 23, 24, 58, 59, 60, 97–102). The approaches are worlds apart in terms of methodology. The group approach of 'Ringi' (management approval) and 'Nemawashi' (consensus) (see *Becoming World Class*, p. 24) has served the Japanese well in terms of pooling talent and resource while being bureaucratic and longwinded. The Western view is to place much more faith in individuals and fast decision making, of course. Both systems have their virtues and neither can replicate the other because of the surrounding host cultures. How can we improve the quality of decision making in the West without losing the advantages of speed and clarity?

My answer, proven in practice, is to increase the knowledge of managers of the decision-making process, of how they and their colleagues arrive at decisions and how the quality can be improved. The best tool (again a tool helping a process) in my view is Action Profiling[R17] which measures how the individual:

- treats information gathering;
- deals with the decision-making process;
- commits to action (see Figure 5.9).

The Action Profile[R18] assessment is based upon a simple model of decision-making initiative. It includes:

– the process and staging of decision making;
– interaction during that process;
– the overall intensity or level of the decision-making energy (dynamism);
– ability in decision making; and
– the level of identification with the environment and initiatives of
  others.

The Action Profile[R] assessment is based upon highly detailed observation of minute variations of non-verbal signals, specifically movement. This gives the assessment its objectivity, its accuracy and its capacity to identify deep-seated motivational forces in the personality. Methods for teaching the system of observation have been developed, and there now exists a group of highly dedicated Action Profile[R] practitioners located in Europe, North America and Africa. Standards, ethics and quality are governed by an international association, Action Profilers International (API).[19]

Although measuring different outputs from people, Action Profiling[R] has a high degree of correlation with MBTI[TM] (significance beyond 0.5) and the instruments combine in measuring preference for certain types of thought process rather than talent, aptitude or competence. In addition, like the Action Profile[R] pattern, the MBTI[R] has no good or bad types, just different preferences for certain activities.[20]

It also offers a further bridge of knowledge between the written output

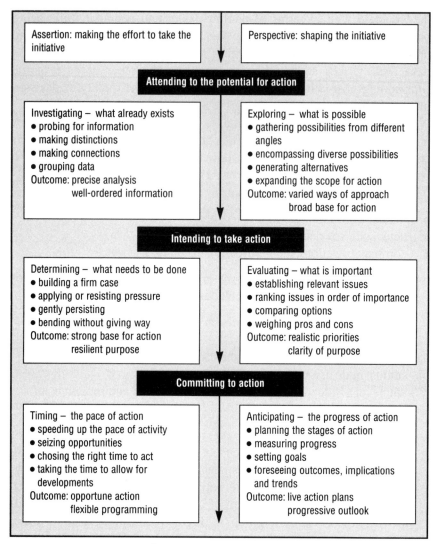

Fig. 5.9 *The Action Profile[R] framework of initiative: action*

(via psychometric tests) and the growing appreciation of NLP (neuro-linguistic programming) and our normal powers of observation.

This can sound overly complex and potentially enters a world where managers can feel out of control (particularly those happy with facts and figures and unhappy with the soft touchy-feely stuff). However, we all appreciate, with experience, that differing types bring different things to the management process and referring to Figure 5.9, by inspection, we will know that some are stronger than others at critical points of the process.

CONCLUSIONS ON CHANGE TOOLS AND TECHNIQUES

Business process re-engineering

Valuable analytical tool, but stuff of operational excellence, not long-term competitiveness. Human factor the missing ingredient.

Total quality

Vital stepping stone. 'I have two jobs: first to do my job; second to improve my job.'

Recipes or initiatives?

No single ingredient that produces successful change. At the other extreme too many uncoordinated initiatives confuse.
Make sense of the change:

Shared goals
Shared cultures
Shared learning
Shared effort
Shared information

Change is a function of structure and process, and process is lubricated by learning.

Classical change process

Sigmoid curve	Facing reality
Lewin model	Mapping tool
Managing transitions	Helping the organization through aligning initiatives
Who's driving?	top-down
	bottom-up, or
	middle-up-down
The learning business	Transferring individual learning to group learning
	Proactive input from employees

The vehicle
Teams   Better than groups
                                   Complementary skills
                                   – technical expertise
                                   – problem solving
                                   – interpersonal skills
Knowing yourself and others
    Use of tools
    Belbin
    Myers Briggs™ – linked to transition management
    Action Profile® – better decision making
    Emotional intelligence

Next: does all this help? What evidence is there that investment in such 'People Management Practices' aids competitiveness?

COMPETITIVENESS – ARE WE THERE IN THE INDUSTRIALIZED WORLD?

The 'world class' formula has been known for some time. The ingredients can be agreed upon by most observers. As we have seen, the tendency has been to go for may be just one or two ingredients exclusively rather than a proper recipe. The enthusiasm has been for systems, typically, for re-engineering, lean production and TQM, all of which in the right context (that is, as part of a recipe) can have good effect in producing competitiveness.

Impact of people management practices on company performance

Michael West and colleagues of the Institute of Work Psychology at the University of Sheffield[21] have conducted a seven-year longitudinal study on market environment, organizational characteristics in over a hundred UK manufacturing companies. The aim of the study published by the Institute of Personnel and Development is to determine what factors principally determine company effectiveness.

The key findings against questions raised are:

Question 1
Do employees' attitudes predict company performance?

- Job satisfaction explains 5% of the variation between companies in change in profitability (after controlling for prior profit). Organizational commitment also explains 5% of the variation.
- In relation to change in productivity, job satisfaction explains 16% of the variation between companies in their subsequent change in performance. Organizational commitment explains some 7% of the variation.

Question 2
Does organizational culture significantly predict variation between companies in their performance, and if so, which aspects of culture appear most important?

- Culture factors accounted for some 10% of the variation in profitability between companies between the two periods measured during the study. The variable which most explained change in profitability was concern for employee welfare.
- In relation to change in productivity, the results were even more striking. Human relations values explained some 29% of the variation between companies in change in productivity over a three to four year period. Concern for employee welfare was by far and away the most significant predictor. This is clear confirmation of the importance of organizational culture in relation to company performance.

Question 3
Do human resource management practices explain variation between companies in profit and productivity?

- In examining change in profitability (after controlling for prior profitability), the results reveal that Human Resource Management practices taken together explain 19% of the variation between companies in change in profitability. Job design (flexibility and responsibility of shopfloor jobs) and acquisition and development of skills (selection, induction, training and appraisal) explaining a significant amount of the variation. This demonstrates the importance of HRM practices.
- In relation to productivity, HRM practices taken together explain 18% of the variation between companies in change in productivity. Job design and acquisition and development of skills explaining a significant proportion of variation.

This is the most convincing demonstration of which we are aware in the research literature of the link between the management of people and the performance of companies.

Question 4
Which managerial practices are most important in predicting company performance?

- The results reveal that strategy explains 2% of change in profitability in companies and less than 3% of change in productivity in companies. These results are not statistically significant.
- Emphasis on quality explains less than 1% of the change in profitability within companies over time and less than 1% of the change in productivity. Of course it may be that these factors explain more of the variation between companies over a longer period of time.
- Emphasis on and sophistication of technology explains only 1% of the variation between companies in change in productivity over time and 1% of the variation between companies in change in profitability.
- In relation to R&D emphasis and expenditure, 6% of the variation in change in productivity is accounted for by R&D, though this is not a statistically significant finding. And 8% of the variation in change in profitability between companies is accounted for by R&D expenditure.

Compared with these four domains (R&D, technology, quality and strategy) HRM practices which explain 18% of the variation in company productivity and 19% in terms of profitability are the more powerful predictors of change in company performance.

The Institute of Personnel and Development (IPD, 1997) comment:

The results suggest that if managers wish to influence the performance of their companies, the most important area they should emphasize is the management of people. This is ironic, given that our research has also demonstrated that emphasis on HRM practices is one of the most neglected areas of managerial practices within organizations. The implications are clear.

HOW CAN WE MEASURE EFFECTIVENESS?

The issue of having effective teams I would argue is key, and the fundamental is that these teams are truly effective – not teams in name only.

The issue of performance here is coincident with that of *communication*

– how linked in is every employee or supplier or other stakeholder with the enterprise? – notoriously difficult in terms of measurement. Hence effective teams can be the route to effective communication.

Voice or Exit

In measuring whether we are competitive or not, some ground breaking work has been done in both the USA and UK using Hirschman's (1970) famous distinction, *'developing productive relationships means stressing "voice" rather than "exit"'*. Hirschman's argument was that if there are practices and procedures whereby shareholders, employees or suppliers meet with management to consider how jointly to improve performance (voice), those groups will be less predisposed to selling, leaving the firm or ending the commercial relationship when dissatisfied (exit).

It has been well demonstrated that such practices or procedures are a strength that promotes better company performance.[22]

The studies by Susan Helper, Professor, Department of Economics, Case Western Reserve University, Cleveland OH and Dr Mari Sako, Professor in International Business at School of Management Studies, Oxford University, have looked at the implementation of 'voice' or 'exit' philosophies in the auto industries in Japan, the USA and Europe with particular reference to supplier/customer relationships against measures of performance. The same distinction was used in parallel studies looking at the impact of worker representation on performance within the auto industry in Europe. I will argue when we look at changing employment trends in Chapter 9 that the issues of 'voice' or 'exit' are becoming indistinguishable between supplier/customer and employee/employer in Western business.

Types of supplier–customer relationships

Simply put, in an 'exit' relationship a customer who has a problem with a supplier finds a new supplier: in a 'voice' relationship, the customer works with the original supplier to resolve the problem.[23]

In most cases a 'voice' relationship is more efficient, since the flow of information between the parties makes techniques such as value analysis and value engineering more effective. However, a company that wants to have a voice relationship with its suppliers must make a commitment that it will continue to buy the suppliers' products for some length of time. The parallel in building trust can easily be made to the employment relationship between employer and employed.

The surveys by Susan Helper, Richard Lamming and Mari Sako on auto industry suppliers obtained 675 responses in the USA; 472 responses in Japan and 262 in Europe (including 116 from the UK)[24] in 1993/94: an unusually comprehensive database of 1409 responses.

To evaluate performance the following definition of 'voice' relationship or 'partnership in supply' was used in all cases:

- the supplier provides the customer with details of its manufacturing (and other) process steps;
- the supplier believes that there is a high probability that it will continue to provide products to the customer for more than three years;
- if another supplier offers a lower price for a product, the supplier expects the customer to help it to make necessary process improvements to match the competitor's expertise, rather than automatically re-source the business, or engage in arbitrary bargaining.

The respondents were asked about their situation in 1993/94 and four years before (around 1989/90) against the above definitions.

Suppliers sharing process information

Figure 5.10 shows that within the control period the USA and UK have matched if not exceeded Japan's performance in this area with the field being led by suppliers of Japanese customers in the UK.

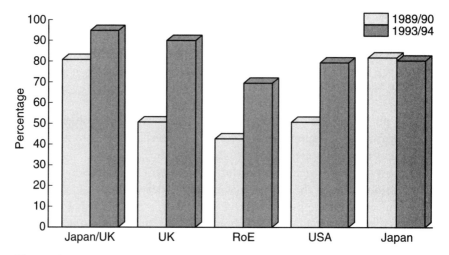

Fig. 5.10 *Percentage of suppliers providing customers with detailed breakdown of process steps*

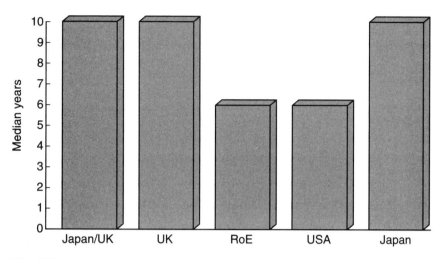

Fig. 5.11 *Gap in perceived customer commitment 1993/94*

Figure 5.11 shows a measure of customer commitment in terms of the duration over which the supplier believes there is a high probability that it will continue supplying to the same customer. The median level of commitment was ten years for the UK and Japan, six years in the USA and seven years in the rest of Europe (RoE).

Solving problems with customers

Suppliers were asked how the customer would react if a competitor offered a lower price for a product of equal quality.

An increasing proportion of UK suppliers (from an average of 39 per cent in 1990 to 78 per cent in 1994) said their customers would help them to match a competitor's effort (see Figure 5.12). The expectation of such a partnership-style reaction was particularly high (65 per cent in 1990 rising to 86 per cent in 1994) among those UK suppliers supplying the Japanese car manufacturers in the UK. In the USA and the rest of Europe, the move towards partnership according to this measure was not as dramatic, from an average of 34 per cent in 1989 to 53 per cent in 1993 in the USA, and from 33 per cent in 1990 to 53 per cent in 1994 in the rest of Europe.

To summarize, an increasing proportion of suppliers in the UK, the rest of Europe and the USA have provided their customers with a detailed breakdown of process steps, so that the gap between the USA and Europe on the one hand and Japan on the other in this respect has been more or less eliminated. At the same time, customer commitment, measured by

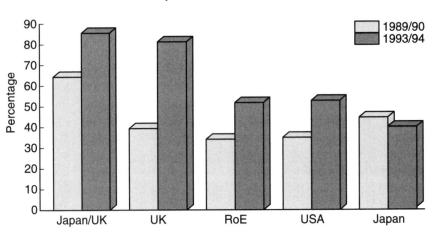

Fig. 5.12 *Europe and USA move towards partnership*

suppliers' future projections, is higher in Japan and in the UK than in the USA or the rest of Europe. With respect to the orientation towards joint problem solving, suppliers' expectations of partnership-style response have increased in the UK, the USA and Europe but declined slightly in Japan.

Suppliers trading with Japanese car manufacturers in the UK – constituting 19 per cent of the UK sample – are clearly in the lead in establishing partnerships along all the three dimensions. Thus, there has been a limited, yet noticeable, convergence in the nature of supplier–customer links in all the regions.

Impact of 'voice' relationships on performance

The studies showed better performance overall for partnership-type arrangements than for non-partnership but there were clear differences in terms of maturity of those relationships. For instance, in comparing the USA with Japan, US auto suppliers with 'voice' relationships obtained 28 per cent more awards from their customers, greater market share growth and 10 per cent were more likely to accept JIT delivery without a cost increase. In Japan the corresponding figures were 18 per cent more awards; nil market share advantage; and 50 per cent more likely to accept JIT delivery without a cost increase.

The researchers are at pains to point out that 'voice' is not a cosy relationship – more than 51 per cent of voice suppliers would have to absorb part of any increase in material cost against 29% of non-voice suppliers. In contrast 16 per cent per cent of non-voice suppliers were able to pass price increases to customers against 7 per cent for voice suppliers.

Tensions and benefits

The studies recognize the real tensions in supply strategies for customers – between the need to *select* the best supplier at any point in time (a goal more likely to be met by using the exit strategy) and being able to *create* good suppliers by working with them over a long period of time (more likely with the voice strategy).

However, the partnership strategy, which must be attributed at least in part to the advent of Japanese firms in Europe, has led to a significant improvement in some aspects of supplier performance and promises much more.

Voice or exit within the enterprise

Is worker participation good for business?

Professor Sako (1997a) has used similar logic to examine the effect of voice and exit relationships in employee relations terms. She identifies the three camps in the debate over whether worker participation is good for business or not.

> First, there are the adamant defenders of managerial prerogative, who argue that both types of employee voice are unnecessary to run a good business. This camp is authoritarian and at best would use downward communication (such as company newsletters) but no other forms of employee involvement (the *authoritarian* view). Second, there are those who are in favour of direct participation (quality control circles) (QCC) because it harnesses individual employees' skills and knowledge to the full, but are opposed to representative participation especially if it is to be imposed by legislation ... (the direct *participation* view). Lastly, there are those who believe that good business performance can best be achieved by giving employees an influence both at the day-to-day operational level and at the policy level i.e. via joint consultative committees (JCC) (the *synergy* view).

Mari Sako recognizes in the preamble some parallels and differences in approach between the USA and the UK.

> Recent empirical studies of human resource management identify a 'bundle' or a package of practices (including direct worker participation) which improve firm performance. These innovative or transformed work practices are adopted especially by firms which face international competition, such as in the car industry. There is ample empirical support for the synergistic relationships, or complementarity, among such things as teamwork, job rotation, problem-solving groups, and performance-related pay. The HR 'bundle' examined in the US, however, does not include representative participation. The latter is a separate policy concern, arising out of a worry over the declining union density and the corresponding increase in the 'representation gap'.
>
> In Britain, as in the US, much of the recent interest in participation has come from looking at the Japanese example. Problem-solving groups and continuous improvement teams are considered a central core of 'lean production' which must be adopted if companies are to survive in international markets .... Direct worker participation for enterprise efficiency exists as a common feature in Japanese transplants in Britain and the US. But while US-based Japanese transplants remain mainly non-union with fewer representative participatory mechanisms, British-based Japanese firms have had joint consultation committees as part of the single-union deal ... . However, even in Britain, the emulators of Japanese transplants have focussed mainly on adopting direct participatory practices on the shopfloor without much regard to the support mechanism off the shopfloor ... . In contrast in Japan, direct participation, which has diffused widely, is typically complemented by joint consultation between employee representatives and management both at the plant and enterprise levels .... Management has had an incentive to implement joint consultation to conduct the annual wage negotiations, and to demonstrate to workers that strategic decisions are made without compromising their commitment to employment security.

The questions relating to the three 'camps' defined above were an adjunct to the longer survey on suppliers (see above – also sponsored by the International Motor Vehicle Programme (IMVP)) but confined to the UK and Europe.

Outline conclusions

Combining JCC and QCC improves quality:

> As is evident in [Figure 5.13], there is no support for the *'authoritarian'* view; significant differences exist between plants with neither QCCs nor JCCs and those with at least one of these participatory practices. As between the two other views, there is greater support for the *synergy* view on two accounts. First, even those plants with JCCs but without QCCs (the second bar in the Figure) do better than those with neither, countering the argument that representative participation may be irrelevant or damaging to plant performance. Also, in direct support of the *synergy* view, combining QCCs and JCCs improves quality over and above having just *direct participation*.
>
> How can this result be best interpreted? In order to answer this question, we need to understand what is happening to employees' willingness to share their ideas with management when QCCs and JCCs are implemented. It is often said that employee involvement improves communication and the quality of decision making in an organization. But from the employees' viewpoint, being asked to take part in QCCs without representative participation *for higher-level issues is like being asked to contribute without having a 'real say'*. If representative

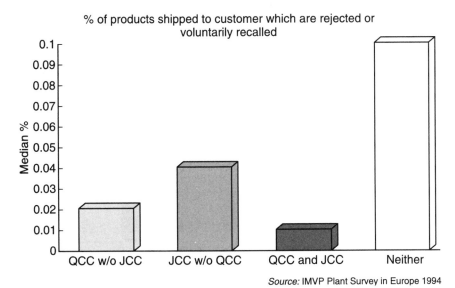

Source: IMVP Plant Survey in Europe 1994

Fig. 5.13 *Combining JCC and QCC improves quality*

participation through JCCs is combined with direct participation, employees are more likely to feel that their voice is heard, and only then are they willing to give their hearts and minds to QCC-type activities.

To examine empirically this line of argument plant managers were asked to show their degree of agreement with the statement: 'Workers sometimes feel reluctant to share their ideas about improved work methods with management.'

As Figure 5.14 shows the best strategy is to combine the two forms of participation.

How and why is worker participation spreading?

If worker participation has business benefits, and if managers are aware of such benefits, that creates a necessary condition for the diffusion of participatory practices. Of the two 'ifs', the first one was already addressed in the last section. What about the second 'if'? The related surveys of the IMVP are able to provide a clue.

The questionnaire asked the respondents how important each of a list of eight items was in their manufacturing strategy. The ranking of the items according to the proportion of those who said they were important or

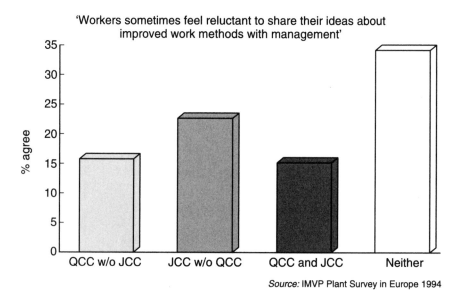

Source: IMVP Plant Survey in Europe 1994

Fig. 5.14 *Combining JCC and QCC maximizes information sharing*

extremely important is shown in Table 5.6. In the UK, 'increase employee involvement' emerged as the most important, followed by 'improve quality', 'reduce overhead', and 'reduce inventory.' Of course, these items are not mutually exclusive, and it is quite likely that employee involvement is important to achieve better quality and reduce inventory. Moreover, it was not made explicit what was to be included in employee involvement, so that some responded with mainly problem-solving groups in mind while others had financial participation or representative participation in mind. However, what is clear is that UK managers felt that employee involvement was of utmost importance, while managers in the USA and the rest of Europe considered it of less importance [perhaps in Europe because of greater institutional worker participation? – my emphasis]. Interestingly, Japanese managers considered employee involvement of least importance, either because it has been diffused for a few decades already (thus losing the marginal improvement which could be derived from it), or because it has actually lost its effectiveness with the shortening of model cycles, the advances in technical knowledge necessary on the part of workers to make relevant suggestions, and the decline in the quality of shop-floor labour.[25]

Table 5.6 *Important factors in the manufacturing strategy of auto parts suppliers. % Important and Extremely important (Ranking in brackets)*

Factors	UK	Rest of Europe	USA	Japan
Increase employee involvement	97(1)	80(4)	90(2)	48(8)
Improve quality	91(2)	87(1)	91(1)	96(1)
Reduce overhead	83(3)	80(3)	82(3)	89(2)
Reduce inventory	81(4)	78(5)	81(4)	83(6)
Develop new products	79(5)	86(2)	70(5)	89(3)
Product simplification/ standardization	59(6)	62(6)	62(6)	79(7)
Increase automation	39(7)	52(8)	57(7)	85(5)
Reduce wage growth	37(8)	61(7)	53(8)	86(4)

Source: IMVP Supplier Surveys

NB. The questionnaire asked: 'In your business unit's manufacturing strategy, what has been the importance of the following factors?' Respondents were asked to indicate the degree of importance on a 5-point scale for each of the eight items listed.

Real hard evidence of managers adopting involvement strategies is shown in Figure 5.15 where the proportion of British plants with direct participation rose from 3% in 1990 to 34% in 1994 with an increase also being shown in Europe.

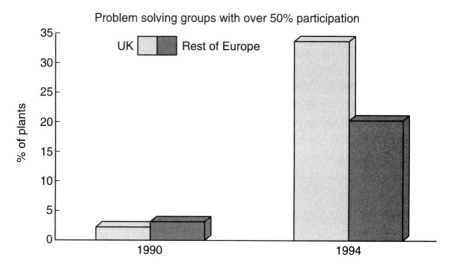

Source: IMVP Plant Survey in Europe 1994

Fig. 5.15 *Direct participation*

Similarly there has been a marked increase in the UK of representative participation (Figure 5.16).

Policy over employment security

The IMVP survey asked plant managers whether their plants had a 'policy of no layoffs resulting from productivity increases' (see Figure 5.17). This is a limited form of guaranteeing employment security, which addresses workers' fears of doing themselves out of a job by working harder or making productivity-enhancing suggestions (turkeys voting for Christmas). Employment security rarely means jobs for life. Nor does management make a commitment never to lay off any workers under any circumstances. This is why this practice is prone to be criticized for being a 'good times only' policy. The test of such a policy is indeed in a

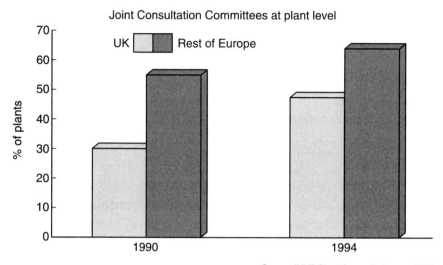

Fig. 5.16 *Representative participation*

downturn, when the employer should be seen to be making every effort to avoid layoffs. It is not the ultimate absence of layoffs, but employees' perception of the firm's degree of effort in avoiding them, which matters. Thus, in Japan (the country of lifetime employment) and at Japanese companies in Britain, some workers were made redundant in the early

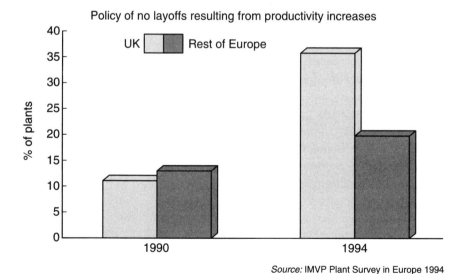

Fig. 5.17 *Employment security*

1990s recession, but most companies were able to preserve the norm of lifetime employment. This retention of management commitment in the eyes of the employees was much helped by their having a representative form of employee participation. It is undoubtably easier to show that layoffs are a last resort and retain workers' confidence in management by allowing employees to be party to a discussion on corporate performance than excluding them from such discussion.[26]

Conclusions on voice or exit within the enterprise

The automotive sector is probably the world's most commoditized industry in that consumer choice is global and competition is rarely fiercer. Hence market advantage is difficult to sustain. Whereas this IMVP study is necessarily confined to that sector, I would argue that its findings translate across into other industries and the service sector.

The IMVP survey in Europe showed that without the force of legislation, both direct and representative forms of employee voice are spreading in the British automotive parts supply industry. One main driver, Mari Sako concludes, is the manager's belief that *'employee involvement is of utmost importance in improving their manufacturing performance'*.

But tensions remain …

Just as the issue of 'voice' or 'exit' in supplier/customer relations gives rise to real tensions, so it applies to choices within the firm.

Take cost reduction as an objective. One possible policy to achieve this objective would be to reduce the number of employees, or to outsource or to reduce unit cost by exploiting economies of scale. This is the exit model – or conventional mass production approach.

An alternative strategy would be to work together with existing employees, customers and suppliers to think of ways of reducing costs. This could be seen as the voice model:[27] 'Exit certainly has the merit of bringing about efficiency savings immediately. But "voice" is more likely to lead to better communications, and the resulting richer flow of information facilitates long-lasting improvements in manufacturing performance.'[28]

What is also clear from this research, and my own experience of working with varying participatory structures, is that the efficacy of voice depends *on the way in which labour and management interact*, not whether unions exist or not or whether formal structures for consultation are in being or not.

The difference between the effectiveness of joint consultation (or employee voice) at Komatsu UK in the late 1980s early 1990s was like cheese compared to chalk at Northern Electric 1992–94 or Anglian Water 1996–98. Both the latter organizations had well-oiled institutional regimes on joint consultation with histories of joint determination going back to the 1940s, but the ethos and culture had not generally progressed from the age of adversarial relations to the age of empowerment. At Komatsu we managed to have an atmosphere of shared destiny because of the competitive environment and deliberate adherence to 'voice' as the way forward. This means management has to drop the habit of producing a solution to then be negotiated with trade unions and employees and adopt a deliberate policy of sharing information early to allow a range of options to be considered by all stakeholders before a way forward is decided.

Mari Sako concludes that the IMVP survey evidence may indicate either of the following: either, this 'voice' is a fad associated with attempts at learning from Japan, which would end with high attrition rates by the next recession; or, it is the beginning of a secular and steady trend towards the adoption of representative as well as direct participation, which would become sustainable once a majority has such a system in place. Japanese industrial firms have travelled this latter route of voluntary adoption for both their joint consultation committees and their quality control circles.

The Commission on Public Policy and British Business (CPPBB) 1997 study, *Promoting Prosperity*, which contributed much to the new UK Labour Government's thinking on the 'Business Agenda', concluded from Mari Sako's work: 'Those companies which had "voice" relationships with employees and suppliers outperformed – in hard cash terms of higher productivity and greater profitability – those which did not.'[29]

Returning to the thread running through this book – it is not so much the efficacy of which system you adopt but how you do it. TQ, BPR, Lean Production, Teams, Joint Consultation – all are laudable and effective in their own right but without 'voice' ethos or trust never reach their promise in terms of competitiveness.

TRUST

We will turn to the relationship between high and low trust and economic performance in the context of nations and regions in Chapter 8; however, in this chapter our perspective is that of the enterprise. Helpfully Mari Sako (1997b) has developed her work on 'voice' and 'exit' in terms of examining whether trust improves business performance and as a second question, 'how can trust be created in business where there is none?'.

The controversial issue of belief in trust as a means of improving performance is as old as the hills. Even in the industrial age the guru giants can be seen in opposite camps. Frederick Winslow Taylor epitomized non-trust by infinite division of labour and quality control by inspection. Edwards Deming contradicted the philosophy by eliminating inspection, giving responsibility to the worker, driving out fear and creating the next 'station' as the customer 'demonstrating trust at each and every step'.

Trust is seen both as something that facilitates high quality – vital in competitive markets and also as a vital component for the success of partnerships, strategic alliances and networks of small firms.

In the wider context I will refer in Chapter 8 to the ground-breaking work of Francis Fukuyama (1995) who attributes national industrial competitiveness to trust as a societal-level cultural norm and social capital.

According to Fukuyama, people's capacity to institutionalize trust in the realm of work and business accounts for the industrial success of Japan and Germany. By contrast, the 'missing middle', namely the absence of intermediate social groups in the area between the family and large, centralized organizations like the Church and State, accounts for the relative economic backwardness of Latin Catholic countries (like Italy, France and Spain) and Chinese societies.[30]

Fukuyama produces an appealing plausible link between trust and business performance. Mari Sako used the studies on 'voice' and 'exit' to support and develop the idea with empirical evidence.

In exploring the concept of trust in the context of customers and suppliers Professor Sako subdivides the subject into three:

Contractual trust (will the other party carry out its contractual agreements?)

Competence trust (is the other party capable of doing what it says it will do?)

Goodwill trust (will the other party make an open-ended commitment to take initiatives for mutual benefit while refraining from unfair advantage taking?)

Outputs in business performance terms

In looking at these three elements of trust Mari Sako relates to three types of output in business performance terms:

1. Reducing transaction costs (from transaction cost economics – TCE), hence if 'goodwill' trust is high then 'contractual' trust safeguards are less necessary then we can do without the lawyers! Similarly Edwards Deming would argue you can do without the inspectors!
2. Investment to increase future returns trusting a new supplier requires an investment, a leap of faith – just as trusting a new employee requires the same. Investment in trust relations may further reduce transaction costs and improve quality.
3. Continuous improvement and learning.

The logic continues that high trust, particularly the goodwill sort, gives rise not only to lower transaction costs or to higher net benefits from investment but also to more rapid innovation and learning.[31]

In other words, suppliers in high-trust relations are likely to exploit opportunities to the mutual benefit of both the customer and the supplier, which would otherwise not have been exploited had transactions depended solely on contracts or 'incentives'. These outcomes are achieved through an orientation towards joint problem solving to improve quality, to reduce costs, and to innovate production and management methods. Such collaboration between a customer and a supplier leads to learning-by-transacting. This implies that even after trust is built and established, trading partners that are performing well are likely to interact intensively. *Trust is therefore like a renewable resource which atrophies with disuse and multiplies with use.*[32]

What is also clear from this analysis of outputs is the parallel with employment – this is exactly what is prescribed in Chapters 1 and 2 of this book in terms of creating a learning business!

Survey evidence

In attempting to address the question of whether trust enhances performance, Mari Sako uses the data collected with Susan Helper via the IMVP programme. Some of the results are shown below.

The survey asked respondents to evaluate how much trust they could place on their customer. The items used to measure trust and opportunism in the questionnaire are shown in Table 5.7. Specifically, the concept of 'contractual trust' is operationalized by the reversed statement: 'We prefer to have everything spelt out in detail in our contract.' This preference for detailed formal contracts is presumed to arise from the supplier's distrust that the customer would not stick to promises unless formally spelt out in a contract. The concept of 'competence trust' is captured by a reversed statement: 'The advice our customer gives us is not always helpful.' 'Goodwill trust' is encapsulated by the statement: 'We can rely on our customer to help us in ways not required by our agreement with them.' The survey also asked about suppliers' perception of fairness which is a basis for the sustenance of goodwill trust. Lastly, customer opportunism was captured by the statement: 'Given the chance, our customer might try to take unfair advantage of our business unit.'

Table 5.7: *Trust and opportunism in Japan, the USA and Europe*

	Japan (N = 472)	USA (N = 671)	Britain (N = 123)	Germany (N = 51)	Latin Catholic Europe (N = 52)
Contractual trust We prefer to have every-thing spelt out in detail in our contract*	24	17	15	27	14
Competence trust The advice our customer gives us is not always helpful*	48	31	36	29	40
Goodwill trust We can rely on our customer to help us in ways not required by our agreement with them	39	37	43	50	64
Fairness We can depend on our customer always to treat us fairly	68	42	40	54	55
Customer opportunism Given the chance, our customer might try to take unfair advantage of our business unit	24	56	33	26	26

Note: The figures show the percentages responding 4 or 5 on a five point scale (5 = strongly agree; 4 = agree; 3 = neither agree nor disagree; 2 = disagree; 1 = strongly disagree). The statements (*) for contractual trust and competence trust are reversed so the figures are the percentages responding 1 or 2.

In order to examine inter-country differences in trust, the data was divided into the following locations of the responding supplier companies: Japan, the USA, Britain, Germany and the Latin Catholic countries in Europe (namely Italy, France and Spain). The sample size (268 out of 1415) for the European countries is quite small and the results must be interpreted with caution. But Britain was separated out to examine the supposed similarities with the USA. Germany and the Latin Catholic countries were distinguished in order to examine whether there is any evidence of a contrast between the 'spontaneously sociable' and the 'missing middle' countries identified by Fukuyama (1995). The survey asked about inter-organizational trust (suppliers' trust of customers). Therefore, we would expect organizational trust in Germany to be higher than in Latin Catholic countries *where high interpersonal trust does not extend to trust between organizations.*

Mari Sako analyses the results as follows. As shown in Table 5.7, 'contractual trust' is the highest in Germany and Japan, while the suppliers in the Anglo-American and Latin Catholic countries prefer less contractual flexibility. Japanese suppliers exhibit the highest level of 'competence trust' towards their customer companies, while results for the other countries are mixed, with Latin Catholic suppliers exhibiting a rather high level of 'competence trust' in contrast to German suppliers. 'Goodwill trust' as measured in the survey is the highest among the Latin Catholic and German suppliers, followed by the German and Catholic suppliers, while the majority of Anglo-American suppliers do not expect fair treatment from their customers. Lastly, customer opportunism is more prevalent in the USA and Britain than in Japan, Germany or the Latin European countries. Although the results are broadly as expected, the anticipated distinction between Germany and the Latin Catholic countries is not evident in the survey.

The results we are now familiar with from the voice versus exit analysis earlier are used to demonstrate the performance of trust relationships (see Figures 5.18, 5.19 and 5.20).

Hence there is some support for the hypothesis that trust is conducive to good supplier performance and that this positive link is stronger for goodwill than for other types of trust.

Now to the holy grail.

How can trust be created?

This is the question that has dogged management in low trust adversarial environments that I can recall throughout my 30 plus years in manage-

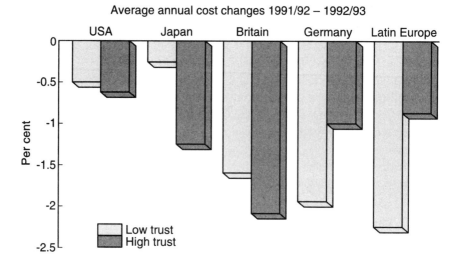

Fig. 5.18 *High trust suppliers controlled costs better in UK and Japan*

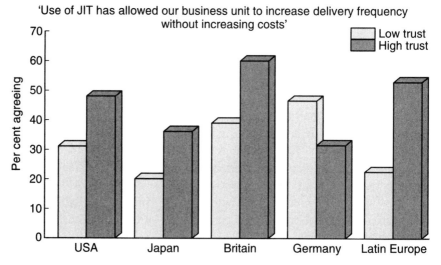

Fig. 5.19 *High trust suppliers were better at just-in-time delivery*

ment. Alan Fox (1973) described this as a vicious circle of 'low trust dynamics' in which low trust generates less open communication (leading to misunderstandings) and tighter control to eliminate any scope for discretion which in turn reinforces the low trust attitude. Breaking the vicious circle is all the more difficult because a trusting first step, for example in the form of disclosing confidential information, increases one's vulnerability to the other's opportunistic behaviour.

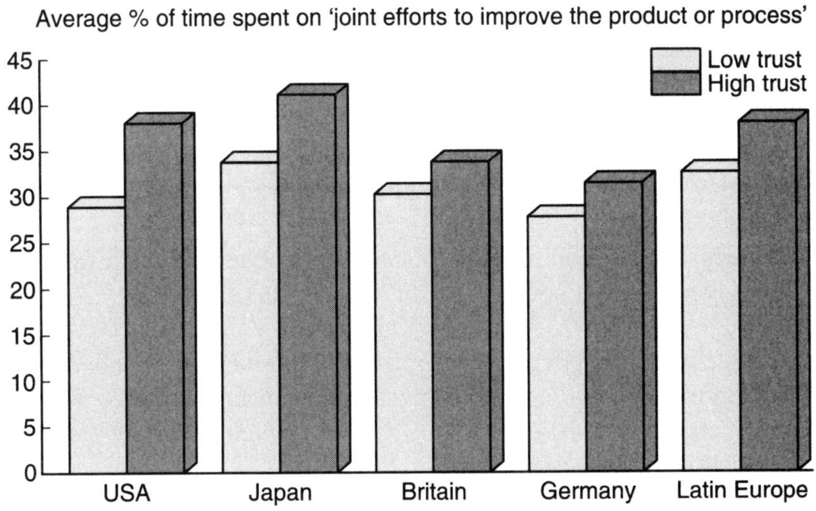

Average % of time spent on 'joint efforts to improve the product or process'

Fig. 5.20 *High trust suppliers were better at joint continuous improvement*

Using well-documented prescriptions Mari Sako measured the empirical data from the survey against:

- legalistic remedies, including the use of formal contracts (helps contract and competence trust but moderates goodwill);
- a rational calculative approach (that is, long-term relationship);
- gift exchange (technical assistance enhances goodwill and competence trust).

Again she finds that allowance must be made for cultural differences such as the 'embeddedness' demonstrated by Japanese companies who are more disposed to trusting their trading partners than British companies.[33]

This may be the product of experience. For instance, Japanese suppliers in the automotive industry may trust their customers more today because they have had more customer commitment, more technical assistance, and so on over a much longer period of time than most US suppliers, and their trusting behaviour has been honoured by being given growing orders. In contrast, a typical (though more eloquent) US supplier executive asserted that their customer 'would steal a dime from a starving grandmother'.

At another level, beyond the firm Fukuyama (1995) argues convincingly that the density of networks at levels between the state and individual firms accounts for the prevalence of institutionalized trust in certain societies such as Japan and Germany.

In conclusion, after allowing for national and regional differences Professor Sako argues that the evidence shows:

1. as we have seen, in terms of linking trust to business performance, the focus should shift from minimizing transaction costs to a focus on learning and innovation with 'goodwill trust' having the strongest impact on performance;
2. in terms of creation of trust, management should move away from safeguards against abuse of trust to enhancers of trust.

The latter are like 'gift exchange' based on loose reciprocity over time. According to the survey evidence, the trust enhancers may take the form of customers' technical assistance to suppliers, which does not function as a safeguard against opportunism.

One effective safeguard is information sharing (that is, two-way flow of information), while the unilateral provision of information by customers, regardless of *whether suppliers reciprocated simultaneously or not*, was found to enhance trust. Other safeguards, such as legal contracts, were found to have differential effects in different countries, with the USA experiencing a low trust dynamics and the Latin European countries experiencing a positive impact of longer contracts on enhancing trust.

Thus, while law in certain countries may help jump-start trust relations in business, in the end 'goodwill trust' has to be found not by resort to law but through learning-by-interacting to fill in the gap left by incomplete contracts. At the same time, gift exchange as an enhancer of trust, in the form of technical assistance for example, may depend on a social norm of loose reciprocity, but in business there is no such thing as blind faith. The process of gift exchange may be started, and can only be sustained, *by intense communication and monitoring of each other's behaviour to find opportunities for continuous improvement*, but these are quite different from 'safeguards'.

This latter conclusion is reinforced by my own experience and also presents a conundrum for those involved in such change in the West. Just as I described in *Becoming World Class* how British managers misinterpreted the close attention and 'support' by their Japanese bosses and Japanese peer group as overwhelming supervision, so 'empowered' employees and independent suppliers may not take kindly to 'intense communication and monitoring' even though it is intended as mutual support.

CONCLUSIONS ON COMPETITIVENESS – HAVE THE GOOD IDEAS TRAVELLED?

The short answer is yes. There is plentiful evidence that world class practice is travelling and having competitive effect. The benchmarks taken by global industries such as motor manufacture are truly global – see the worldwide comparisons championed by Womack Jones and Roos in *The Machine that Changed the World*. Those plants most closely associated with learning from Japan are at the top of the list (see Figure 5.21).

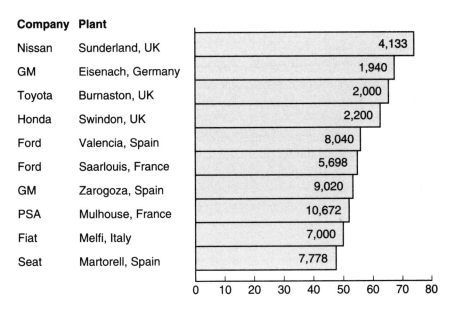

Company Plant

Company	Plant	Workforce
Nissan	Sunderland, UK	4,133
GM	Eisenach, Germany	1,940
Toyota	Burnaston, UK	2,000
Honda	Swindon, UK	2,200
Ford	Valencia, Spain	8,040
Ford	Saarlouis, France	5,698
GM	Zarogoza, Spain	9,020
PSA	Mulhouse, France	10,672
Fiat	Melfi, Italy	7,000
Seat	Martorell, Spain	7,778

Fig. 5.21 *Europe's most productive car plants. Vehicles per employee, 1996 (figure at end of bar is total workforce)*
Source: Financial Times 27.8.97

Between sectors too ...

A study of foreign inward investment into Europe and its effect on work practices and growth[34] concludes that almost a third of the productivity growth in UK manufacturing industry since the mid-1980s can be ascribed to the 'ripple through' effects of changes in work practices triggered by inward investment. Manufacturing productivity in the UK has risen significantly faster in the past ten years (3.75 per cent p.a.) than in the previous decade (2.8 per cent) and at above the rate of most of its international competitors with only Japan exceeding this figure.

The significance of the process of 'osmotic transfer' of new ideas being behind the leap in productivity growth is that the improvements are also transferred between companies which are in totally different sectors. My experience in the resurgence of the North East of England supports this. Japanese inward investment spawned Quality North.[35] This in turn spawned 'Manufacturing Challenge' which then begat 'Service Challenge' to catch the service sector up with the learning and networking that was going on in manufacturing (see also Chapter 8 for comparison with South Carolina, USA).

Further evidence of improvement is documented in a McKinsey study of the performance in quality terms of European auto-component suppliers (see Figure 5.22).[36]

The authors say customers of UK companies make 512 complaints about quality for every million parts compared with 1050 for Germany and 780 for France. Management techniques are partly behind the UK's high standing combined with the willingness of shop floor workers to adapt quickly to changing circumstances.

In running one of the world's largest businesses, Jack Welch says the priority is to transfer the best ideas from everyone, everywhere for renewal.[37]

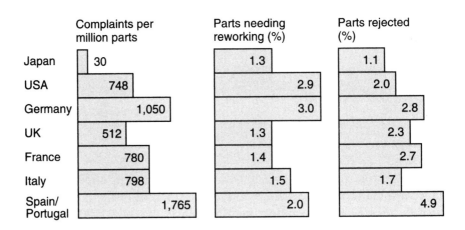

Fig. 5.22 *Comparison of process quality indicators*
Source: Romnel *et al.* (1997) *Quality Pays*

The challenge is that there is excess global capacity in almost every industry. Pricing pressures are dramatic across sector after sector. Change is getting faster. Our intellectual capital isn't US-based. Our culture is designed around making a hero out of those who translate ideas from one place to another, who help somebody else. They get an award, they get praised and promoted.

The way we do this is transportable and translatable. The fact is, all we are talking about is human dignity and voice – giving people a chance to speak, to have their best idea. That is a global desire of all people who breathe. If you find a way to get rid of the hierarchical nonsense and allow ideas to flourish, it doesn't matter if you're in Budapest or Beijing.

If this is so why aren't we all world class already!

Simply because not all have received and implemented the message. Professor Chris Voss of the London Business School in a study with Phil Hanson of IBM in 1994 found that 20 per cent of UK firms were 'laggers' despite an increasing number of leaders in terms of world class performance. Myopia across Europe is commonplace.

Chris Voss found that while 70 per cent of UK companies thought they performed at world class levels, only 2.3 per cent actually did so. The pattern was repeated elsewhere in Europe.

What about suppliers – led by example?

A recent study of medium-sized UK companies concluded that 73 per cent of middle market companies disagree that they should operate in partnership with their larger customers, preferring instead to maintain an adversarial commercial relationship.[38]

There is clearly much still to do to reach world class.

Notes
1. Eccles, 1994.
2. Hammer and Champy, 1993.
3. BPRC/DTI Study, 1997.

4. 'Competitiveness through Partnerships with People.' DTI, DfEE, Incl. TEC National; IPD, CBI, EEF, IIP, ESRC, TUC, IMC, IPA, MCI, RSA, IOD & IM.
5. Katzenbach and Smith, 1994: 18.
6. Ibid.: 45.
7. Ibid.: 48.
8. West and Lawthom, 1994.
9. *Personnel Today*, March 1996.
10. Ibid.
11. IPD, 1995.
12. Belbin, 1996.
13. Barger and Kirby, 1995.
14. Ibid.: 128, 129.
15. Ibid.
16. Ibid.: 204, 205.
17. For description of theory and practice see Ramsden and Zacharias, 1993.
18. Ibid.: (xvi), (xvii).
19. Ibid.
20. Ibid.: 364.
21. IPD, 1997.
22. For example: Blair, 1995; Kay, 1993; Sako, 1996.
23. Helper and Sako, 1995.
24   Sako, Lamming and Helper, 1995.
25. Sako, 1997a.
26. Ibid.: 8.
27. Helper, 1997.
28. Sako, 1997a.
29. CPPBB, 1997: 89.
30. Fukuyama, 1995: 55, 56.
31. Sabel, 1991.
32. Sako, 1997b.
33. Dove, 1993.
34. Barrell R. and Pain N. Foreign Direct Investment Technological Change and Economic Growth within Europe NIESR
35. See Morton, 1994: 91   and Moss Kanter, 1995: 365.
36. Romnel *et al.*, 1997.
37. Welch, J., CEO General Electric. Interview with Richard Waters, *Financial Times*, October 1997.
38. Coopers & Lybrand, 1994: 78.

6 Beyond Change. The Role of Leadership and Strategy

In Chapter 1 we looked at how individuals and teams made the learning organization. This theme was then developed into how companies could create knowledge for competitive advantage. To capitalize on knowledge, change must be embraced otherwise the host culture will reject the idea and not create the environment for growth.

Examples of change from round the world were looked at in detail in subsequent chapters and some broad-brush conclusions can be drawn:

- Change is hard.
- Change is resisted at every level due to fear of the unknown and protection of what we have (I have heard it said that the only person in favour of change affecting themselves is a baby with a wet nappy!).
- Creating a culture of change receptive to new ideas takes time and is values driven.
- Making change happen is a mixture of top-down, bottom-up and innovation in the middle.
- Systems, techniques, tools, teams, thirst for learning are all vital factors, however …
- Little will happen without leadership, signals, example and change embraced from the top.

This is 'motherhood and apple pie' of course. All in industry and government would agree. Often the perceived lack of 'walking the talk' at the top of organizations adds to the 'reasons for resisting' change. But it is necessary for us to get beyond this, beyond why don't *they* change to why don't *we* change. I believe we need to take a fundamental look at:

- what Boards are designed to do
- how we select for Board membership
- how we get the most from the members – is the sum of the whole greater or less than the parts?
- whether the Board should be a team – what are the obstacles?

WHAT BOARDS ARE DESIGNED TO DO

Bob Garratt in *The Fish Rots from the Head* (1996) quotes the 'Standards for the Board' from the Institute of Directors (IOD), London 1995. It is what Bob Garratt calls the four 'Directoral Dilemmas':

1. The board must simultaneously be entrepreneurial and drive the business forward while keeping it under prudent control.
2. The board is required to be sufficiently knowledgeable about the workings of the company to be answerable for its actions, and yet to stand back from the day-to-day management and retain an objective, longer-term view.
3. The board must be sensitive to the pressures of short-term, local issues and yet be informed of the broader trends and competition, often of an international nature.
4. The board is expected to be focused on the commercial needs of the business while acting responsibly towards its employees, business partners, and society as a whole.

This is not the place to go into depth over corporate governance or the discrete differences between Chairman and CEO, the respective roles of non-executive and executive members, how many and where their loyalties should lie. That has been covered *ad nauseam* by others and to me can be a sideshow to the real issue – how does the Board manage the *directoral dilemmas*?

Also, to use another Bob Garratt term, how does the Board become a *Learning Board*? How does the Board move from fixing day-to-day crises and being absorbed in historical measurement to perceiving the future through learning from the external environment?

Using the Chris Argyris model[1] of double loop learning, Bob Garratt draws the two loops for the Learning Board (see Figure 6.1), defining the 'business brain' as needing both to listen to what operations in the company are telling them is going on and at the same time monitoring the complexity and chaos of the continual changes in relevant external environments.

The necessary balance between these learning loops can be further understood if we examine subject matter for Boards. Bob Tricker (1980) developed a model of a Board's roles in 1980 (Figure 6.2).

Bob Garratt has developed the Learning Board model from these, reversing the order of strategy and policy on the right-hand side because he argues that policy is a function of reaction to the external environment

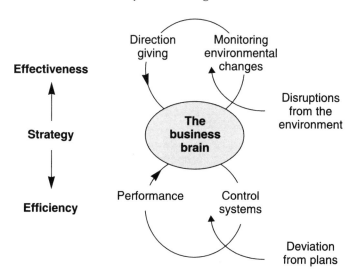

Fig. 6.1 *Double loop of learning*
Source: Garratt, B. (1996) *The Fish Rots from the Head*, HarperCollins LtdJ164

and strategy is about achieving the political will once policy is agreed (see Figure 6.3). He also replaces the central activity of the Board (appointing and rewarding the CEO) with the Learning Board as a recognition of the real importance of the effectiveness of the whole Board, not just one man or woman.

This move also helps with the earlier dilemmas in providing a focus on learning for the benefit of the whole organization – the Board as a 'central processor' of the organization while allowing all parts of the enterprise to simultaneously learn to survive. Giving the opportunity for Professor Reg Revan's maxim to be achieved:

$L \geqslant C$ for survival:
Learning must be greater than or equal to the rate of change.

Bob Garratt has taken this logic further in defining tasks for the Board. The left-hand side of the Learning Board model is christened *Conformance*:

- Accountability (conformance to legislation, regulation, shareholder and stakeholder wishes and audits)
- and Supervision of Management (conformance to key performance indicators, cash flow, budgets and projects)

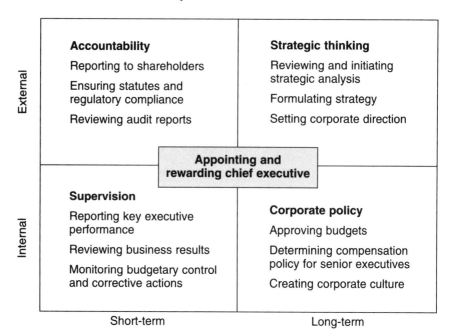

Fig. 6.2 *Bob Tricker's early model of a Board's roles*
Source: Tricker, R. I. (1980) *Corporate Governance*, London: Gower Press

The right-hand side – *Performance* – involves Policy formulation and Strategic thinking which drive the whole enterprise forward.

In a clever way this relates to the neuro-linguistic programming (NLP)[2] terminology of the left- and right-hand elements of the human brain in that the left-hand side of the 'business brain' deals with sensory, measurable aspects of business output whereas the right-hand side reflects the 'global' view or big picture in terms of policy and strategic thinking.

An example in practice – Peterborough Hospitals (see also Chapter 4)

In my second stint as Chairman of an NHS Hospital Trust I had the opportunity to use this logic to reconfigure how the Board fulfilled its role.

I inherited a Board that had a 'distance management' approach. The non-executives liked to meet separately and didn't want internal or external players to attend Board meetings. In Bob Tricker's terms[3] it was a 'Country Club' style Board where surroundings, status and relationships between non-executives were regarded as of a high order.

A workshop was eventually held after some resistance (oh, we've had one of those before – it wasn't successful), facilitated by my alter ego

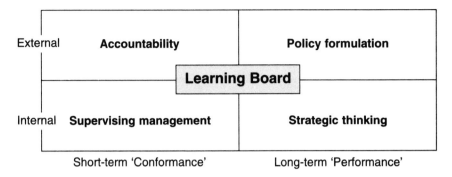

Fig. 6.3 *Learning Board model*
Source: Garratt, B. (1996) *The Fish Rots from the Head*, HarperCollins Ltd

Kelvin Cox when we analysed what we did against the Tricker/Garratt models. After a struggle the outcome was positive. We creamed off the conformance issues to a sub-committee of the Board – widening the coverage to take in all stakeholder measures – not just finance and efficiency but including measures such as patient care and staff satisfaction to give overall effectiveness. The conclusions were still presented to the Board, but summarized and giving the Board – now widened to include managers below Board level (and public and staff as observers) – time to delve into matters of policy and strategy instead of leaving these to the executive members as in the past. The distinction between Conformance and Performance was really useful and has helped shape a more dynamic Board that deals with all the issues – not just the ones that either the non-executives are most comfortable with or the issues that are fed to them by the executives because of perceived interest. The team process has been taken one step further with the Peterborough Board in 1998 with the wider members' understanding and sharing of their Myers Briggs profiles.

The balance between conformance and performance has been instinctively arrived at in the most successful companies. Walter Goldsmith and David Clutterbuck (1997) have studied what has enabled some of the world's most successful companies to remain on top through the 1980s and 1990s.

Lord Blyth, CEO of Boots PLC, is quoted on p. 57 of *Winning Streak Mk II*:

We don't review the performance numbers of the business at board meetings. The board gets a note of the figures in advance of the meeting and they ask questions about the numbers before the meeting. We don't spend more than ten minutes talking about the numbers in an historical sense. Nearly all the conversation is about critical challenges and growth opportunities.

Before moving on to the next vital issue – that of selecting for Board membership – it's worth noting the change the debate on corporate governance has made to the perceptions of Board role, in particular in relation to public sector Boards.

Local government and nationalized industries have had the great and the good as members on Boards, Authorities and Councils for as long as anyone can remember. The added value has been variable to say the least. I have worked both as an officer reporting to such bodies and as a Board member. The ethos was: feed the members enough of the right detail to distract them from interfering in the running of the business! A colleague tells me of a case with one local authority where the elected members were getting too interested and too close to some embarrassing issues for comfort. A diversionary tactic worked well. A paper on 'How should our town be signposted?' excited such interest that it was an agenda item for the next 18 months!

HOW DO WE SELECT FOR BOARD MEMBERSHIP?

Having closely examined the purpose of the Board the same rigour has to be applied to who is to be on the Board.

The corporate governance debate has concentrated on structural issues of Chairman/CEO roles, how many non-executives, what stakeholder interests are to be represented and defended, but little that helps the Board become a dynamic team.

What style of Board do we want? Let us return to Bob Tricker's model (Figure 6.4).

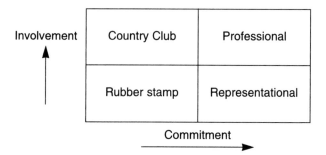

Fig. 6.4

Regrettably, until recent times the terms low commitment and low involvement have accurately described many Boards. The sketch picture of non-executive members being appointed for their name, status, connections and representational abilities has been all too familiar. Executive members playing games to achieve their own ends rather than serving the interests of stakeholders has been prevalent.

I would argue that this has been because the answers to the two questions so far:

What is our Board designed to achieve?

And what should be our Board style?

have not been effectively addressed.

Assuming that the aspiration for Tomorrow's Company is to have a professional Board, then factors other than connections, name, status, representing whatever, have to be used.

Recently I was asked to become a non-executive on a Board outside my own company. I was impressed when the reason highlighted was not one of connection or specialism but to fill a personality gap that had been identified by the Board. They were short of a 'Resource Investigator' in Meredith Belbin's definition. This told me they were looking to build a team, not a collection of individuals.

Executive member selection is open to similar blight. Managers in organizations are rewarded for producing the numbers. Traditionally those who have climbed the greasy pole have managed the 'conformance' elements of the business and are more than likely to be 'sensors' in Myers Briggs terms, that is, those whose decision making is based on hard quantifiable facts and figures. In terms of managing the right-hand side of the business brain, this is totally justifiable.

However, probably they have been immersed in the engine room of the business where the right-hand brain is dominant. At Board level (and preferably below) the left-hand brain of performance, that is, policy and strategy, becomes more important for the long term than conformance. Stokers below decks are unaware of approaching icebergs. The horizons have to be widened to take in other stakeholder needs and intuition is needed for future direction. Boards need intuitives and 'feelers' at executive level as well as sensors and 'thinkers' – it is a question of balance to ensure short-term conformance and long-term performance.

A parallel danger has been Board cloning. Margaret Thatcher was often quoted as asking 'Is he one of us?' Perhaps a reason for her demise before she was ready to go was in having too many 'of us' around her. On the Rolls-Royce IPG Board (see Chapter 4) we went through a personality profiling exercise – initially to help with more effective recruitment, later to aid teamwork. It was a great surprise to many round the boardroom table that they had very similar profiles – no wonder they rarely questioned each other's assumptions and no wonder they thought I was different, if not strange!

Along with this uncanny genetic-like selection goes parenting. Boards in authoritarian climates have operated in parent–child mode to subordinates since time immemorial.

Just as with the horrifying evidence from family life that the abused become abusers, it's easy to note how historical patterns are repeated in management hierarchies.

To me, then, board selection techniques are as vital as recruitment techniques when the modern organization builds a team.

Having selected a Board with due regard to corporate governance, stakeholders, conformance and performance, the questions then are:

> *How do we get the most from the members? Is the sum of the whole greater or less than that of the parts?*

> *Should the Board be a team?*

Many Boards meet at infrequent intervals, often due to a combination of the nature of the business and geographic spread of the members.

It's hard for such Boards to perceive the need for teamworking. It is harder to achieve, even when the organization has adopted teamworking as a modus operandi below board level.

In my mind there is a definite parallel between the self-managing worker teams we are trying to develop across the base line of the organization and our top management group. We are really trying to create the same behaviours of openness, collective problem solving, multiple leadership, and mutual trust and respect in both situations. So there are important parallels. But somehow it is still different and more difficult at the top.

(George Fisher, CEO Motorola,
quoted by Jon Katzenbach and Douglas Smith[4])

Some Boards settle for being a working group rather than a team. The differences are highlighted by Katzenbach and Smith (see Table 6.1).

The Board needs to examine what added value it expects. If it wants the

Table 6.1 *Differences between Working Group and Team*

Working Group	Team
Strong, clearly focused leader	Shared leadership roles
Individual accountability	Individual and mutual accountability
The group's purpose is the same as the broader organization mission	Specific team purpose that the team itself delivers
Individual work products	Collective work products
Runs efficient meetings	Encourages open-ended discussion and active problem-solving meetings
Measures its effectiveness indirectly by its influence on others (e.g. financial performance of the business)	Measures its performance directly by assessing collective work products
Discusses, decides, and delegates	Discusses, decides, and does real work together

Source: Katzenbach, J. and Smith, D. (1994) *The Wisdom of Teams: Creating the High Performance Organization*, McGraw-Hill

'Team' benefits, then hard work is needed to create a team from such high performing individuals.

Katzenbach and Smith set out the obstacles to acceptance of the team concept:[5]

1. *The purpose of the team is identical to the purpose of the Company.* Yes, the executives at the top are responsible for the Company's purpose; however, the same is true of potential teams elsewhere in the organization, although to a lesser degree. However, teams lower down the organization have more helpful tasks as potential products of their team work. Perhaps the answer is to articulate more clearly what the expected outputs need to be from executive teams.
2. *Membership in the team is automatic.* Membership is hierarchically dependent and not a product of selection on the basis of complementary skills, common commitment and mutual accountability (as can happen with 'naturally' occurring teams). In contemplating teams, boards often baulk at the potential size of the inclusive team and form subsets of ad hoc 'kitchen cabinets' without being open about it. This is often a function of linear thinking based on role or hierarchy. If the variable of personality type, left- and right-hand brain contribution, the need to integrate 'conformance' with

'performance' is injected then teams 'fit for purpose' rather than 'as of right' can evolve.

3. *Role and contribution of team members, including the leader, are defined by their hierarchical and functional position.* 'My job' is far more clear cut and easier to commit to than 'our job'. Individual accountability and personal achievement are deeply ingrained in successful executives. (See Chapter 1 for discussion on educational influence.) The expected contribution coincides with that individual's formal job title or description. The measure of the dynamic team in my view is where the contribution transcends this strait-jacket and allows individual members to contribute to the full range of board business. Teams at the top, like teams elsewhere, must develop a sense of mutual trust and interdependence – it is hard to rely on peers who are neither boss nor subordinate. Without development of mutuality the leader's life can be very lonely and very exposed.

4. *Spending extra team time is inefficient.* The top management group frequently has a common goal of *minimizing* their time together, sticking to well-prioritized agendas in order to allow time for leading their own discrete teams and getting 'the job' done. Teamwork-type tasks are done by folk below with results reflected upwards. Hence the executive's contribution typically covers two aspects, (a) work done by other people and (b) the executive's own judgements and experience. I would argue that effective time spent building the board team pays handsome dividends.

5. *Team effectiveness depends only on communications and openness.* These are important ingredients of teamworking but do not add up to forming a team with mutual accountability and what is called emotional intelligence (see Chapter 5).

Katzenbach and Smith argue that acceptance of these five assumptions drives executive groups to the working group approach without any consciousness that a choice is being made.[6]

For the sum of the whole to be greater than the sum of the parts the Board *has to* work as a team. Boards can operate as working groups, arriving at decisions using effective discussion and then assigning individual members for implementation. However, there is not necessarily any joint responsibility for the outcome of such decisions and in such a case there is no commitment to team performance.

Training and development

Bob Garratt argues[7] that having dealt effectively with selection, board tasks and composition:

A board needs to commit itself to the idea of having three parallel streams of training and development under way simultaneously:

– The training and development of individual directors

– The training and development of the board as an effective working group (or team)

– The continuing development of the enterprise as a whole.

This then connects the Learning Board to the Learning Organization.

But how? Director development programmes exist in abundance around the world, concentrating on educating the individual on governance, strategy, understanding functions with the inevitable concentration on mechanics and efficiency.

My experience is that Bob Garratt's first two streams can be simultaneous and can give synergy to one another. Just as in other change programmes mentioned in this book, movement here is a function of process. By a number of Board members developing together unique bonds are created while participating in the learning process.

Breaking the ice

Substantial Board development occurred at Gateshead Hospitals, Rolls-Royce IPG and latterly Anglian Water, all starting from the point of sharing knowledge about personality profiles. At Gateshead in 1993 we shared the results of the Belbin personality inventory (see Chapter 4) and then formed subgroups based on this information to pursue various projects, having constructed the teams based on preferences, not position or job title. This had the effect of creating the 'Unitary board' where all felt able to contribute equally and the CEO did not feel in a lone position. I would argue that this is a real measure of an effective team – does the CEO feel exposed and isolated when the going gets tough? Or is the problem shared?

Similarly at Rolls-Royce IPG we eventually pooled Myers Briggs personality preference data and decision-making styles using Action Profile[R] (see Chapters 4 and 5). The first product was to legitimize diversity

– those with different profiles (for example 'feeling' types) not only were encouraged to be true to their type but also the team recognized that their contribution was needed for effective management. Also, intuitives ('N' preference) were able to bring their perspective without being 'put down' by sensors challenging for historical facts when judging the future.

There was an amusing moment when the whole Board discovered how 'private in intention' they were in terms of getting on with the daily and functional task. (For a definition of 'intention' see Figure 5.9.) One of my colleagues said there was probably truth in the rumour that if someone died on the director's floor they wouldn't be discovered for two weeks! Not a unique perception – I heard of another company where the director's oak panelled floor was known as the 'Chapel of Rest'!

Why is such 'soft stuff' necessary for director development? Essentially because the nature of business and the world of work is changing so rapidly. Daniel Goleman in *Emotional Intelligence*[8] suggests that by the millennium a third of the American workforce will be 'knowledge workers', people whose productivity is marked by adding value to information. Peter Drucker, who coined the term 'knowledge worker', points out that such workers' productivity depends on their efforts being coordinated as part of an organizational team: 'teams become the work unit rather than the individual himself or herself'[9] (this challenge is taken up in Chapter 9).

Emotional intelligence as opposed to IQ is the skills that help people harmonize in teams. Goleman defines these skills as knowing and managing one's emotions (not necessarily controlling); motivating oneself through marshalling emotions; having empathy with others; and handling emotional relationships. High performing organizations, according to Goleman, tend to have high levels of emotional intelligence among their members and strong links between emotional capabilities and skills.[10]

> The single most important element in group intelligence, it turns out, is not the average IQ in the academic sense, but rather in terms of emotional intelligence.
>
> The key to a high group IQ is social harmony. It is the ability to harmonize that, all other things being equal, will make one group especially talented, productive and successful, and another – with members whose talent and skill are equal in other regards – do poorly.[11]

If all this sounds too ethereal for Board development, Daniel Goleman retorts: 'How can we learn together if we can't get along together?'

There is another relevant dimension for pressured executives which is beyond just getting on better with their colleagues. Bob Garratt empathizes:

> Directors ... feel that there is a lack of balance in a number of personal areas: between mind and body, work life and home life, work and recreation, work life and spirit. The vast majority of directors I meet around the world think that they are out of balance on all these dimensions and are struggling to find the time to rebalance matters. Having a Personal Development Agenda at least legitimizes the aspiration.[12]

This is a long way from yesterday's notion that for a director 'if you are god you are not trainable'. My colleague Chris Mellor, Group Managing Director of Anglian Water, points out that if we were aspiring sportsmen no one would think twice about one-to-one coaching, mentoring and development, so why not for directors?

Using the mirror

I have only described the first faltering steps on the 'team' journey, simply because it is so difficult for Boards to accept that they not only can benefit from such development but that they can as a Learning Board set the tone for the whole organization. That it is a longish journey with an uphill task is graphically shown by Katzenbach and Smith in the Team Performance Curve[13] (see Figure 6.5).

Their definitions of the stages along the curve are as follows:

Working group: Sum of 'individual bests'. Group meets to share information, best practices or perspectives and to make decisions to help each individual perform within his or her area of responsibility.

Pseudo-team: Perceived incremental performance need but not focused on collective performance and is not really trying to achieve it. No interest in shaping a common purpose – the sum of the whole is *less* than the potential of the individual parts.

Potential team: Perceived incremental performance need and effort to improve. However, lacks clarity about purpose, goals or products. No collective accountability.

Real team: People with complementary skills, equally committed to a common purpose, goals and working approach for which they hold themselves mutually accountable.

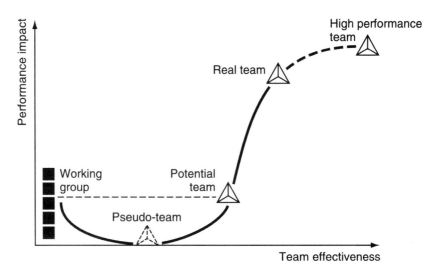

Fig. 6.5 *The team performance curve*

Source: Katzenbach, J. and Smith, D. (1994) *The Wisdom of Teams: Creating the High Performance Organisation*, McGraw-Hill

High performance team: As above but with members who are also deeply committed to one another's personal growth and success. It outperforms all other like teams and all reasonable expectations.

The process doesn't end there of course. Bob Garratt recommends a thorough system of Board development with an ongoing programme of regular facilitated away-days to take stock and move on to the next step.

Other observers would agree. Lynn McGregor produced an unpublished discussion paper entitled 'New Realities for Leading Boards' in 1994 based on a survey of 100 Board members, eight Institutional shareholders and her experience over 15 years of assessing Board and top-level potential. As a further mirror on Board performance I reproduce her comparative table on 'Levels of competence: differences between poor and advanced boards' (Table 6.2). This, with an honest self-appraisal, would give Chairmen/CEO a measure on where their particular Board is and an idea of the distance that needs to be travelled along the Team Performance Curve to give world class performance.

If the reader is still unconvinced on the need for Board development then a start point is the UK Institute of Directors report 'Development of and for the Board' (1990) which showed that 92.4 per cent of UK directors had no training and development for the job – most did not even know

Table 6.2 *Levels of competence. Differences between poor and advanced Boards*

(5) Poor Boards	(4) Mediocre Boards	(3) Competent Boards	(2) Good Boards	(1) Advanced Boards
Nearly out of the League	Fourth and Third Division (somewhere between poor and competent Boards)	Third Division (Second and First in the UK Step change from 4)	Premier League (All of 3. Plus the following:)	On the way to world best (All of 3 and 4 plus the following:)
1. No sense of vision or direction. Strictly short term. Crisis management. 2. Poor financial performance. Consistent loss of market share. 3. Can't deliver either at all or on time. Poor systems and structure which don't work. 4. Weak Board dominated by incompetent key players. Lack of trust, morale or goodwill. Climate ripe for either potential or actual malpractice. 5. Negative and difficult relationships with shareholders and other stakeholders. Large numbers of increasing complaints. 6. Demotivated and ineffective employees.	1. Usually characterized by an emphasis on survival and cost cutting. Intolerance of risk. 2. Lack of confidence, morale or enthusiastic competitive energy. 3. Low level of thinking and decision-making. Board members' talents not fully utilized, Poor grasp of priorities. 4. Financial performance on borderline. Low growth. Too many unpleasant surprises for comfort. 5. Out-of-date Board structure and composition. Some inappropriate Board members. 6. There is potential for improvement but people don't take time to do something about it because they are too busy.	1. Healthy bottom line results. The Board delivers what it says it's going to deliver on time. 2. Enthusiastic shareholders, happy customers, suppliers and other stakeholders. High calibre, motivated and effective employees. 3. Products and services serving the perceived general well being of society. 4. Good vision, leadership and strategic direction. Effective identification, distribution and execution of major Board tasks. 5. Effective working practices which orchestrate the talents, experience, skills, energy and time of every Board member and the Board as a whole. 6. Aware of change and need to change but not sure how to. May not grow people fast enough and may be too complacent for change.	1. Increased levels of confidence in the ability to respond, both to market forces and to the increasingly searching demands of stakeholders and key institutional (and others) investors. 2. A powerful, coherent Board, seen to be performing beyond its expected capacities with improvement reflected in well above average bottom line results. 3. Innovative working practices which enable step changes to be made to go from second to first division. 4. Willingness of Board as a whole to continuously improve performance. Regular reviews of how performance affects results. 5. Significantly improved quality and speed of decision making. 6. Ability to be questioned, challenged and to change.	1. Outstanding results in the areas of finance, technology, products and services, and social innovation. 2. Clearly defined role within a global context. Advanced socially responsible and wealth-creating global vision. 3. Inspired leadership in constructive and creative partnership with shareholders and stakeholders. 4. In forefront of best practice in most areas. Ahead of the game. Able to think the unthinkable and make significant shifts. 5. Able to influence and help improve the system as a whole. 6. Continued capacity to grow, learn and be challenged.

what the job was. Bob Garratt in his involvements with Boards worldwide finds this pattern is universally true.

A later survey by Warwick Business School and the Foundation for Manufacturing and Industry for Coopers and Lybrand in 1997 found that company directors in UK middle-sized companies were neglecting their own training and career development. As a result they lack a depth and breadth of business experience and suffer from a 'high degree of insularity'. Only 8 per cent of the 308 companies in the sample stipulated the provision of minimum days for Board director training.[14]

A further measure of dysfunction at Board level is the well-publicized 'fallings out' in recent times at notable companies such as Cable and Wireless (C&W), E Map, United Utilities, BP, Glaxo, Cowie Group and Saatchi. Matthew Lynn, studying this pattern in *Management Today* in February 1997, includes a quote from Ian Smith, MD at management consultants Monitor Europe: 'There is often an escalating impasse between directors because of the low quality of the dialogue within the boardroom. The collective IQ of the board is often lower than that of individual members … often people just find themselves taking up duelling positions.'

In the same article Colin Sewell-Rutter, Director of Results Partnership, put his finger on the issue: 'The single most important source of problems within the Boardroom is the lack of a shared vision, and shared corporate goals.'

A more fundamental point is raised as to whether the structural improvements to Board membership brought about by the corporate governance debate (that is, as a result of the Cadbury recommendations for more non-executives on the Board) has meant a greater distance between executives and non-executives due to a vast difference in 'insider' knowledge.

What has happened is that in many cases more non-executives have been introduced by unitary Boards for all the right reasons of protecting stakeholder interest but the product has sometimes been perversely unhelpful. These non-executives, very busy people now forming 50 per cent and more of total Board membership, either don't have the inclination, time or are not encouraged by the executives to become involved in the business. This low level of involvement was tolerable with a minority of non-executives but with a majority it can lead to instability and more frequent challenges to Chairman and CEO based on distance and lack of understanding.

Based on the experience at both Gateshead and Peterborough Hospitals where by definition non-executives are in the majority, my prescription is for non-executives to become involved and be given some limited responsibility. This was first tried in my experience on the Tyneside Training and Enterprise Council Board where I was deputy chair from 1990 to 1993. Here non-executive members 'adopted' areas of the business, taking care not to become 'lobbyists' or to undermine executive management. The pattern worked and has been successfully repeated on both the hospital Boards.

Training for non-executives is also vital – why not involve them in the 'away-day' pattern and sharing of personality profiles? After all as the business brain they to have to balance short term and long term, 'conformance' and 'performance'. It is they who often ultimately will decide on direction and policy through the key appointments of Chairman and CEO.

Leadership and teams

A further potential dysfunction relates to a tendency to place too great a faith in one individual such as a 'saviour' CEO brought in to turn around the company.

This discourages a collegiate approach, creates an unreal distance in status and often salary between the CEO and the rest of the Board and leaves the company vulnerable on succession. Arie De Geus in *The Living Company* (1997) points to the success of the Leeds Permanent Building Society which was run without a CEO for 18 months and increased its profits by 22 per cent during this time!

Arie De Geus comments: 'The machine [the Company] is too complicated, too sophisticated to be in the hands of one individual. It is extremely dangerous for business. Yet companies are remunerating it as if it is a beautiful thing.'

The conflict in the mind between where the world class organization should place its faith gets to the heart of the issue for the future.

While espousing teamwork and a collegiate approach flowing from 'stakeholder corporation' thinking the West still articulates undiluted faith in the panacea of charismatic leadership from the top. The evidence is often to the contrary. James Collins and Jerry Porras (1995) spent six years studying exceptional companies – visionary companies – to see what accounts for their success (to be explored further in Chapter 7).

What are visionary companies? They are the premier organizations in their field, firms that have a long record of having an impact on the world: Ford, Sony, Procter and Gamble, Merck, Motorola, Johnson and Johnson.

These are companies that have distinguished themselves as a special and elite breed of institution. With an average founding date of 1897 and stock-return performance of 15 times the general market since 1926, they are companies that have stood the test of time.

Collins and Porras make the telling distinction between leaders of 'time telling' and 'clock building':

- Having a great idea, or being a charismatic, visionary leader is like 'time telling'.
- Building a company that's healthy long after the visionary leader is gone or after the great product is passé is 'clock building'.

Charismatic leaders can be a myth. Although many visionary companies have had high-profile leaders like Henry Ford or Sam Walton, charismatic leadership is not necessary for success. 3M (see Chapter 3) for example, has never had a charismatic CEO. The best leaders, Collins and Porras argue, charismatic or not, make it a point to develop managers and processes. In their view the firm is not a vehicle for products or personalities; products are a vehicle for the company.

These highly successful companies have created vision and values that permeate generations of management and everything they do. It is not even in some cases bound up in a carefully crafted mission statement – it is all about living the values. I suppose it is the reverse of the bad parenting I talked of earlier; it is good parenting which builds on solid foundations.

Collins and Porras unearthed some interesting material on succession. Of the 18 visionary companies studied, only four times – in a combined life of 1700 years – did one of them go outside the firm for a CEO! That doesn't mean these companies don't go in for radical change. GE is a classic example. Under Jack Welch, a GE man all his working life, the group has accelerated with an average return on equity of 26.29 per cent under his leadership. Visionary companies like GE (see Chapter 3) develop, promote, and carefully select managerial talent from inside the company. That helps them preserve the ideals they believe in and ensures a long line of quality leaders. As the GE story shows, there's no inconsistency between promoting from within and stimulating significant growth and change.

It is impressive of course, and convincing; however, it doesn't help those who inherit organizations that have had a chequered past or need to be 'turned around' where injecting new leadership is needed. However, Collins and Porras are strong on process rather than the parachuting in of a charismatic leader.

For instance, 'Where to begin':

Pin down core ideology
Pin down purpose – what would the world lose if the company ceased
to exist?
What type of progress do you want to stimulate?

- BHAGs (Big Hairy and Audacious Goals) like Boeing
- Evolutionary like 3M
- Self-improving like Marriotts or all three features like Motorola?

Alignment to preserve the core and stimulate progress.

As for the charismatic leader model, we think the world is heading in
exactly the opposite direction. Just look at the twentieth century. Nearly
the entire world has moved towards democracy. [See also Table 7.1.]
Democracy is a process. The very essence of democracy is to avoid
over dependence on any single leader and put the primary focus on the
process. Even Churchill – perhaps the single greatest leader of this
century – was secondary to the nation and its processes, kicked out of
office at the end of World War II. Hitler, Stalin, Mussolini, Tojo – these
were charismatic leaders who did not understand they were
fundamentally less important than the institutions they served. ...
moreover *all* leaders die.[15]

Leadership is often seen as an alternative to teamwork. Jay Bourgeois,
Professor at the University of Virginia's Business School, puts limits on
team activity. 'You probably don't want to have a group decision when
you're landing an aircraft at Heathrow. Sometimes a project is best carried
out by a single person.' Sounds attractive but if in one pair of hands it is
all or nothing. The contrast is the example Daniel Goleman quotes in
Emotional Intelligence[16] of pilot McBroom.

Melburn McBroom was a domineering airline pilot with a temper that
intimidated those who worked with him. One day in 1978 McBroom's
plane was approaching Portland, Oregon when he noticed a problem with
the landing gear. He continued to circle at high altitude while he fiddled
with the mechanism, obsessed with the landing gear. The plane's fuel
gauges steadily approached the empty level. But his co-pilots were so
fearful of McBroom's wrath that they said nothing even as disaster
loomed. The plane crashed, killing ten people. Today the story of that
crash is told as a cautionary tale in the safety training of airline pilots.

The cockpit is a microcosm of any working organization. Goleman

makes the point that in 80 per cent of airline crashes pilot error could have
been prevented if teamwork, open lines of communication, cooperation,
listening and speaking one's mind – rudiments of social intelligence – had
been applied. I wonder how many company failures and lost opportunities
for growth could be attributed to the industrial versions of Pilot
McBroom?

Goleman argues for a value to be put on emotional intelligence – using
heart as well as head, contrary to tradition in industry. He quotes Shoshana
Zuboff, a psychologist at Harvard Business School:

> There was a long period of managerial domination of the corporate
> hierarchy when the manipulative, jungle fighter boss was rewarded.
> But that rigid hierarchy started breaking down in the 1980s under the
> twin pressures of globalization and information technology. The jungle
> fighter symbolizes where the corporation has been: the virtuoso in
> interpersonal skills is the corporate future.

The business of achieving the contribution of individuals in teams is
what leadership is all about. C.K. Prahalad, co-author of the best selling
Competing for the Future, warns that the fashion for teams might lead to
some kind of tame consensus management and argues the case for 'stars'.

Sir John Harvey-Jones does not feel that stars and teams are mutually
exclusive concepts. 'Look at wolves,' he says, 'they're not lone at all.
They hunt in a pack with each member of the pack taking up the role
which he or she is in the best position to fill in relation to what's going on
at the time – that's also how the British Army SAS unit operates.'[17]

The same thought is echoed by John Kay, Director of the Said School
of Management Studies at Oxford University.[18] He and colleagues applied
econometrics to the performance of clubs in the English football league
over a 20-year period. By and large they found that in performance terms
you got what you paid for and those clubs who paid most for players
obtained the best performance.

But some football clubs showed superior performance even without
superstars. During this period, Liverpool FC was most conspicuous in not
only being the most successful of all clubs but with far less expenditure
on players.

Liverpool FC was one of the few cases where there was evident value
to the team – the whole was worth more than the aggregate of the parts.
How did Liverpool FC do this? They made a virtue (or value) of the
passing game, not the shooting game. The player with the ball at his feet
decides which way to go based on:

the extent to which his rewards reflect individual or team performance and what he thinks his colleague will do with the ball

The route normally chosen (that is, in accordance with values) creates either a passing team or a shooting team. John Kay's research showed that it is easier to change from a passing game to a shooting game than to go in the opposite direction. Liverpool have found that the passing game, barring accidents, pays off in the long term – at lower cost.

John Kay concludes: 'Designing structures which achieve a balance between cooperation and competition, which combine team behaviours and individual motivation is one of the hardest parts of building organizations – or designing economic systems.' Perhaps that's where Leadership comes in.

Professor Amin Rajan of City University Business School has produced a report on creating leadership in the City of London.[19] He draws the distinction: 'Management is about now, leadership about the future; one implements goals, the other sets them; one relies on control, the other inspires trust; one deals in rational processes, the other in emotional horizons.' The study points out that in developing leaders it is a continuum, a journey from childhood experience, emotional intelligence, workplace experiences and mentoring through to 'knowing thyself and others'. Rajan concluded that there were the following five key ingredients of successful companies:

- Their leaders are visionary, enthusiastic champions of change who have communicated their business goals throughout the company and generated the necessary commitment at all levels.
- They have flexible, motivated employees capable of performing multiple tasks at differing levels of responsibility.
- They learn from their customers, competitors, suppliers and academia.
- They have a culture of innovation that seeks continuous improvement in products and working methods.
- Their business processes and practices seek to achieve low-cost product customization while retaining a clear edge in price, quality and service. They have inverted traditional manufacturing logic by securing for batch production all those advantages commonly associated with mass production and standardization.

Rajan concluded: 'these companies have a style that reconciles the diverse needs of customers, shareholders and employees'. Through strong face-to-face contacts their leaders generate a sense of excitement and mutual trust which enthuses managers and employees to go that proverbial 'extra mile' for one another, creating the essential motivation for high productivity. Ian Gibson CBE, Chief Executive of Nissan Motor Manufacturing UK, believes that in today's more complex business climate, leadership has to be redefined. Organizations, he says, have gone from 'diamond', ordered crystalline structures with fixed boundaries and linkages, to 'mud', amorphous, changing shapes, blurred edges and definitions (incidentally both made of carbon!).

Teams can easily become amorphous whereas organizations create their own rigidities.

Leadership, he says, is giving people skills, goals and the room to excel.

These thoughts are not new; Los-Tzu is claimed to have said:

The bad leader is he who the people despise.
The good leader is he who the people praise.
The great leader is he (of) whom the people say 'we did it ourselves'.[20]

LEADERSHIP AND STRATEGY

If leaders no longer direct people in their everyday work (and lives), how do they make a difference? Professor Amin Rajan's research[21] shows that top leaders in the City see themselves as chief coaches. If this is so he questions whether they can justify their pay differentials.

Goldsmith and Clutterbuck in *Winning Streak Mk II* (1997) focus on three 'cornerstones of sustained performance' which stem from attitudes at the top of the most successful companies that they studied:

- A challenge culture
- Simple (but not simplistic) solutions to complex problems
- A highly developed sense of 'rightness'

These are all contributions of leadership and can lead to 'vision', 'policy' and values (see Collins and Porras).

Winning Streak Mk I was published in 1983 when eight characteristics of highly successful companies were defined: *Leadership, autonomy, control, involvement, market orientation, zero basing, innovation and integrity.* Those were the days when crystalline structures (to take Ian Gibson's definition) were perceived to be the solution.

Today, Goldsmith and Clutterbuck find that the critical issues are ones of balance in an increasingly complex world, not wholesale addiction to a formula that transcends time. They find it is a case of striking the 'correct' balance in ten areas:

1. *Control versus autonomy*
2. *Long-term strategy versus short-term urgency*
3. *Evolutionary versus revolutionary change*
4. *Pride versus humility*
5. *Focus versus breadth of vision*
6. *Values versus rules*
7. *Customer care versus customer count*
8. *Challenging versus nurturing people*
9. *Leaders versus managers*
10. *Gentle versus abrupt succession*

There are more parallels between this study and *Built to Last* by Collins and Porras in particular the critical issues above: 1 to 10. For a comparison see 'No Tyranny of the OR' from *Built to Last*.

On the one hand:		**Yet, on the other hand:**
Purpose beyond profit	AND	pragmatic pursuit of profit
A relatively fixed core ideology	AND	vigorous change and movement
Conservatism around the core	AND	bold, committing, risky moves
Clear vision and sense of direction	AND	opportunistic groping and experimentation
Big Hairy Audacious Goals	AND	incremental evolutionary progress
Selection of managers steeped in the core	AND	selection of managers that induce change
Ideological control	AND	operational autonomy
Extremely tight culture (almost cult-like)	AND	ability to change, move, and adapt
Investment for the long term	AND	demands for short-term performance

| Philosophical, visionary, futuristic | AND | superb daily execution, 'nuts and bolts' |
| Organization aligned with a core ideology | AND | organization adapted to its environment |

The distinction appears to be almost one of semantics between Goldsmith and Clutterbuck, who are saying it's an issue of balance and the 'OR' has to be evaluated in each one of their critical issues, and Collins and Porras who say it's not balance (which in their mind implies going to the midpoint) but moving from choices (OR) to the genius of the 'AND'. 'In short, a highly visionary company doesn't want to blend yin and yang into a grey indistinguishable circle that is neither highly yin or highly yang; it aims to be distinctly yin *and* distinctly yang – both at the same time all the time.'[22] In other words, dealing with the dilemma of 'doing and 'being' (see Chapter 1).

This then is what leadership is about, running profitable companies today that have aspirations for a bright future because tomorrow's issues are addressed today.

This links to the eternal debate on strategy. However, as we saw from Bob Garratt's analysis, policy or vision has to be developed before strategy. Strategy is about how you get to the goal, not the goal itself.

Jack Welch of GE (see Chapter 3) is famous for specific vision or goals for each GE business to be No. 1 or No. 2 in their discrete markets. To liberate internal forces he has added 'boundarylessness' as a value to break down the internal barriers of hierarchy, geography and function to promote teamwork. He is not a fan of detailed strategic planning.

Trying to define what will happen three to five years out, in specific quantifiable terms, is a futile exercise. The world is moving too fast for that. What should a company do instead? First of all define its vision and its destiny in clear broad terms. Second maximize its own productivity. Finally be organizationally and culturally flexible enough to meet massive change. The way to control your destiny in a global environment of change and uncertainty is simple: Be the highest value supplier in your marketplace.[23]

STRATEGY BELONGS WHERE THE ACTION IS

Goldsmith and Clutterbuck remind us that the 1970s and 1980s concept of large central strategic planning departments were a product of the dictum 'structure follows strategy'. Strategy became the responsibility of strategists and managers were expected to stick to managing. Those were the days of 'crystalline' structures.

Two factors combined to make organizations reject this approach.

Firstly it didn't work. Phalanxes of MBAs trained in the same strategic theories tended to come up with the same answers whatever organization they worked in, so there was little opportunity for companies to differentiate themselves through the originality of their strategic approach. Managers who didn't have responsibility for generating strategy had no ownership of strategy ... Secondly, the return to fashion of leadership ... encouraged entrepreneurial people to demand that the centre should return accountability for strategy to those who had to make it work.

Goldsmith and Clutterbuck make the point that high performance companies rarely fell into this trap. The mantra was *strategy belongs where the action is*:

- the people running a business unit are usually best placed to understand how their markets are developing [using left-hand brain – my notation]
- strategic planning is a continuous evolutionary process and
- ownership and implementation of strategy are indivisible.[24]

As usual we discover that this is not a new idea. The Japanese under the influence of Edwards Deming evolved the system of Policy Deployment or 'management by policy' which I described in *Becoming World Class*, pp. 33, 148–51. The logic is one of cascade, consultation, involvement and consensus on policy and strategy (see Figure 6.6).

Policy deployment

My fellow adventurer, Peter Wickens, provides a helpful definition of Hoshin Kanri:

Objectives are integrated with the business strategy and permeate throughout, not only top-down but upwards and laterally, and this can only be done by involving people at all levels. The very process is part of their development. Top management, as a team, needs to begin the process by determining the corporate objectives; but in cascading

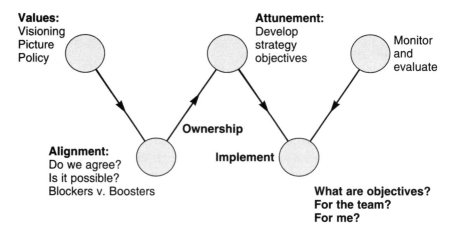

Fig. 6.6 *Policy deployment process (Hoshin Kanri)*

through the organization the process has to be not one of top-down imposition, but of asking people what they can do to contribute, discussing it, assessing the impact on their colleagues and agreeing not only the objectives but also the means of achieving them and the measurements to be applied. At all stages discussions between those affected takes place. The Japanese use the term hoshin kanri (policy deployment) for this process and the discussion and debate over the objectives is termed 'catchball'. It is a superb process for determining what really are the key objectives and for ensuring that they are genuinely shared.[25]

For a distinction between Hoshin and Kaizen see Chapter 1, p. 6.

Policy deployment, albeit not new, can be refreshing. In Anglian Water we tried this approach for the first time in 1997. The company had been following a process of empowerment for several years (see Chapter 4) but strategy was the province of executives and a central strategic planning department. This all changed and strategy and business planning were linked with Finance in 1996. With a confusing and increasingly complex business environment the route wasn't clear and managers didn't understand the conclusions that executives had drawn for future strategy. It was decided to cascade the 'picture' to all middle managers and first-line supervisors over a series of workshop days inviting contribution and response, linking the themes and process to two live programmes – IT roll-out and coaching techniques for managers. The two immediate products were a much better common understanding of the environment and the options on strategy and a buy-in to the agreed way forward. There were several by-products, not the least of which was that directors, in presenting the overall vision, confessed to understanding it themselves for the first time following simplification and delivery! An echo of Goldsmith and Clutterbuck's findings:[26]

> When a large European aerospace manufacturer decided to share its business plan with every one of its 22,000 employees, it was a bold step. Before then, only an inner cadre of 20 or so people had access to the whole plan. Communicating it more widely meant that it had to be turned into plain language and presented using straightforward, easily understood graphics. Some months later, a couple of members of the inner core admitted that this was the first time they had understood the plan fully and that one of the benefits of the exercise was that they were much clearer about what they had to do.

These pragmatic approaches would, I think, be approved of by Professor Henry Mintzberg (1988), the 'scourge of strategic orthodoxy' (Clutterbuck and Crainer, 1990) who puts forward the need to differentiate between strategic planning and strategic thinking, the former being analysis, the latter synthesis.

He identifies three key fallacies of strategic planning:

1. Its attempt at prediction in the era of discontinuity
2. Its typical detachment in practice from operations
3. Formalized approaches don't forecast discontinuities

He advocates a process instead:

(a) Use of planning as a process of operationalizing strategy
(b) The recognition of the ability of all employees to promote strategic change
(e) Use of planners as catalysts helping managers challenge convention
(d) Use of diversity – creative thinkers and analytical planners
(e) Avoid formalizing the process.

Using Mintzberg's process approach Gary Hamel and C.K. Prahalad (1994) have gone a giant leap further and challenged managers to reconfigure whole markets and industries – not be enslaved to them. They argue that changes in technology and the growth of international competition have eroded the traditional boundaries between markets and industries – the companies that survive into the next century will be those that first perceive these changes, define their core competencies by differentiating from the competition, and act accordingly.

Their motto is strategy as stretch with the object of using the human potential in the business: 'It is not cash that fuels the journey to the future, but the emotional and intellectual energy of every employee.'[27]

They point out how, like David and Goliath, the fortunes of well-established, well-resourced companies have changed only to be overtaken by those with less visible resources, for example:

Volkswagen versus Honda
Upjohn versus Glaxo
CBS versus CNW
Xerox versus Canon
RCA versus Sony
Westinghouse versus Hitachi
Pan Am versus BA
IBM versus Compaq
Firestone versus Bridgestone
Sears versus Wal-Mart

As an example of enormous stretch they instance the famous story of Komatsu which I detailed in *Becoming World Class* (pp. 29–36):

When Komatsu set its goal to match Caterpillar's world class quality in 1960, its product quality was less than half that of its exemplar. A more realistic goal for Komatsu might have been a 20% p.a. improvement in quality, but this would have left it far short of what it needed to wrest share from Caterpillar in export markets. Komatsu did achieve world-class quality levels and won the Deming prize a mere three years after announcing its quality quest.[28]

The strategic intent then was to 'catch up with and surpass Caterpillar'. Thirty years later Komatsu made another strategic leap. Ghoshal and Bartlett (1994) covered this change in a section of a *Harvard Business Review* article, 'From strategic intent to corporate purpose: the remaking of Komatsu'.

By 1989, when Tetsuya Katada (my mentor at Komatsu and a visionary leader) became President, worldwide demand for construction equipment was down, competition was up, and Komatsu's profits were in steady decline.

As Katada saw the situation, Komatsu's management had become so obsessed with catching Caterpillar that it had stopped thinking about strategic choices. For instance, its product development efforts were biased toward Cat's high-end bulldozers rather than toward smaller, lower-priced products like hydraulic excavators, for which market demand was growing. Katada worried that Komatsu's top management had stopped questioning the business the company was in.

Managers, Katada decided, 'can no longer operate within the confines of a defined objective. They need to go out and see the needs and opportunities and operate in a creative and innovative way, always encouraging initiative from below.' In other words, he told the company, 'I want everyone to stop concentrating simply on catching up with Caterpillar.'

Under a new banner of 'Growth, Global, Groupwide' (the Three Gs), Katada encouraged management at all levels to find new growth opportunities through expanding geographically and leveraging competencies.

More than a strategy, Komatsu now had a corporate purpose to which its managers could commit and in which they had a voice. In the first three years after Katada articulated the Three Gs, Komatsu's sales, which had been declining since 1982, perked up. That surge was driven almost entirely by a 40 per cent growth in Komatsu's non-construction equipment business.

The shift was from the goal of operational excellence (using TQ, Kaizen) which had served Komatsu well for 30 years to strategic positioning (using Hoshin Kanri). This is the subtle difference between World Class and Beyond World Class in reinventing business and creating new markets.

Professor Michael Porter (1996) believes that companies confuse operational excellence with strategy (in this sense he is in agreement with James Maxmin – see Chapter 4). 'Operational improvement is doing the same thing better', Porter says. Strategy, by contrast, involves choosing. 'Choice arises from doing things differently from the rival. And strategy is about trade-offs, where you decide to do this and not that.'

'Companies start out with a clear position, and over time they're drawn into a competitive convergence where they and their rivals are all basically doing the same thing. Those kind of competitions become stalemates.'

At this point, Porter introduces the second part of his thesis.

To Porter the issue of leadership in strategy is to make choices (see Figure 6.7) – to establish the trade-off between activities that have no

Flawed strategic thinking

- Best practice mentality is pervasive
- Industry conventional wisdom homogenizes competition
- 'Customer focus' is misinterpreted to mean serving *all* customer needs
- Managers believe that there are no longer trade-offs

Organizational barriers

- Making trade-offs is perceived as organizationally risky (no choice v. bad choice)
- Leaders are reluctant to disappoint valued managers or employees

The growth trap

- Growth pressures, or the apparent saturation of the target market, often lead managers to broaden the company's strategic position
  – Line extensions, new features, imitating competitors' popular services
- Too often, efforts to grow undermine strategy by blurring uniqueness; creating compromises; reducing fit

The greatest barriers to strategy are often internal

Fig. 6.7 *The failure to choose*
Source: M. Porter, 1996

long-term competitive future and those that show promise – and this is all internal to the company. He is sceptical of the Japanese Corporate Model, believing that Japanese leaders still concentrate on operational efficiency, see Figure 6.8. As we have seen from the Canon, Sony, Toyota and Komatsu examples this is not universally the case. The issue of contrast to me seems to be that Western companies, in part, practise operational excellence in terms of 'Kaizen', are enthusiasts for reducing labour force numbers, are poor at 'Hoshin Kanri' but are further ahead in terms of making strategic choices. Because they have reduced their resources so far they have less generation of ideas and less real strategic choice. The Japanese on the other hand are better at Kaizen and Hoshin Kanri but are overmanned and less strategic in their thinking. Surely there is some synergetic middle way?

To summarize: the key to survival is effective process in using all resources available to the enterprise. Process is not to be confused with

- Japanese companies pioneered most of the modern tools for operational effectiveness
- As a result, many companies enjoyed cost and quality advantages that lasted many years
- Japanese companies rarely developed distinctive strategies
  - Imitation has been the rule
  - All rivals offer most varieties and features, employ all channels, match production processes, etc.

  But,
- The gap in operational effectiveness has narrowed or become a disadvantage
- Growth is slowing in the industries in which Japan competes

Many Japanese companies are caught in a trap of their own making

Fig. 6.8 *Re-evaluating the Japanese corporate model*
Source: M. Porter, 1996

narrow definitions of business process re-engineering and operational excellence.

Sumantra Ghoshal and Christopher Bartlett (1995) propose three processes that have all featured in this chapter:

- One that promotes creativity and entrepreneurs
- One that builds competence across boundaries
- One that promotes continuous renewal

Very similar messages came from Gary Hamel when asked by Tony Jackson of the *Financial Times*:[29] How does a company become an industry revolutionary?

First, create new passions. In the past we've driven the emotions out of strategy. The field is dominated by people who trained as economists and engineers – the two disciplines which have the least grasp of what it is like to be a human being!

Second, new voices must be brought into the strategic process. There is too little genetic diversity – and this is most acute at the top of organizations. What you need is a hierarchy of imaginations – more young people, more from the geographic periphery.

Third, companies must create new forms of conversation about strategy; teams which are a deep diagonal slice across the organization. Boundarylessness gives idea creation.

Finally, companies need new perspectives. At any given point every industry is governed by certain orthodoxies. New wealth is created by challenging them.

Imagination, Hamel believes, is more widely distributed in organizations than top management generally allows.

Hamel believes we are on to the second revolution in using worker brain power. The first was the quality revolution a decade ago where the old command and control approach to organizing work gave way to a system involving input from the workers themselves (Kaizen approaches). The second revolution is progressed by companies that recognize that workers have brains and must apply this potential to broader tasks – to strategy (Hoshin Kanri can be the vehicle).

This is Beyond World Class when companies overcome the educational shackles we saw in Chapter 1 where their workforces find it difficult to get beyond tacit learning into explicit and from 'discovery' to 'development'. To achieve this is to realize the power of harnessing intellectual capital to make strategic choices.

Notes
1. Argyris, 1993.
2. Coined by Richard Bandler and John Grinder in *Frogs into Princes* (1979).
3. Tricker, 1980.
4. Katzenbach and Smith, 1994: 212, 214.
5. Ibid.: 217–21.
6. Ibid.: 221.
7. Ibid.: 191.
8. Goleman, 1996: 159.
9. Drucker, 1994.
10. Goleman, 1996: 160.
11. Based on research by Yale psychologists Robert Steinbergand and Wendy Williams (1988).
12. Garratt, 1996: 197.
13. Katzenbach and Smith, 1994: 84.
14. Foundation for Manufacturing & Industry, 1997.
15. Collins and Porras, 1995: 227.
16. Goleman, 1996: 148.
17. Interview in *Human Resources Magazine* by Godfrey Golzen, April 1996.
18. *Financial Times*, 17 January 1997.

19.   Rajan and van Eupen, 1996.
20.   Senge, 1990: 341
21.   Rajan and van Eupen, 1996.
22.   Collins and Porras, 1995: 45.
23.   A conversation with Roberto Goizueta and Jack Welch in *Fortune* 11 December 1995.
24.   Goldsmith and Clutterbuck, 1997: 66.
25.   Wickens, 1995: 230.
26.   Goldsmith and Clutterbuck, 1997: 69.
27.   Hamel and Prahalad, 1994: 127.
28.   Ibid.: 137.
29.   The Management Interview, *Financial Times*, 24 April 1997.

7 The Organization and Society

*We stand at the gates of an important epoch, a time of ferment,
when spirit moves forward in a leap, transcends its previous
shape and takes on a new one. All the mass of previous
representations, concepts, and bonds linking our world together
are dissolving and collapsing like a dream picture. A new phase
of the spirit is preparing itself. Philosophy especially has to
welcome its appearance and acknowledge it, while others, who
oppose it impotently, cling to the past.*

(G.W.F. Hegel, in a lecture on 18 September 1806)

Our journey has taken us through the elements of my three-legged stool:

- The Individual learning and change
- The Organization learning and change including leadership, policy
  and strategy

and now to

- The Organization and Society

In some senses it appears a non-issue. After all, we all make up society,
don't we? Whatever the policies of our corporations, they contribute to
what we are pleased to term society. But then so does the behaviour of
individuals, good and bad.

Since the start of the industrial revolution entrepreneurs have
considered, to a greater or lesser degree, their impact on society – other
than as profit generators for shareholders. Many successful corporations
have put a high priority on producing a worthwhile impact beyond the
factory gates. Some even saw enterprise as a vehicle for social change –
for the better, such as the UK's famous chocolate makers Cadbury and
Rowntree or Robert Owen the nineteenth century pioneer–entrepreneur of
radical social reform.

What is expected today is not the odd beacon, an occasional obsessive
with an over-developed social conscience, or a single minded environ-

mentalist crusader but what the UK Royal Society of Arts, Tomorrow's Company inquiry called 'the licence to operate'.

The concept of the place of business in society has been accelerating all over the world due to a number of changing factors:

- Globalisation: leaving aside the debate as to the extent of overhype (to which we will return in Chapter 8), the transnational nature of many businesses, the perceived loss of influence by national governments over international finance and flow of money, give a feeling of growing helplessness of the population in the face of multinational corporations.
- The environmental lobby extends its impact almost on a daily basis challenging corporations, governments and individuals as never before.
- The consumer lobby has escaped from monopoly products by step changes liberalizing markets and information technology revolutionizing access – essentially giving more choice.
- The information revolution itself has enormously widened access to what is going on and what should be happening. It has also shifted the 'ownership' of the enterprise with the acceleration of intellectual capital (assets in the brains of employees, suppliers and so on).
- Those closer to the enterprise have suddenly found 'voice'. Employees, suppliers and those who thought they had the power – shareholders – but rarely exercised it.
- Underpinning all this, I would argue, is the growth of liberal democracies worldwide. It may seem far fetched, but the worldwide tolerance of autocracies is exhausted whether these be national or industrial autocracies. Francis Fukuyama (1992) in his acclaimed first book *The End of History and the Last Man* produced a stunning table on the growth of liberal democracies (Table 7.1).

Fukuyama studies the breakdown and internal collapse of the last great autocracies within the communist soviet block and the seeming triumph of capitalism as the one route towards the fulfilment of man within the framework of liberal democracy.

He argued that liberal democracy may constitute the 'end point of mankind's ideological evolution' and the 'final form of human government' and as such constituted the 'end of history'.[1] Not surprisingly this thesis attracted criticism as well as adherence. Fukuyama countered critics by pointing out that today's stable democracies, like the USA, the UK, France and Switzerland, were not without injustice or

Table 7.1 *Liberal democracies worldwide*

	1790	1848	1900	1919	1940	1960	1975	1990
United States	x	x	x	x	x	x	x	x
Canada			x	x	x	x	x	x
Switzerland	x	x	x	x	x	x	x	x
Great Britain		x	x	x	x	x	x	x
France	x		x	x		x	x	x
Belgium		x	x	x		x	x	x
Netherlands		x	x	x		x	x	x
Denmark			x	x		x	x	x
Piedmont/Italy			x	x		x	x	x
Spain								x
Portugal								x
Sweden			x	x	x	x	x	x
Norway				x		x	x	x
Greece			x			x		x
Austria				x		x	x	x
Germany, West				x		x	x	x
Germany, East				x				x
Poland				x				x
Czechoslovakia				x				x
Hungary								x
Bulgaria								x
Romania								x
Turkey						x	x	x
Latvia								x
Lithuania								x
Estonia				x				x
Finland				x	x	x	x	x
Ireland					x	x	x	x
Australia				x	x	x	x	x
New Zealand				x	x	x	x	x
Chile			x	x		x		x
Argentina			x	x				x
Brazil						x		x
Uruguay				x	x	x		x
Paraguay								x
Mexico					x	x	x	x
Colombia				x	x	x	x	x
Costa Rica				x	x	x	x	x
Bolivia						x		x
Venezuela						x	x	x

Table 7.1 *cont'd*

	1790	1848	1900	1919	1940	1960	1975	1990
Peru						x		x
Ecuador						x		x
El Salvador						x		x
Nicaragua								x
Honduras								x
Jamaica							x	x
Dominican Republic								x
Trinidad							x	x
Japan						x	x	x
India						x	x	x
Sri Lanka						x	x	x
Singapore							x	x
South Korea								x
Thailand								x
Philippines						x		x
Mauritius								x
Senegal							x	x
Botswana								x
Namibia								x
Papua New Guinea								x
Israel						x	x	x
Lebanon						x		
Totals	3	5	13	25	13	36	30	61

serious social problems. However, he argued that these were ones of incomplete implementation of the main principles of liberty and equality on which modern democracy is founded rather than of flaws in the principles themselves. He maintained that the *ideal* of liberal democracy could not be improved upon. Also that he wasn't saying that events were at an end but 'history – understood as a single coherent, evolutionary process, when taking into account the experience of all peoples in all times'.[2]

This concept Fukuyama inherited from the great German philosopher G.W.F. Hegel, the concept then having been developed by Karl Marx.

Both Hegel and Marx believed that the evolution of human societies was not open ended but would end when mankind had achieved a form of society that satisfied its deepest and most fundamental longings. Both thinkers thus posited an 'end of history': for Hegel this was the liberal state, while for Marx it was a communist society. For them it meant that there would be no further progress in the development of underlying principles and institutions, because all of the really big questions had been settled. 'Hegel ... believed that work was the essence, the true essence of man' (Karl Marx).

This helps form the bridge between Fukuyama's work and the subject matter of this chapter.

There are two other factors that link it inextricably to society quite apart from the stakeholder pressures that come to bear on business.

The first is the continuation of 'End of History', that is, the extension of liberal democratic principles into the world of work.

The second is the replacement of the 'work ethic' in capitalist societies with the valid concept of the world of work being the development medium for the fulfilment of purpose for the individual.

These two factors are linked. Just as the development of liberal democratic governance in a political sense has been an existential product of the experience and development of the individuals in that society, so it follows that the evolving principles and systems of governance in industry must be a product of the experience and development of *all* stakeholders in the business.

The vital difference in taking this approach is to create the possibilities stemming from tapping the potential within and between the partners or stakeholders rather than the nannying emphasis of much of today's literature on stakeholder philosophy – 'business ought to', 'governance rules dictate' and so on.

Before leaving this foray into philosophy, a word about process as opposed to structure. The thinking of Hegel and Marx led their followers into the subsequently failed structural solutions of Nazism and Communism. Chronologically, in between the two, came the father of existentialism, Søren Kierkegaard, who reacted strongly against Hegel's system-building rationalistic 'philosophy of pure thought'.[3] Kierkegaard objected that Hegel had no answer in his systems approach to 'What is happening to man?' and 'Why do we exist?' Hence followers of Hegel and Marx were happy to subjugate the individual to the needs of the state (or society as you will).

Existentialism is a reaction to and revolt against the 'dehumanization and objectivation' (Tillich) of man in our modern technical society, which frustrates and demoralizes him. Modern mass society isolates the individual in the very midst of the rootless crowds of the big cities – Existentialism is the product of the free individual against all that threatens or seems to threaten his unique position as a free subject who, though a being in the world and so a part of nature, at the same time stands out from the background of nature.[4]

I divert into this area of philosophy (or maybe later seen as psychology) because I now realize in retrospect that it was the origin of my adherence to 'process rather than systems philosophy' throughout my career in the management of change. Process in this sense meaning that the individual has some control over change rather than being an accessory to a remote systems approach. I was entranced by the writings of Søren Kierkegaard at university when I spent a period working in Denmark over 35 years ago. The philosophy and thinking of existentialism has stayed with me ever since. However, existentialism can be seen as anti-system. 'An existential system is impossible. It cannot be formulated' (Kierkegaard) and therefore cannot be a holistic philosophy. The truth is a systems approach *is* needed but one that 'embraces the total human condition from the inside' (Sartre) – one that allows for ownership and development of the systems by the individuals themselves. This is the very essence of what this book tries to convey – how the individual can be in control of change.

WHY A STAKEHOLDER APPROACH?

It is a question of opportunities rather than threats. The factors of change listed earlier in the chapter have relevance:

- Globalization can give the 'osmosis' factor highlighted in the last chapter where ideas translated with ease round the world that are industry specific can trickle down supply chains or into other unrelated sectors locally.
- Environmental sensitivities can with positive approaches lead to new business (for example, Body Shop) or at least prevent losses (such as the consumer reaction against Shell over Brent Spar).
- Consumer groups can help rather than hinder. I was always struck by the enlightened approach of Komatsu asking consumers what they wanted in the next product development on launching the latest model!
- Intellectual capital. Professor Kjell Nordstrom of Stockholm Business School posits that Marx has now been vindicated. Leading edge companies are now owned by the workers. Not in quite the sense that Marx intended but knowledge-based companies have 70–80 per cent

of their assets (intellectual capital) 'owned' in the brains of their employees.

- The 'death of deference' as the RSA (1995) Inquiry put it means on the one hand more demanding employees, customers and communities who expect their individual needs and values to be respected but on the other gives an opportunity for greater dialogue and contribution that can aid the objectives of the enterprise.

The RSA Inquiry adds two more forces of change that impact on the stakeholder debate.

- *New employment patterns* are emerging, with the rise in importance of the knowledge worker, the growing numbers of self-employed people and small businesses, the erosion of the traditional concept of the job as full-time, permanent and male, and the consequent changes in the role and outlook of trade unions.
- *New organizational structures* are emerging, with the introduction of the networked organization, the reduction and streamlining of corporate centres, the subcontracting of whole functions, and the growing use of independent specialists.[5]

We will return to the issues of how this leaves the individual in Chapter 9.

The RSA inclusive approach criteria

(Incidentally, they use the term 'inclusive' approach in preference to stakeholder.)

(a) Vision

Tomorrow's Company competing at world-class levels through adoption of an *inclusive* approach.

How an *inclusive* approach to all key business relationships makes the difference between success and failure. The RSA describe a framework in which Tomorrow's Company:

- defines and communicates its purpose and values;
- develops a unique success model and applies it through matching measurements;

- places a positive value on each of its relationships;
- works in partnership with stakeholders;
- maintains a healthy reputation – a strong licence to operate.

(b) An inclusive approach to business leadership

This means:

- Accepting the need for change.
- Almost all company directors rate long-term 'trust' relationships higher than short-term adversarial relationships as a source of competitive advantage (Figure. 7.1).
- Reinterpreting directors' duties, that is, to stakeholders not just shareholders (see Chapter 6 on Board development).
- Creating a new success language (beyond 'conformance'). Establishing a measurement framework (for example, Balanced Scorecard[6]).
- Bring reporting into line, that is, inclusive. Annual reports that mean something to all stakeholders, not just obeying company law.

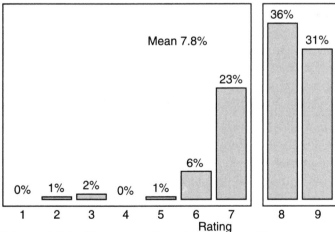

Fig. 7.1 *Relationships. Inquiry themes – boardroom values*
Source: MORI
Base: Captains of Industry 101

(c)   An inclusive approach to people

Understanding the pre-conditions for success, Tomorrow's Company:

● anticipates and responds to changes in employment patterns and in individuals' expectations;
● supports individuals in developing their capabilities;
● motivates people to make the best possible contribution;
● adapts its organizational structure to enable people's contributions to be used fully;
● participates in exploring the future of work.

(However, it should be noted that the RSA Inquiry sidesteps the issues of contribution of collective bargaining, consultation and trade unions in general.)

(d)   An inclusive approach to investment needs

The *first priority* is for investors and those who advise them to apply the *inclusiveness* test in their assessment of companies. The best fund managers and analysts concentrate the minds of company leaders not only on immediate performance but also on future prospects.

The *second priority* is for financial institutions themselves to adopt an *inclusive* approach to their whole range of relationships, to ensure that their own competitive position is not weakened by adversarial behaviour.

It appears that much of the discussion of *inclusive* factors which occurs within the company/investor relationship takes the form of a *dialogue of the deaf*:

● *The perception within companies* is that their discussions with investors lead them to neglect long-term strategies in the interests of immediate financial returns. Investors are perceived as placing a relatively low priority on the business fundamentals – such as customer loyalty, investment in people and supplier relationships – which will determine long-term success.
● *The perception within the investment community* is that companies are preoccupied with immediate returns and are reluctant to volunteer information about the fundamentals.[7]

(e)   An inclusive approach to society

Business leaders can help create a climate for success, by:

- developing community partnerships;
- working with government to manage the competitiveness agenda;
- improving business representation and networking structures;
- enhancing supply chain performance;
- clearing the way for the growth of small businesses.

DOES THE FORMULA WORK?

The RSA cite many business leaders who give anecdotal evidence of the various aspects of the inclusive company having a beneficial impact. Also, the observers would support the RSA conclusion.

Studies by Bain and Company have shown that where employees stayed longer with the company, so did the customer. And customer loyalty is one of the best predictors of profitability. The studies concluded: 'The longer employees stay with the company, the more familiar they become with the business, the more they learn and the more valuable they can be. It is with employees that the customer builds a bond of trust and expectations, and when those people leave, the bond is broken.'[8]

Professor John Kay of Said School of Management, Oxford University, writing in *The Foundations of Corporate Success* states that stability in relationships with employees, customers and suppliers are important factors in responding positively to change and therefore commercial viability.

In terms of bottom line results Kleinwort Benson's Tomorrow's Company Investment Fund selects for its portfolio only those companies which fulfil strict 'inclusive approach' criteria. Looking at performance over the past three years (1994–97) the model portfolio outperformed the FTSE 100 by almost 35 per cent.[9]

Mark Goyder, Director of the Centre for Tomorrow's Company, points to further evidence that attitudes are shifting. A MORI poll published by the centre of 88 UK business leaders found that 72 per cent agreed that a successful business will better serve the needs of its shareholders by focusing on the needs of its customers, employees, suppliers and the wider community. Only 17 per cent thought focusing on shareholders was the only way to succeed.

Forty per cent went further, identifying themselves with the statement that 'business cannot succeed without recognizing that it is *accountable* to other stakeholders as well as shareholders'. In the past the word 'account-ability' was usually avoided when discussing the relationships between business and its stakeholders, he says.

Concludes Goyder: 'This is a significant shift in attitudes. I vividly recall the climate in 1992 before the Tomorrow's Company Inquiry began. We consulted business leaders informally then, and for two-thirds of them there had to be a relentless focus on shareholders, and nothing else.'

The approach is not without its critics. For reasons the RSA are conscious of, the term 'stakeholder' is open to misinterpretation in that the only people who *own* the business are shareholders and therefore are the only 'stakeholder' to be able, by policy, to grow the business or cease trading. Hence the RSA choice of 'inclusive' which regrettably doesn't attract accolades as an alternative. Also the Involvement and Participation Association would argue that the trade unions should be seen as stakeholders and as such are not included in the RSA scope. The main criticism of the stakeholding approach is the supposed liability for confusion and potential deflection of concentration from the 'bottom line'. Proponents would retort that the results can be seen over the long term from stakeholder or 'inclusive' companies such as Marks & Spencer and Boots or indeed the evidence from the Kleinwort Benson Fund above – the bottom line is the winner over the long term rather than just the short-term horizon.

Tony Jackson of the *Financial Times* observes that:

In real life, managers need to hold several ideas in their heads at the same time. A public company must satisfy its shareholders. It cannot do so for long if it exploits its customers, employees, suppliers or the surrounding community.

The stakeholder–shareholder argument is thus a false dichotomy. To put it another way, pity these poor chief executives. If they do not deliver value to shareholders, they will be sacked. But if they do not deliver value to everyone else in the long run, they will be sacked just the same.[10]

Taking a wider political stage, Will Hutton, author of best selling *The State We're In*, joins with Professor John Kay to spell out their seven principles of stakeholding.[11]

1. OPEN economies and democratic societies are the basis for wealth creation.
2. WE must all be *included* in the workings of the economy and society.
3. OWNERSHIP confers obligations including paying tax.
4. THE good economy is one where you do the right thing without being policed.

5. BUSINESSES are social institutions not creatures of the stock market.
6. GOOD businesses are bound to make healthy profits but they must share their prosperity.
7. SUCCESSFUL market economies rely on a host of intermediate organizations.

Hutton's work in particular is a politically aimed polemic credited with starting the 'stakeholder capitalism' argument in the run-up to the UK Government election victory for Labour in 1997.

Both Kay and Hutton try to find the middle ground between the extremes of old style socialism and unbridled market focus of the Reagan/Thatcher era. 'The key stakeholder value is inclusion rather than the equality sought by the Old-Left or the individual autonomy of the New Right.'[12]

Much of the essence of the argument got lost in dogmatic stances prior to the UK general election. Will Hutton was cast as 'Old Labour' by the embattled Tories because of his perceived suspicion of free markets, enthusiasm for public spending and unconstrained assault on the City of London.

John Kay has managed to maintain the intellectual basis for the argument, stating:[13]

- Stakeholding is the most important economic issue of the age – a great deal more so for the economic future of Europe than whose head is on the coinage. At stake is the sustainability of the market revolution.
- Capitalism has scored some extraordinary victories in the past two decades. It has won the battle of ideas against socialism and witnessed the collapse of the centrally planned regimes. Yet market economics remains unpopular.
- The common left-leaning liberal response is to express contempt for markets and those who trade in them, and to seek to minimize their influence on human affairs.
- The right wing reaction is to tell sensitive souls they must not be so squeamish. This rhetoric has its own phrase – 'wealth creation' – to explain why behaviour which, at first sight, seems morally contemptible is necessary for all that is morally worthwhile.
- What is needed, argue the wealth creators, is wider education in the importance of commercial values and respect for private property. Those who refuse to understand can, if intelligent, be marginalized in universities. If unintelligent, they can be sent to prison.

Experience in the US demonstrates that security guards and prisons are a costly and ineffective means of dealing with excluded minorities. If capitalism lacks legitimacy, capitalism itself will be undermined.

This is coterminous with the 'licence to operate' argument and the rising tide of democracy.

The John Kay contribution is a preamble to a review of another polemic on stakeholding, by John Plender, leader writer of the *Financial Times*. Plender (1997) distances himself from Will Hutton's declinist tendencies and perceived reconstructed socialist policies, taking an inherently optimistic view. Plender is ready to embrace markets, if not entirely uncritically.

His argument is that if economies are seen to depend on trust, cooperation and the existence of shared and *inclusive* values rather than the naked pursuit of self-interest then the issue of the word legitimacy of capitalism would largely disappear. Hence the left critique and the right defence are beside the point.

Plender comes nearest to my own thinking and, I would argue, experience of successful capitalism based on the partnership principle where participants own solutions by contributing freely of themselves, developing potential on the way.

An 'existentialist' solution if you like!

In particular, to bring us back to the level of the organization, Plender acknowledges that:

the stakeholder concept operates at several levels. At the level of the firm, it asserts the need to recognize the value in a much wider set of relationships than those acknowledged by the conventional principal-agent model of capitalism, with its heavy emphasis on property rights. Those relationships, whether described in the sociologist's language of social capital or the economist's jargon of implicit contracts, are an all-important element in the competitive advantage of firms. It is the job of the manager to foster them in the long-term interests of the company and the wider interests of society. The emphasis on the cohesive nature of the relationships between the various economic actors does not preclude shareholders' exercise of discipline over management. But it does imply a different definition of objectives and thus a different approach to monitoring.[14]

But he also recognizes that stakeholder solutions at one level contribute to others. For companies this is often in what economists call lower 'transaction costs' (see also Chapter 5 for discussion on the impact of supplier/customer relationships on lower transaction costs), for instance in Germany, Switzerland or Japan where due to higher levels of trust (also see Fukuyama) transaction costs are lower:

> The co-operative ethos of German and Swiss culture, for example, encourages a universal commitment to investment in training. In Japan it leads to a legal profession that is tiny by the standards of the rest of the developed world; and the Japanese do not have to fear for their safety if they walk the Tokyo streets late at night, which means that law and order impose a lesser burden on the national budget.

Plender also takes a pragmatic view of the perceived failure of the traditional Japanese and German versions of stakeholding in today's global competitive state.

> What gave the stakeholder concept additional marketability was that it coincided with a realization that the success of the Japanese owed much to stakeholder values. Most large Japanese companies are run primarily in the interests of employees; secondarily in the interests of stakeholders such as suppliers and banks; and lastly for shareholders, whose interests have rarely, until recently, been given a second thought. Impetus also came from the realization that more and more of the value in the modern corporation lay in human capital and in the nature of the relationships with employees and suppliers.[15]

> The extent to which the Japanese and Germans are retreating from the stakeholder model can be greatly exaggerated. Under the pressure of economic forces they are merely picking and choosing selectively from an Anglo-Saxon model which is itself beset with problems. The point is rather that these countries' versions of stakeholding have become flawed in current circumstances because the interests of the various constituents have become very unbalanced. Investors and depositors have historically been financially disadvantaged in relation to the other stakeholders. This was because the heavily regulated and bank-dominated financial systems of Japan and Germany were intentionally designed to deliver a low cost of capital to industry.[16]

This concurs with my own view that it is foolish to be judgemental about these successful economies because of short-term fluctuations.

Plender also echoes the point I made on the growth of intellectual capital in sophisticated service industries, referring to the work of Paul Milgram and John Roberts of Stanford University.

> Employees in these newer areas of business often make a costly investment in knowledge and skills that are specific to the firm and not transferable if they change jobs. The decisions taken by the firm therefore put the employees' human capital at risk in much the same way as investors' capital is at risk. There is thus an enhanced moral as well as economic case for taking the employees' interests into account in the firm's decision making.[17]

In essence Plender argues that stakeholding is really a question of balance – not dissimilar to the conclusions of Chapter 6 on leadership.

EXAMPLES OF THE STAKEHOLDER CORPORATION

Inspired by Tony Blair's decisive Singapore speech in early 1996 which put stakeholding on the political map, David Wheeler and Maria Sillanpää wrote *The Stakeholder Corporation* (1997). They drew on much of the material and thinking that I have referred to from Will Hutton, John Kay and John Plender and their own experience with Body Shop where they have been engaged as consultants on audits of social and environmental performance.

Prime Minister Tony Blair endorsed the front cover thus: 'Stakeholding is not a new idea – it is one of the oldest strategies for creating value. Many successful businesses have a strong commitment to maximizing stakeholder loyalty.'

Wheeler and Sillanpää follow a pattern similar to that of the RSA Inquiry on Tomorrow's Company illustrating the influences on today's business (Figure 7.2).

The authors widen the potential stakeholders from a handful to a constellation – admittedly with a variation in intensity! Wheeler and Sillanpää set out the case for the stakeholder corporation, not least because the place of business in the modern world is vastly different from the time when the basic rules for competition were laid down. In particular they refer to the well-documented rise of the transnational corporation.

> According to the US-based Institute for Policy Studies, of the 100 largest 'economies' in the world today, 51 are global corporations. There are now 40,000 corporations whose activities transcend national

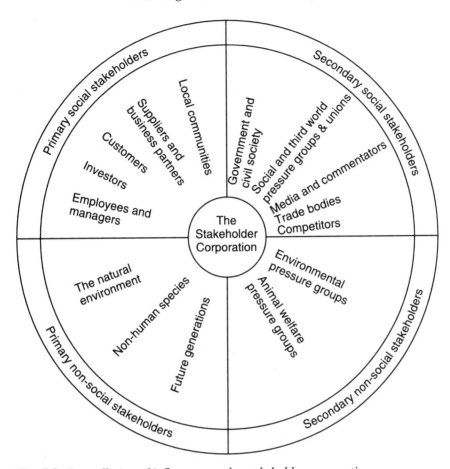

Fig. 7.2 *Constellation of influences on the stakeholder corporation*
Source: Wheeler, D. and Sillanpää, M. (1997) *The Stakeholder Corporation*, Pitman, p.5
Reproduced with permission of *Financial Times* Management

boundaries; the top 200 of these have sales equivalent to more than a quarter of the world's total economic activity.

On a strictly financial basis, Mitsubishi has a sales turnover bigger than Indonesia (the country with the 22nd biggest economy in the world). General Motors outweighs Denmark (number 23 in the list of national economies). Ford is bigger than Hong Kong and Turkey (the 25th and 26th largest economies). Toyota and Royal Dutch Shell outrank Norway (29th). IPS also calculates that between 1982 and 1995 the revenues of the top 200 corporations rose as a percentage of world gross domestic product from 24.2 to 28.3 per cent. The table below [Table 7.2] lists the world's top twenty corporations; eleven are Japanese.[18]

Table 7.2 *The world's top twenty global corporations ranked by 1995 sales*

Rank	Company	Business	Country	Sales ($ million)
1	Mitsubishi	Trading	Japan	184,510
2	Mitsui & Co.	Trading	Japan	181,661
3	Itochu	Trading	Japan	169,300
4	General Motors	Automobiles and trucks	USA	168,829
5	Sumitomo	Trading	Japan	167,662
6	Marubeni	Trading	Japan	161,184
7	Ford Motor	Automobiles and trucks	USA	137,137
8	Toyota	Automobiles	Japan	111,139
9	Royal Dutch Shell Group	Energy	Netherlands/ UK	109,853
10	Exxon	International oil	USA	197,893
11	Nissho Iwai	Trading	Japan	97,963
12	Wal-Mart	Drug & discount stores	USA	93,627
13	Hitachi	Electricity & electronics	Japan	84,233
14	Nippon Telephone & Telegraph	Telecommunications	Japan	82,002
15	AT&T	Telecommunications	USA	79,609
16	Daimler-Benz	Automobiles	Germany	72,253
17	IBM	Computer systems	USA	71,940
18	Matsushita Electric/ Industrial	Appliances	Japan	70,454
19	General Electric	Electrical equipment	USA	70,028
20	Tomen	Trading	Japan	67,809

Source: Wheeler, D. and Sillanpää, M. (1997) *The Stakeholder Corporation*, Pitman
Reproduced with permission of *Financial Times* Management

The authors conclude: 'Large corporations are among the most powerful economic influences on the planet. They have immense capacity for creating wealth and doing good; equally they have unlimited ability to abuse their economic power.'

However, it is not just the large corporations that have influence – the majority of people are still employed in small business and family owned concerns; indeed it is the expansion of this sector that has been seen as the salvation for unemployment in many mature economies.

SO WHAT IS THE BRAVE NEW WORLD OF TWENTY-FIRST CENTURY CAPITALISM?

Having charted the rise and fall of bureaucratic corporations through the ascendancy of the 'downsizers, rightsizers and capsizers' (autocratic to corporatist to autocratic) the authors (Wheeler and Sillanpää, 1997) ask where today's heroic style business leaders are taking management of people:

> And while middle managers in major corporations the world-over quaked in their corporate boots, they were offered scant comfort by the gurus. *Liberation Management* is not much fun when you are the person who used to fill *The Empty Raincoat*.
>
> The primary cause of all this uncertainty – the need to slash management costs in the face of cut-throat competition in the global marketplace – is not going to go away. The danger is that all too often the result in management terms will not be a quest for better team playing or a kinder style of leadership, it will be a return to the tough, autocratic tendency which characterized the early years of the industrial revolution. A customer-focused entrepreneur like Richard Branson of Virgin can become an icon for the young with his relaxed dress, daring stunts and his David and Goliath reputation for taking on the 'bad guys'; but that should not disguise his very hard-nosed approach to business, with no-frills management and vigorous exploitation of his Virgin brand. Bill Gates may encourage informality and meritocracy at Microsoft, but none of his managers and staff are in any doubt about the implications of failing to deliver.

To me this is real. However persuasive the RSA Tomorrow's Company formula, it cannot be a soft option. The business results have to be there – dare I say – in the short term as well as in long term. Hence the new drivers for twenty-first century business have to be given a more prescribed value. We should take seriously the results of the RSA Inquiry from research on 3000 businesses in North America and Europe: 'intangible' factors like intellectual property, innovation and quality were the strongest drivers of competitive performance. A beautiful example of a company that takes this seriously is Skandia Assurance which published a separate supplement to their annual report on Intellectual Capital. The following extracts illustrate the logic.

> One of the principal tasks is to continue creating long-term, sustainable growth in shareholder value. This includes nurturing and developing Skandia's intellectual capital – capital that is seen in the difference between the company's market value and its book value.
>
> A true and fair view of Skandia's development requires a broader description of our business than what can be read in our financial accounting. This year's Annual Report Supplement, *Customer Value*, therefore describes our undiminished commitment to creating a greater customer focus, developing a knowledge-sharing organization, and devising even more highly developed work procedures, services and systems.
>
> In this year's 1996 Intellectual Capital Report, Skandia has chosen to visualize its customer capital. [See Figures 7.3 and 7.4.]

In addition to the RSA evidence of the bottom line benefits of a stakeholder approach (Kleinwort Benson example earlier in this chapter), Harvard Professors John Kotter and James Heskett[19] have conducted studies on comparative benefits of a stakeholder approach to those with a 'shareholder' first philosophy. Over an 11-year period, large established companies which gave equal priority to employees, customers and shareholders demonstrated sales growth of four times and employment growth of *eight times* that of 'shareholder first' companies.

Examples of employee 'stakeholding' have existed since the beginning of the cooperative movement nearly 200 years ago – not all successful by any means. As Wheeler and Sillanpää put it:

> Clearly, co-operatives can work, but where they mingle ownership with executive responsibility they are not necessarily known for their dynamism, entrepreneurial flair or customer service. Democratic decision-making can be a laborious affair. While they have proven increasingly successful in areas like banking, credit and housing provision, there is no doubt that in retailing and wholesaling they

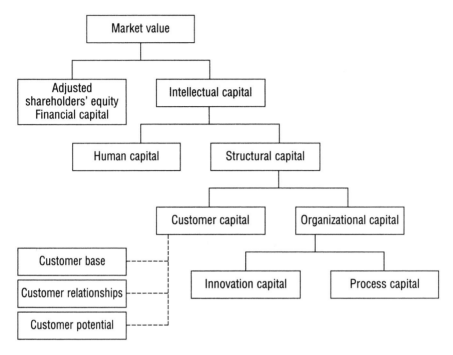

Fig. 7.3 *Skandia value scheme*

have struggled to turn participation into enduring competitive advantage.[20]

However, the proponents of worker share participation would point out that in today's delayered business it is all the more important as an outlet for growth and ambition:

One company which has transformed its internal culture through employee participation in share ownership is Reflexite – a high technology firm based in Connecticut. In 1984 company founders Hugh and Bill Rowland rejected a sellout to 3M, instead backing the judgement of senior executive Cecil Ursprung that an employee stock ownership program (ESOP) was the answer. Combining growing ownership with a quality improvement plan in 1989 proved to be a winner for Reflexite – efficiencies flowed without threats to job security and workers got votes as well as shares in their business. Between 1984 and 1994 the value of the ESOP increased from $150,000 to $19 million – equivalent to 42 per cent of the company. Reflecting on the implications for structure and responsibility,

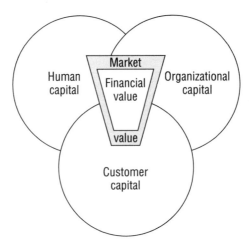

Fig. 7.4 *Vizualizing value creation*

Ursprung noted, 'To get the maximum amount of participation in decision making, you have to have the flattest organization possible, because the main purpose of managers and supervisors is to tell people what to do. And so the growth in managerial and supervisory jobs in this company hasn't matched the company's growth overall. There are people at Reflexite who in a very traditional sense have difficulty seeing their next step up the ladder and their perception is accurate.'[21]

A reality in many modern organizations.

The UK experience with ESOPs is not as helpful – the limited schemes in common use do not usually engender the type of fundamental shift in the psychological contract between workers and their company which is achieved by a cooperative or common ownership model. The examples of John Lewis in retailing and Scott Bader in chemicals show that with transference of ownership this transition can occur.

Another example of a company increasingly valuing intellectual capital, and this time putting a price on it, comes from Volkswagen.

Volkswagen has emerged as one of the most outspoken sceptics of over-reliance on 'shareholder value', saying openly that 'workholder value' should carry equal weight.

As a way of demonstrating this philosophy in practice, employees now receive part of their wages in 'time' shares. These are not denominated in money but in working hours. The monetary equivalent of the time shares, plus interest, is to be reinvested in the company, so that employees become quasi-shareholders. The scheme can be used to finance early retirement, buy extra holiday, or even as protection against redundancy. Daimler-Benz, Germany's largest industrial group, is also keen to limit the influence of shareholderism. As chairman Jurgen Schrempp put it, 'Shareholder value must not be pushed at the expense of future viability and future earnings potential. Our future lies not only in chips, machinery, buildings and concepts but also in the heads and hearts of our employees.'[22]

HOW CAN MANAGEMENT ADOPT A SYSTEM THAT GIVES SUSTAINABILITY?

Not all companies can or wish to adopt a share ownership approach (like John Lewis) or become crusaders for the environment (like Body Shop), but many recognize for long-term survival the need to be sensitive to their environments and to involve their principal stakeholders.

1. **My first prescription is to adopt *double-loop learning*.** We saw the need in Chapters 1 and 2 for the individual and the organization to see all development through a learning perspective. We also discussed in Chapter 6 the need for the company Board to deal with both 'conformance' and 'performance' issues (see p. 163). The business brain was centred in the double-loop of learning. Companies that encourage partnership with suppliers, customers and the community automatically gain double-loop learning which feeds back into business viability. Boards that concentrate on the short term, on conformance issues of 'producing the numbers', tend to use single-loop learning. Boards of companies that take a stakeholder approach tend to last longer (see *Built to Last*, Collins and Porras), have greater profit consistency over the long term (see *Winning Streak*, Goldsmith and Clutterbuck) and invent their own future (see *Stakeholder Corporation*, Wheeler and Sillanpää, and *Competing for the Future*, Hamel and Prahalad). Exemplar companies have a clear perspective of where they are currently in relation to the market place, society and the environment and in particular where they want to be as the world changes and opportunities evolve. This is not obtained by the single learning loop, focusing on conformance or just producing the numbers. It is about double-loop learning and ensuring both left- and right-hand brains are functioning, talking to each other, and

being given equal weight. A spin off is that involvement in this way develops the human resource.

We have all seen the result of narrow focus by elements of the value chain in companies. Ross Perot, when he was at General Motors, wrote a particularly hard-hitting memorandum to General Motors executives. *'You hate your customers, you hate your dealers, you hate your workers and your shareholders, you even hate each other – how can you have a bright future?'*

To give today's management a formula for 'inclusive' continuous improvement, the Quality movement and the Stakeholder approach have joined forces in what is termed:

2. **Total Quality Management.** The European Foundation for Quality Management (EFQM) and the US Malcolm Baldrige National Quality Award (MBNQA) have set criteria that link strategic business objectives with human resource development, customer satisfaction and even (in the case of EFQM) impact on society.

The EFQM model makes explicit the connections between leadership, processes and business results (see Figure 7.5).

As we have seen from other examples of the systems approach, having a system does not guarantee success – it is the process with which it is implemented and the ownership of those involved that makes it a success. The EQA (EFQM) model can make the bridge between the outside world, business strategy, enablers and results.

Percy Barnevik, Chairman and CEO ABB (ASEA Brown Boveri Ltd), states in the foreword to *The European Way to Excellence*:[23]

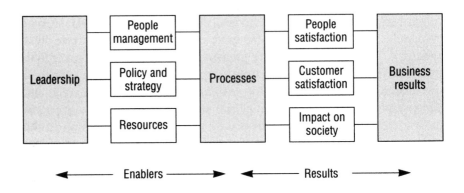

Fig. 7.5 *Connections between leadership, processes and business results (EQA)*

The move within European business to embrace Total Quality Management is part of the effort to adapt to change because, at its core, quality management is about becoming more competitive by changing the way we do business to match our changing markets. And because markets are changing faster than ever – new technologies, competitors, suppliers, governments, regulations, etc. – the winners are those who can keep up with or stay ahead of the changes.

To spur us on Percy Barnevik lays down the real challenge: can we change fast enough? Who will be the winners? It brings us back to a familiar theme: Quality, Cost and Delivery are not enough today; speed of response and anticipation through linking into the outside world is the key – the difference between Kaizen and Hoshin Kanri.

Imagine that the world changes in the next six years as much as it did in the past six years. Imagine that it changes even faster. What will those changes look like? What impact will they have on Europe's business? Who will be the winners? In my view, only one thing is sure: those who can move fast to take advantage of the opportunities presented by an ever-changing world will be the ones who win in the long term.[24]

SO WHAT DOES THE EQA (EFQM) MODEL ADD?

The EQA Model, which is owned and developed by EFQM, has new characteristics which provide a response to the criticisms and shortcomings in respect of the initial ideas of Total Quality Management. The main shortcoming of these initial ideas lies in the fact that they often relied heavily on 'quality departments', 'quality directors' and 'quality projects'. As a result they often remained disconnected from other functions and processes in the organization, resting on a superficial, possibly doctrinal dimension.

The EQA Model is one of the outcomes from the insight that in creating good management of quality, one has to create true quality of management. The EQA Model underlines the fact that TQM has to be more closely linked to strategic management, which implies deeper involvement of top management. This legitimizes the effort, the change and the formalization of goals. In addition the EQA Model (see Figure 7.6), by combining basic management subjects like Leadership, Policy and Strategy, and Processes, emphasizes the fact that Total Quality

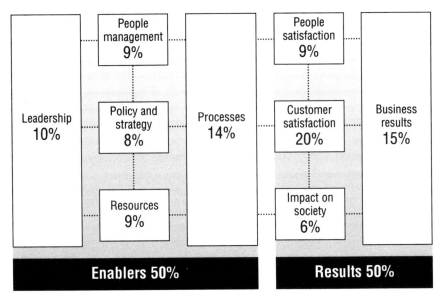

Fig. 7.6   *The EQA Model*

adheres to integral management approaches. In addition, it is grounded in ideas about the generation and processing of information (in particular measurement results focusing on stakeholders such as customers, employees, society and financial stakeholders) and feedback mechanisms relating to improvement and learning. The EQA Model positions Total Quality as a real strategic resource serving the real goals of an organization rather than just being a simple technique.

One of the characteristics of the EQA Model is that it tries to be as non-prescriptive as possible. Its elements should therefore be seen as areas for attention rather than criteria. On first sight the EQA Model shows nine elements but perhaps the most important feature is that all the elements are seen as interrelated. The percentages in each criterion reflect the weight factors used when applying for The European Quality Award. For organizations the EQA model is not only a guide for what must be understood by TQM but also a tool for self-assessment.

WHAT ABOUT THE MALCOLM BALDRIGE MODEL?

The Malcolm Baldrige National Quality Award Criteria's Framework has three basic elements (see Figure 7.7):

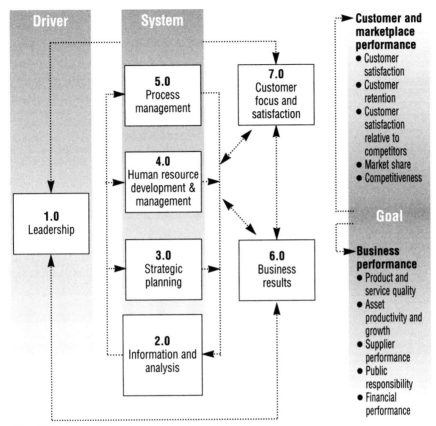

Fig. 7.7

- **Driver**
  Senior executive leadership sets direction, creates values, goals, expectations and systems, and pursues customer and business performance excellence.
- **System**
  The system comprises a set of well-defined and well-designed processes for meeting the company's customer and overall performance requirements.
- **Goal**
  The basic aims of leadership and the purpose of the system are two-fold:
  - *Customer and marketplace performance*
    Customer and marketplace performance means delivery of ever-improving value to customers, high levels of customer satisfaction and a strong competitive position.

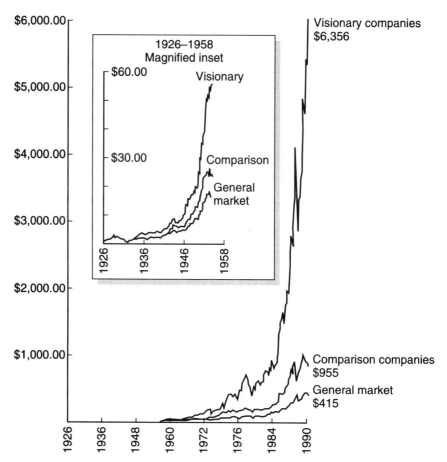

Fig. 7.8 *Cumulative stock returns of $1 invested, 1 January 1926 – 3 December 1990*
Source: Collins, J. and Porras, J. (1995) *Built to Last*, Random House. Reproduced with permission.

 – *Business performance*
   Business performance is reflected in a wider variety of financial
   and non-financial results, including human resource development
   and corporate responsibility.

3. **The Triple Bottom Line.** Social and environmental accounting has
spawned an imaginative formula termed the Triple Bottom Line. This
attempts to bring together in accounting terms economic prosperity,
environmental quality and social justice. The goals were made clear in the
Harvard Business Review of Jan./Feb. 1997 by Stuart Hart in 'Beyond
Greening. Strategies for a Sustainable World': 'Beyond Greening has an
enormous challenge – and an enormous opportunity. The challenge is to

develop a sustainable global economy, an economy that the planet is capable of supporting indefinitely'.

This to me is the essence of the matrix from p. ix in the introduction of this book developed into Figure 10.5, p. 276. (For more detail of the Triple Bottom Line see John Ellington's *Cannibals with Forks*, 1997 Capstone.)

MODELS, OK BUT WHAT ABOUT RESULTS?

Details were given earlier in this chapter of superior performance from 'inclusive' companies as defined by the RSA in Tomorrow's Company research and as selected by Kleinwort Benson.

Collins and Porras in *Built to Last* showed that visionary companies with core ideology and values were 'clock builders' not 'time tellers' and not only lasted the course but gave on average seven times the stock returns of their comparator companies between 1926 and 1990.[25] (See Figure 7.8.)

An example of such vision and values is given by the authors concerning Johnson and Johnson who in 1943 nailed colours to the mast by establishing a clear pecking order of responsibility: Customers, Employees, Management, Community, Stockholders.

Our credo

WE BELIEVE THAT OUR FIRST RESPONSIBILITY IS TO THE DOCTORS, NURSES, HOSPITALS,
MOTHERS, AND ALL OTHERS WHO USE OUR PRODUCTS.
OUR PRODUCTS MUST ALWAYS BE OF THE HIGHEST QUALITY.
WE MUST CONSTANTLY STRIVE TO REDUCE THE COST OF THESE PRODUCTS.
OUR ORDERS MUST BE PROMPTLY AND ACCURATELY FILLED.
OUR DEALERS MUST MAKE A FAIR PROFIT.

OUR SECOND RESPONSIBILITY IS TO THOSE WHO WORK WITH US—
THE MEN AND WOMEN IN OUR PLANTS AND OFFICES.
THEY MUST HAVE A SENSE OF SECURITY IN THEIR JOBS.
WAGES MUST BE FAIR AND ADEQUATE, MANAGEMENT JUST, HOURS REASONABLE,
AND WORKING CONDITIONS CLEAN AND ORDERLY.
EMPLOYEES SHOULD HAVE AN ORGANIZED SYSTEM FOR SUGGESTIONS AND COMPLAINTS.
SUPERVISORS AND DEPARTMENT HEADS MUST BE QUALIFIED AND FAIR-MINDED.
THERE MUST BE AN OPPORTUNITY FOR ADVANCEMENT—FOR THOSE QUALIFIED
AND EACH PERSON MUST BE CONSIDERED AN INDIVIDUAL
STANDING ON HIS OWN DIGNITY AND MERIT.

OUR THIRD RESPONSIBILITY IS TO OUR MANAGEMENT.
OUR EXECUTIVES MUST BE PERSONS OF TALENT, EDUCATION, EXPERIENCE AND ABILITY.
THEY MUST BE PERSONS OF COMMON SENSE AND FULL UNDERSTANDING.

OUR FOURTH RESPONSIBILITY IS TO THE COMMUNITIES IN WHICH WE LIVE.
WE MUST BE A GOOD CITIZEN—SUPPORT GOOD WORKS AND CHARITY,
AND BEAR OUR FAIR SHARE OF TAXES.
WE MUST MAINTAIN IN GOOD ORDER THE PROPERTY WE ARE PRIVILEGED TO USE.
WE MUST PARTICIPATE IN PROMOTION OF CIVIC IMPROVEMENT,
HEALTH, EDUCATION AND GOOD GOVERNMENT,
AND ACQUAINT THE COMMUNITY WITH OUR ACTIVITIES.

OUR FIFTH AND LAST RESPONSIBILITY IS TO OUR STOCKHOLDERS.
BUSINESS MUST MAKE A SOUND PROFIT.
RESERVES MUST BE CREATED, RESEARCH MUST BE CARRIED ON,
ADVENTUROUS PROGRAMS DEVELOPED, AND MISTAKES PAID FOR.
ADVERSE TIMES MUST BE PROVIDED FOR, ADEQUATE TAXES PAID,
NEW MACHINES PURCHASED,
NEW PLANTS BUILT, NEW PRODUCTS LAUNCHED, AND NEW SALES PLANS DEVELOPED.
WE MUST EXPERIMENT WITH NEW IDEAS.
WHEN THESE THINGS HAVE BEEN DONE THE STOCKHOLDERS SHOULD RECEIVE A FAIR RETURN.
WE ARE DETERMINED WITH THE HELP OF GOD'S GRACE,
TO FULFILL THESE OBLIGATIONS TO THE BEST OF OUR ABILITY.

This is the text of the original 1943 Credo as penned by R. W. Johnson, Jr.

Continuing the contrast with Japan, Guiding Principles at Toyota are:

1. Be a Company of the World.
2. Serve the greater good of people everywhere by devoting attention to safety and the environment.
3. Assert leadership in technology and customer satisfaction.
4. Become a contributing member of the community in every nation.
5. Foster a corporate culture that honours individuality while promoting teamwork.
6. Pursue continuing growth through efficient global management.
7. Build lasting relationships with business partners around the World.[26]

In Europe an up-to-date example can be seen in SGS-Thomson, the winners of the European Quality Award in 1997. SGS-Thomson have calculated the business benefits of using the EQA (EFQM) model over the period 1992–95 (Figure 7.9). *It proves it's possible, it proves the benefits.*

BEYOND WORLD CLASS AND SOCIETY

The polemic is that businesses should achieve partnerships with their stakeholders for their own good and the stability and growth of society. If it is of such obvious benefit why doesn't it happen as a rule?

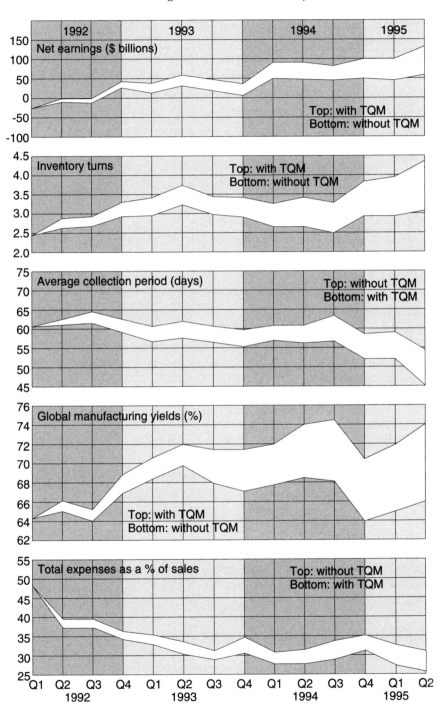

Fig. 7.9 *SGS-Thomson EQA business benefits*

1. Mistaken impression that to focus on stakeholders, waters down focus on profit.
2. Involvement outside the firm looks like escapism, or opting out.
3. Looks like inviting in more complexity to an already complex world.

The truth is that it is proven that partnership gives longevity to the firm, learning about the business, social and natural environment and the licence to operate. Such investment of time pays off to the individual, the firm and community.

How does this work in practice?

In the next chapter we shall examine the impact of individuals, firms, trust and social capital on economic growth.

Notes

1. Fukuyama, 1992: (xi).
2. Ibid.: (xii).
3. Grunebaum, 1970.
4. Ibid.: 363.
5. RSA, 1995: 5.
6. Kaplan and Norton, 1992.
7. RSA, 1995: 14, 18
8. Reichheld, 1993.
9. *Financial Times*, Wednesday 16 April 1997.
10. Tony Jackson, Trying to serve two masters, *Financial Times*, 22 December 1997.
11. *Observer*, 13 October 1996.
12. Ibid.
13. *Financial Times*, Thursday 27 February 1997.
14. Plender, 1997: 23
15. Ibid.: 17.
16. Ibid.: 25.
17. Ibid.: 17–18.
18. Wheeler and Sillanpää, 1997: 31, 32
19. *Observer*, 1 September 1996 and The *Guardian*, 16 November 1996.
20. Wheeler and Sillanpää, 1997: 68.
21. Reder, 1995.
22. *Financial Times*, 25 October 1996.
23. Published by DG III EU Commission 1997.
24. Barnevik, 1997.
25. Collins and Porras, 1995: 5.
26. Goyder, 1998: 87.

8 Economic Revival and Regional Development

The next leg of the economically dependent 'stool' following the individual and the firm is the economic grouping. I use that vague term because there is considerable doubt among the commentators as what the suitable collective noun should be.

NATION OR REGION AS ECONOMIC FOCUS?

Professor Michael Porter (1990) talks of the competitive advantage of nations being built from 'clusters' of similar firms or industries – usually in regional groupings.

Kenichi Ohmae (1996) argues the nation state is dead and the relevant grouping is that of an economic region. Francis Fukuyama, author of *The End of History and the Last Man* argues in his later book *Trust* that the key to economic growth is whether a society or region is low trust or high trust in terms of its culture – this may not be coincident with national boundaries.

Within many industrialized economies there is a mismatch between the signals and the reality. Nations measure their economic performance in terms of GDP and productivity but this masks enormous variations between regions within that state and, Kenichi Ohmae would argue, masks real economic activity in regional groupings that transcend national borders.

GLOBAL FORCES – OUT OF CONTROL?

Ohmae, previously head of McKinsey in Tokyo and a world-renowned business strategist, argues that nation states are dinosaurs waiting to die. He says that not only have nation states lost their ability to control exchange rates and protect their currencies, but they no longer generate real economic activity. The global logic, he argues, is now in the 4 'I's:

Investment is no longer geographically constrained. Most money moving across borders is private money – governments do not have to be involved.

Industry is now global in orientation. Strategies of modern multi-national corporations are shaped by the need to serve attractive markets wherever they exist and to tap attractive pools of resources wherever they sit.

Information technology. The hurdles for cross-border participation and strategic alliance have been demolished. Capability can reside in the network and be made available – virtually anywhere as needed.

Individual consumers have become global in orientation. Chauvinism in consumer choice has all but disappeared.

He adds: 'Region states are different in that they side step the bunting and hoopla of sovereignty in return for the ability to harness the global I's to their own needs.'

Ohmae argues that 'Region' states are replacing nation states as economic loci. These region states can be economic groupings of nations or even a region within a state if it makes economic sense.

Ohmae considers that the political need to give the whole plebiscite the same access to services, benefits and infrastructure actually holds back economic growth. He cites that 44 of Japan's 47 prefectures are now net recipients of government subsidies. The other three – all in the Greater Tokyo area – pay for the rest.[1] This experience is of course repeated worldwide.

Throughout Europe, economically it makes no sense to prop up high unemployment benefits while being unsuccessful in creating new jobs.

The decline of the influence of nation state is also detailed by Will Hutton in his best seller *The State We're In*[2] where he points to a worldwide loss of faith in state intervention, regulation and ownership as instruments. Hutton sees UK national politics as pale imitations of US experience. 'In trying to copy the USA the British have ended up with the worst of both worlds. We have neither the dynamism of the US or East Asia, nor European institutions of social cohesion and long term investment.'

He does later, however, encourage regional determination on the basis of economics as well as for democratic reasons by comparing with success in Germany and Japan: 'The German "mittelstand" (SMEs) companies are clustered in one place, so are the Japanese "Kigyo Shudan" (subcontractors: suppliers). Moreover public intervention has been imaginatively used to create supply-chains of subcontractors, which makes for a virtuous cycle of efficiency, growth and successful urbanization.'[3]

Not all observers agree that globalization is inevitable with policies determined for us from outside.

The Royal Institute of International Affairs produced a challenging Chatham House Forum report at the end of 1996 entitled *Unsettled Times* in which the RIIA set out three provocative scenarios for the industrialized world up to 2015. They are:

Scenario One: Faster, Faster – a world of starkly accelerating change, in unyielding, unprofitable competition, forcing the population into three groups:

- those considered essential to the firm
- larger groups working in affiliation
- and a substantial group who work only occasionally or not at all.

Will Hutton in *The State We're In* analyses the current working population of the UK into 30:30:40

First 30 per cent	Disadvantaged; unemployed, married to unemployed, economically inactive
Second 30 per cent	Marginalized and insecure part-timers, paid half or less than the average wage, fixed term contracts of less than two years service
Third 40 per cent	Privileged: full time employees with security

These definitions are of course open to challenge.

RIIA conclude that those with the lowest skills are the most penalized and that *Faster, Faster* is a scenario that threatens to spin out of control.

Scenario Two: Post-Industrial Revolution

Rapid change as per Scenario One but nations are able to exploit the smooth, endless, technological explosion. Relative economic success amongst the Industrialized World (IW) nations creates the conditions for positive partnerships and thus supranational collaboration develops. The forces as in '*Faster, Faster*' remain potent but this drives the re-creation of the tools of government. Each IW nation emphasizes its distinctive competence, doing so within a common framework of *knowledge-centred commerce*.

Scenario Three: Rough Neighbours!!

This is where '*Faster, Faster*' slips off the treadmill. The nations of the IW fall into difficulty to find Rough Neighbours on the scene. The IW tries to slow down the pace of change, and introduces mild forms of protectionism. It finds itself confronted by a predominantly Chinese-based Asian region and growth in Islamic influence. The IW is fragmented and bruised.

The RIIA starting point is that globalizing features are often products of domestic policies, not something generic imposed from the outside, for example:

- Global features of change are abstract factors such as technology and benchmarks of good management.
- Many features of change are consequences of policies governments have pursued to meet a variety of challenges. For instance, measures to increase internal competition, liberalization of markets, privatization, competitive tendering.
- Trade has been growing at much the same rate for a century. The content may have changed but overall volumes have enjoyed relatively constant growth. (See Figure 8.1.)

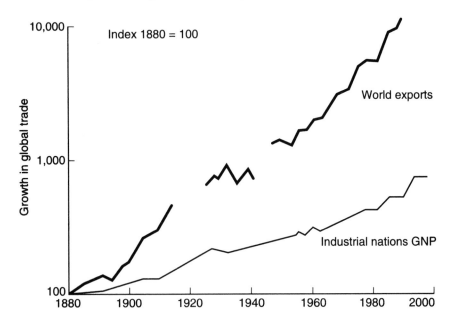

Fig. 8.1 *Global trade and the economic performance of the industrialized nations*

The RIIA attacks the globalization myth and concludes that change is being driven by events that are internal to Industrialized World nations. It is concerned that attention is being deflected by, on the one hand, opposing 'globalization' or on the other, industry getting over-excited by ideas of globalization to the extent of seeking fairy gold. Some industries are suited to an internationalist approach, while others are not.

RELEVANCE OF REGION AS AN ECONOMIC UNIT

To conclude, the RIIA gives an interesting perspective on the changing focus of power 1950 to 2015 (Figure 8.2). In 1950 the trend to national centralization of power was in full swing. The chart on the right suggests the contrasting shape of how these balances may be felt in 2015. The boundary to the perceived limits to action is moving swiftly inwards, acting to circumscribe the options which appear to be open. Relatively more power is won by Regional and Supranational entities, relatively less by national governments. Then why is there so much focus on *national* competitiveness? As though, somehow, it were the nation states and not their enterprises and regional clusters that were in competition.

My conclusion is that the Region, in this particular context, can have the 'hand on the tiller' and create conditions to foster the RIIA Scenario Two. The key is the theme of partnership.

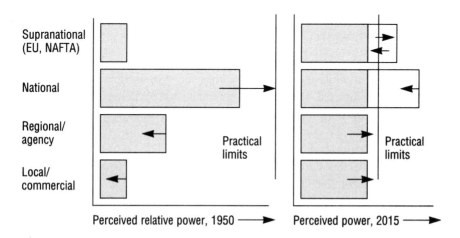

Fig. 8.2 *Changing focus of power, 1950–2015*

THE THEORY OF REGIONAL DEVELOPMENT

Professor Michael Porter's seminal work *The Competitive Advantage of Nations* (1990) brought the expression 'cluster' into the terminology of regional economics. Using his earlier works on competitive strategy and competitive advantage for corporations he applied the theory of the Five Competitive Forces that determine industry competition to a national context (Figure 8.3).

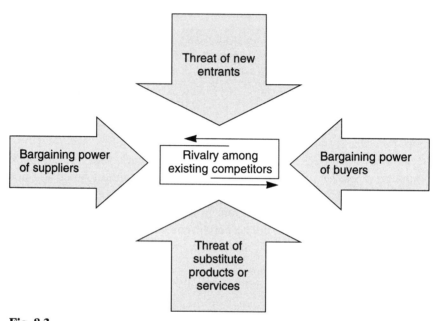

Fig. 8.3

Source: Porter, M. (1990) *The Competitive Advantage of Nations*, Macmillan

Sources of competitive advantage within the corporation come via the Value Chain (Figure 8.4) and this is enhanced by the Value System within an industry including inputs from suppliers and chains (Figure 8.5).

Porter's niche product is in producing a model for determinants of national (or regional) advantage.

The attributes that determine whether a nation can achieve international success in a particular industry are (see Figure 8.6, Porter's Diamond):

● Factor conditions. The nation's position in factors of production such as skilled labour or infrastructure, necessary to compete in a given industry.

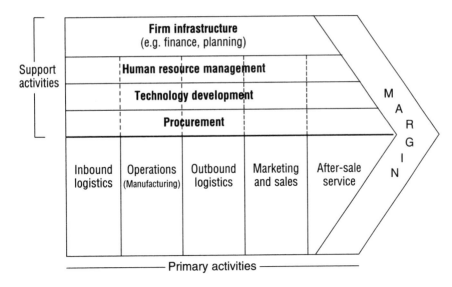

Fig. 8.4

Source: Porter, M. (1990) *The Competitive Advantage of Nations*, Macmillan

- Demand conditions. The nature of home demand for the industry's product or service.
- Related and supporting industries. The presence or absence in the nation of supplier industries and related industries that are internationally competitive.
- Firm strategy, structure and rivalry. The conditions in the nation governing how companies are created, organized and managed and the nature of domestic rivalry.

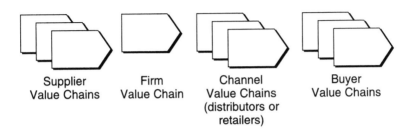

| Supplier Value Chains | Firm Value Chain | Channel Value Chains (distributors or retailers) | Buyer Value Chains |

Fig. 8.5

Source: Porter, M. (1990) *The Competitive Advantage of Nations*, Macmillan

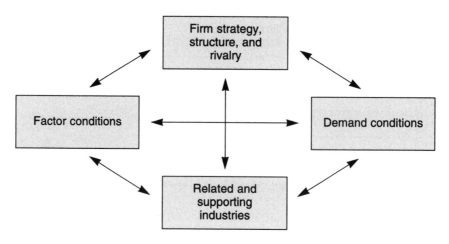

Fig. 8.6 *Porter's 'Diamond'*

Source: Porter, M. (1990) *The Competitive Advantage of Nations*, Macmillan

DETERMINANTS OF NATIONAL ADVANTAGE

Porter's contribution to the debate was fundamental. He challenged the conventional wisdom on national competitiveness that then laid great stress on factor costs (especially labour), economies of scale, economies of scope, and the impact of fluctuating interest and exchange rates. Porter noted that these explanations do not address the real challenge of seeking out, securing and, of particular concern, rejuvenating a nation's true competitive advantage: 'Pursuing factor costs with their short term appeal, will virtually guarantee that the United States – among other advanced nations – never achieves real and substantial competitive advantage.'[4]

His theory stems from a very thorough, detailed and far-reaching four-year study of ten major trading nations. This is a normative approach of observing what works, why it works and understanding how it can be applied.

Like all economic models it is of course open to criticism. It is seen by some as an explanatory framework rather than a deterministic theory; also, it appears an over-extrapolation of the analysis of enterprise competitive advantage to national competition. It appears to imply that all international economic activity is a zero sum game in which one country only gains what another loses.

However, it is robust and has been used by nations and regions to act as a catalyst to determine economic policy with a real focus on what elements of the famous 'diamond' exist, what can be injected and what industry and service sector clusters can be built upon.

My disappointment is first that it appears mechanistic and second that although the prescription for developing economies is convincing, and there is empirical evidence to support the acceleration of the Pacific basin Tiger economies for instance (despite their recent fall), I find the prescription for the mature economies doesn't give confidence for a turn round, neither does Porter give sufficient weight to the rejuvenating aspects of inward investment in the UK, and the US benefits of the supply chain, and the impact of service industry; however, we will return to that subject later in the chapter.

Francis Fukuyama in *Trust: The Social Virtues and the Creation of Prosperity* continues his radical agenda from his *The End of History* where he argued that with the collapse of Eastern bloc communism a New World Order was emerging because of the convergence of economic systems and modes of political organization around the world. The most important contribution in this context is the theme of liberalism in market terms. The new order, such as it is, means unfettered consumerism on a global scale. The antidote is the opportunity that Hamel and Prahalad exhort manufacturers with – to reinvent markets for new products (see Chapter 6).

This theme coincides with Kenichi Ohmae's four 'I's of global logic where, as we saw earlier, his fourth I is Individual consumerism as global in orientation.

The exciting contribution from Fukuyama's later work, *Trust*, is that it adds a real human dimension to Porter's rigorous analysis. He shows that free markets, competition and hard work are not the sole precursors for prosperity. There is another key ingredient – 'trust' – and I would include culture and community.

Fukuyama contrasts ever-rising prosperity in the Far East, seemingly without social problems, with America also in boom but with social problems by the dozen. Middle class fortresses have to be erected against the barbarians. Business costs have shot up because of the need to insure against attacks from lawyers who have turned 'rights' into a protection racket. America has been living off a diminishing fund of 'social capital' which threatens future prosperity.

Rosabeth Moss Kanter in *World Class* (1995) also refers to the decline of 'Social Capital' in the USA.

American cities have been struggling to remain viable in the midst of fiscal crises, racial tensions, ageing infrastructure, reports of deteriorating schools and a decline of 'Social Capital' – the informal connections among people that build trust and a foundation for civic engagement. As a contributor to economic development efforts in my own area and elsewhere, I wondered why any company has to be in any particular place once it joined the world class – and how the local workforce, the middle class, already reeling from re-engineering and recession, could deal with its loss of job security. I wondered how the rise of the 'World Class' changes the meaning of community – a source of identity and well-being that is largely (geographically) rooted.

Fukuyama addresses the nation of social values behind capitalism. Given trust you can settle matters with a telephone call. In its absence industry pays lawyers enormous fees, suffers labour unrest and sometimes settling issues is left to the mafia.

This discussion leads on in the book to 'who do you trust?' Fukuyama addressed the factors of religion and family – particularly in terms of the nature of the enterprise. Protestants appear to be, on the whole, better at capitalism than Catholics. The influence of Shintoism and Confucianism on Far East enterprise is formative.

Rosabeth Moss Kanter refers to the same influence in *World Class*:

> In 1904 the German scholar Max Weber attributed America's growth to values such as hard work and sacrifice for the future, as described in his classic book *The Protestant Ethic and the Spirit of Capitalism*. Almost a century later such a book could also be titled *The Confucian–Buddhist Ethic and the Spirit of Capitalism*.
>
> Asceticism, diligence and thrift were associated in recent decades with rapidly growing Asian nations. Singapore, South Korea and Hong Kong enjoyed the world's highest mean economic growth between the 1970's and 1990's; Taiwan & Japan were not far behind.

Religion and family are interlinked and Fukuyama makes parallels between the Chinese (heavily influenced by Confucianism and the defined family unit) and southern Italian society (Catholic and tight-knit families) where large companies are almost non-existent in contrast to Northern Italy, Japan or Korea where large companies, supported by a supplier infrastructure, are the order of the day. In China and Southern Italy the members of the family are the only people you trust, so firms remain small. They are often very successful but there is no teamwork beyond the family. If larger firms are required the state has to create them in these environments.

The incredible economic power of Germany and Japan is explained by other writers as being a function of a group-oriented society. Traditionally prizing obedience to authority, they both practise what Lester Thurow labels as 'communitarian capitalism'.[5]

Fukuyama would lay success for Japan and Germany at the door of having a high degree of social trust, shared values and consequently, a strong propensity for spontaneous sociability (he would see the same for the USA in the past). Factors others would adduce for Japan and Germany are that they are 'late developers' given enormous help post-war by the USA. Social capital as opposed to familial ties give the conditions, he argues, for the emergence of large organizations.

Not that prosperity and growth have to be associated with the emergence of large organizations. Fukuyama argues that 'at least at an early stage of economic development, firm size and scale do not appear to have serious consequences for a society's ability to grow and prosper'.[6] In fact, of course, small companies are easier to establish, are more flexible and adjust more quickly to changing markets than large corporations. Fukuyama points out that countries with relatively small firms on average, such as Italy, Taiwan and Hong Kong, have grown faster in recent years than their neighbours with large firms. However, firm size does affect the sectors of the global economy that a nation can participate in and may in the long run affect overall competitiveness. Small firms are associated with relatively labour-intensive goods such as clothing, textiles, plastics, electronic components and furniture. Large firms are required to master complicated manufacturing processes needing large amounts of capital, such as aerospace, semiconductors and automobiles.

Fukuyama adds another dimension to the liberal trade theory built upon by Porter. 'Social capital needs to be factored into a nation's resource endowment.'[7] The degree of high and low trust in any particular society also affects the way industry organizes. A high trust society can organize its workplace on a more flexible and group-oriented basis with more responsibility delegated to lower levels. Lean production, discussed in detail in Chapter 5 and in *Becoming World Class*, p. 152, can demonstrate that community and efficiency can go together. Fukuyama's analysis demonstrates that, as in so many things, there is not a 'one size fits all' solution and that managers have choices which need to take into account the issues of trust, social capital, shared values and human personality. 'There is no necessary trade-off in other words, between community and efficiency; those who pay attention to community may indeed become the most efficient of all.'[8]

REGIONAL DEVELOPMENT IN PRACTICE – THE VALUE OF
COMMUNITY

Rosabeth Moss Kanter has taken the analysis a stage further by looking at
five main cities in the USA: Boston, Cleveland, Greenville-Spartanburg/
South Carolina, Miami/South Florida and Seattle/Puget Sound, on the
basis of a large sample questionnaire (2655 responses), company
interviews, employee focus groups, community interviews and
business/civic leaders' forums. The focus was to determine how new
global relationships affected local transactions.

She found that the public concerns have shifted in the USA from
economic issues to social issues. Once focused primarily on the
competitiveness of large business corporations, leaders are more and more
concerned about the strength of communities and the competitiveness of
cities, states and regions. Balancing the decline and fragmentation of
many big corporations, the SME (Small and Medium-sized Enterprises)
sector are looking to higher shares of international growth markets.

The companies small and large that were perceived to be successful –
qualifying for the label 'World Class' – are labelled by Moss Kanter as
'Cosmopolitans': leaders and linked to global chains, with a global
mindset, able to bridge culture differences. Their intangible assets were
seen to be:

Concepts: the best and latest knowledge and ideas
Competence: the ability to operate at the highest standards of any place
    anywhere
Connections: the best relationships which provide access to the resources
    of other people and organizations around the world.

'Locals' are primarily defined by geography, rooted in communities
and some are stuck.

There is great interest worldwide in the entrepreneurial SME sector and
Moss Kanter notes the benchmarking that has happened between the UK
and the USA, in particular between Scottish Enterprises and
Massachusetts and the Silicon Valley. She also notes the mirrored
enthusiasm for foreign investment between South Carolina and the North
East of England with their common view that it raises local standards and
serves global markets.[9]

Moving on to 'World Class' regions Moss Kanter argues: 'What
distinguishes the world class from the merely good is the ability to be a
global centre of thinking, making or trading. World class regions

demonstrate excellence in at least one of these three domains.'[10] She postulates that whole regions need to demonstrate the three 'C's and also *magnets* and *glue*:

Magnets: to attract external resources, new people, new companies
Social glue: social cohesion and social infrastructure for collaboration

COMPARATIVE REGIONAL DEVELOPMENT

South Carolina and North East England

Rosabeth Moss Kanter's work gives the opportunity to compare the growth of two regions in different continents but with the same objectives – revitalization of industry through injection of foreign-owned manufacturing.

The parallels in reading the analysis of South Carolina with my experience of the North East are uncanny. Rosabeth visited the North East of England herself and draws some parallels by inspection but the extensive survey described earlier did not extend beyond the USA.

Foreign investment into South Carolina has been accepted since the early 1950s and over this period of time leaders of inward investment companies, principally from Switzerland and Germany, have integrated with indigenous industry to form a kind of shadow government, more cosmopolitan and more enduring than most local politicians.[11]

As an insider observed, 'In South Carolina there's an incredible network, a fairly small network, of people who get things done and make decisions.'

The parallels with the North East are remarkable. Foreign investment too arrived in the 1950s, however, then from the USA, and Caterpillar in particular set up a plant in Birtley, Co. Durham on the site of an old steel works. However, inward investment was not encouraged due to scarcity of labour and a protection mentality. The pattern of industry was not then going through the radical transformation that was to come in the 1970s and 1980s. The latter period saw the massive decline in basic industries where in 1962 30 per cent of all employment was in coal mining, ship-building, and metal manufacture. By 1997 only 1 per cent of employment remained in these industries in the North East. Gross domestic product in the North declined and as a proportion of UK GDP (Figure 8.7).

The attitude of the UK Government in the 1960s and 1970s towards Regional Development was interventionist, perceiving national

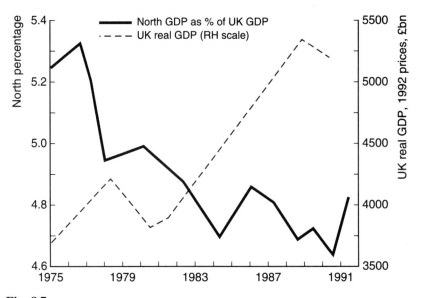

Fig. 8.7

Source: Evans *et al.* (1995) *The Northern Regional Economy*

government's role as to compensate for declining basic industry by
investing in infrastructure and intervening in industrial reorganization.
The Thatcher administration embraced free market economics from 1979,
concluding that economic depression in regions such as the North were a
function of market inefficiencies, lack of entrepreneurial 'culture' and
excessive state intervention. Hence policies emerged of removal of
constraints on free operation of market forces, especially within the labour
market. Financial support was to be targeted selectively and labour market
policies operated nationally such as reduction in trade union power and
encouraging mobility of labour.

While eschewing the interventionist approach, the Thatcher
administration focused on three policies to overcome regional inequalities:

- Inducing inward investment to areas of high unemployment
- Stimulating indigenous growth in the less advantaged regions
- Investing in the socio-economic infrastructure – in particular for
  training and enterprise to be linked later to economic needs via the
  Training and Enterprise Councils

A further shift in policy occurred towards the end of the 1980s with the
recasting of the Department of Trade and Industry as the Department for

Enterprise with the emphasis on indigenous development to replace inward investment as the dynamo of economic growth. The design was to move the emphasis from direct job creation towards job creation via wealth creation.

In summary, in the UK the view of inward investment has shifted in 30 years from an issue of competing for scarce labour resource to relief that inward investment provides jobs, any jobs, to job creation via wealth creation.

From my experience in arriving in the North East to establish the first European manufacturing plant for Komatsu (see *Becoming World Class*, p. 29 onwards) the parallels with South Carolina are obvious.

First, inward investment was welcomed with open arms – admittedly at the lowest denominator in terms of providing jobs – real jobs. There were clear distinctions as to what was a real job in that then chauvinist society. Burtons the tailors had closed factories in the North East in the 1970s with the loss of many thousands of jobs for women with little local protest. However, if Parsons cut its apprentice intake (real jobs) there was an outcry. Komatsu were offering jobs in a traditional North East mould – in medium to heavy engineering. Small wonder that we had 3000 applications for the first 60 posts. For varying reasons we positively discriminated in favour of the unemployed – that, after all, was why Komatsu had been encouraged to go to the North East.

Second, I quickly found that the North East was 'a small village'. Komatsu's contribution to the development of the North East was welcomed and before long people like myself had to be careful about how much 'work time' was being spent on community-related activities, as laudable as they are. Despite the strong and deep Labour Party roots in the North East, a very pragmatic view was taken of involving industrialists in wider matters of regeneration, collaboration, education and so on.

Third, the Northern Development Company, under its Chief Executive Dr John Bridge, set up to accelerate inward investment, worked in close collaboration with the DTI to involve new inward investors in attracting more would-be investors to the region.

Fourth, opportunities arose for inward investors to influence the prevailing mindset of industry and regional government. The new positive approaches to management described in *Becoming World Class* (Chapters 3–6), so-called Japanese management techniques and the School of Human Resources management, were perceived as a breath of fresh air to a region tired of decline, hopelessness and downsizing. There was some success.

The Quality North campaign – a joint brainchild of David Williams, then Marketing Director for Northern Development Company (NDC), and myself, was a typical product of the 'osmosis' factor of inward investment.[12]

NDC reaches over ten thousand companies regionwide with programmes to boost their competence and connections. A Quality North campaign launched in 1990 spreads 'Best in World' quality principles; the area's world class companies like Japan's Komatsu have taught their techniques. Quality North has involved over three thousand organizations in three stages: first, emphasizing quality tools and service; second, forming networks to exchange ideas across companies and partnering between customers and suppliers; finally, engaging three hundred executives as ambassadors to attract new companies to the region while NDC's fit for Europe expert campaign helps companies find international markets.[13]

Successful football and successful local business

The North East today is vibrant because of its champions and as often happens their interests go beyond business. Sir John Hall, a son of a miner, born in the North East, who made his fortune in property development most notably in building the Metro Centre, the largest out of town retail development in Europe, went on to champion Newcastle United Football Club which was at the time relegated and sidelined. His involvement was electrifying for the team and its supporters and this in turn affected the local economy.

A successful football side should contribute towards a healthy local economy. The converse should also be true. If the local economy is buoyant then people will spend more on leisure, the club's receipts will rise, the club can afford better players, and the team improves. Moreover, in cities where a team enjoys strong grass-roots support, a good record should contribute significantly to the local feel-good factor. It is reasonable then, to assume that a top team and a prosperous economy are connected, or even that they go hand in hand, feeding off each other in some sort of virtuous circle.

Hall says, 'It reflects a lot of people's dreams and ambitions.' 'If your team wins on Saturday, you go to work happy on Monday.'
Newcastle experienced something of a football/economic Wirtschafts-

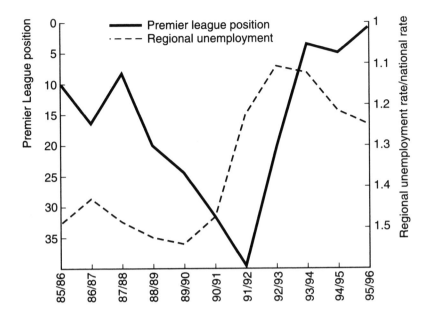

Fig. 8.8 *The link between the state of play of Newcastle United and the state of the economy*

wunder in the early 1990s, with a demonstrable link between the state of play and the state of the economy (see Figure 8.8).[14]

RESULTS OF THE FOCUS ON INWARD INVESTMENT

• The UK has had the lion's share of inward investment into the EU, averaging in excess of 40 per cent since the mid-1980s. The North East has attracted £8.8bn of capital spend – around 10 per cent of UK total Foreign Direct Investment between 1986 and 1997 and direct employment created for 75 000 in 520 foreign-owned projects. There were, of course, many more jobs created with suppliers and the service sector. More than 20 per cent of the North's industrial production is in foreign-owned plants: it has a greater proportion of activity run by foreign multinationals than any other English region.[15]

• The North has experienced the smallest decline in male employment of all UK regions and the growth in female employment is only greater in Scotland and Northern Ireland.[16]

• The North has the second highest gross value added per employee in manufacturing, second only to the South East. See Table 8.1.

Table 8.1

UK manufacturing gross value added	£ per person employed
South East	30,698
North	**30,474**
Wales	28,946
Scotland	26,431
East Anglia	26,358
North West	26,249
South West	25,657
Yorks & Humber	25,143
East Midlands	23,350
West Midlands	23,985
Northern Ireland	22,429

Source: Regional Trends Survey

Unemployment rate

	March 1985	September 1996
United Kingdom	13.5%	7.5%
Tyne & Wear	19.6%	10.3%

Source: T & W Research and Intelligence Unit

Similarly the drop in Tyne and Wear's unemployment rate from 19.6 per cent to 10.3 per cent between March 1985 and September 1996 was greater than the UK's overall decline from 13.5 per cent to 7.5 per cent over the same period.[17]

- On innovation some 33 per cent of foreign-owned manufacturing plants are involved in R&D; 40 per cent in product development.[18]
- On quality and other awards the North has the highest percentage of BS5750 accreditation (see Table 7.3) of any UK region[19] and also the best record nationally in firms achieving the UK Government's Investors in People standard (a measure of company training excellence).
- Last, in terms of new management style the inward investors have made a major impact. Professor Robin Smith of Northumbria University, analysing the changes over a decade in the compilation 'The Northern Regional Economy', points to four major influences that have been at work:

(a) The general economic recession in the early 1990s intensifying competitive pressures in all firms (sometimes accelerating the decline of the Region's traditional industries).
(b) The continuation of a deliberate strategy by inward investors of a relatively sophisticated approach to management in contrast to the traditional or constitutional styles of indigenous firms.
(c) The increasing number of newly privatized or deregulated businesses in the utilities, service and public sectors which had been granted a significant degree of autonomy from previously well-established national industrial relations arrangements and the growth of subcontracting and flexible labour patterns in many firms.
(d) The continuous erosion of trade union membership in all sectors which had probably weakened still further the capacity of unions to influence management style.[20] [This gives an incomplete impression: the trade unions in many cases have had a positive impact on management style in my experience.]

In terms of the prevailing management ideology in the UK the overturning of the traditional unitary theory of paternalism by the pluralism of the 1970s was short lived.

Managers generally now, post-recession and post-Thatcherism, are convinced that industrial organizations must unite behind a common corporate position if they are to survive.[21]

The Japanese practice of extending in-house training and development programmes to suppliers has meant the spread of the new HRM practices on flexible working, team working and quality management. Other companies in the region, even if not directly connected to Nissan, Komatsu and Fujitsu, identify with concepts like flexibility, teamwork and quality, single-staff status and communications. Labour management and union relations assume less importance in the new world of work.

Personnel practitioners now see themselves firmly as part of the management team and not part of the duopoly of what Diane Watson (1988) termed 'Managers of Discontent'.

In summary the North East is a very different place today after the impact of direct inward investment. In 1993 it was named by the World Economic Forum as the *number one new plant location in the world*, based on data collated by the international consultancy Price Waterhouse and Plant Location Int.[22]

Howard Davies, ex-Deputy Governor of the Bank of England, in his

Royal Society of Arts lecture at Darlington UK in November 1996 on Britain's Regional Economies, said:

> I find it interesting that the North of England has done better than the North West [Howard Davies' original home!] in recent years in attracting inward investment and revitalizing its manufacturing sector. This seems to me, in part, to reflect better regional organization and stronger regional determination to address economic problems.

To return to the South Carolina lesson, Rosabeth Moss Kanter identifies four factors behind South Carolina's success:

- Visionary leadership, from lead companies that built a foundation for later successes, working actively to recruit international companies to bring new resources to the area.
- A hospitable business climate and positive work ethic attracting innovative manufacturing companies making long-term investments and helping foreigners feel welcome.
- Customized training and continual upgrading of worker skills through educational improvement.
- Collaboration within the business community and across sectors to bring world class quality, improve operational skills and practices, offer mutual assistance and act in concert on community priorities.[23]

All the above could be describing the success story in the North East of England and some other regions anxious to rejuvenate their economies. Very little of the above has anything to do with national policies, economic planning or levers of power. It has all to do with the intrinsic ability of the inhabitants and incoming investors' vision or, as Moss Kanter would describe it:

- Concepts
- Competencies
- Connections

and I would add the Community formed between the newcomers and indigenous population.

This is, I guess, what she means by social 'glue'.

Rosabeth Moss Kanter instinctively adds the missing ingredient – the human element – just as people issues need to be added to the discredited business process re-engineering system.

Michael Porter, Kenichi Ohmae and Francis Fukuyama all underrate two things in their rigorous approaches:

1. The impact of inward investment in rejuvenating mature economies (particularly where local content rules dictate the use of local suppliers – not just the issue of providing jobs).
2. The intangible issue of community which gives a coalition of interest to improve the local economy. Fukuyama would argue that you either have this in terms of 'social capital' or 'social trust' or you don't.

I believe from the experience of North East England that this social capital can and does grow. Admittedly the foundations have to be there. If this cannot happen, then mature economies with declining industries really don't have a future. These positive examples from the USA and the UK illustrate the powerful potential of the economic region as the crucible for growth and development of the individual, the organization and society.

Notes
1.   Ohmae, 1995.
2.   Hutton, 1995: 15.
3.   Ibid.: 19.
4.   Porter, 1990.
5.   Fukuyama, 1995: 28, 29.
6.   Ibid.: 30.
7.   Ibid.: 31.
8.   Ibid.: 38.
9.   Moss Kanter, 1995: 27.
10. Ibid.: 31.
11. Ibid.: 243.
12. See Morton, 1994: 91 and Moss Kanter, 1995: 366.
13. Moss Kanter, 1995: 366.
14. Rigby, 1996.
15. Ibid.: 31.
16. Darnell and Evans, 1995: 25.
17. Tyne & Wear Development Corporation Report, 1997.
18. Darnell and Evans, 1995: 84.
19. Ibid.: 122.
20. Ibid.: 195.
21. Ibid.: 198.
22. Moss Kanter, 1995: 365.
23. Ibid.: 248.

9 New Patterns of Employment and Unemployment

America has entered the age of the contingent or temporary worker, of the consultant and subcontractor, of the just-in-time workforce – fluid, flexible, disposable. This is the future. Its message is this: You are on your own. For good (sometimes) and ill (often), the workers of the future will constantly have to sell their skills, invent new relationships with employers who must, themselves, change and adapt constantly in order to survive in a ruthless global market.

(Lance Morrow, 'The Temping of America', *Time*, 1993)

My ambition in starting this book was, amongst other things, to show that for success an effective partnership of interests was necessary. The three legs of the stool had to play equal and supportive parts. When this works society prospers. The examples of South Carolina and the North East of England in the last chapter show that in regional economic terms the partnership can work astonishingly well.

Again measuring in economic terms, Mari Sako's work quoted in Chapter 5 shows that for whole industries the partnership concept or, in that case, employee and supplier voice gives remarkable business results. The stakeholder approach gives positive results as detailed in Chapter 7 especially in terms of longevity and staying power as Collins and Porras demonstrate. Add to this the various anecdotal examples of successful change throughout this book from the experience of others as well as my own and there can be no doubt that the partnership route gives a long-term durable solution.

The three-legged 'passive' stool, however, is not enough. It may be stable for balance and support but it is not intrinsically dynamic. It also, of itself, doesn't encourage the separate legs to feel 'in control' of their own destiny. The legs may appear to be of unequal length and thickness and more weight can be felt than is justified or fair. The 'hoops' of education, networks and vision can make for cohesion and support.

We started with the impact of change on the individual at the beginning of the book. I posed the question on page 2:

Are we making it different? Are we planning for successor generations relative to the world they will experience'

It seems to me that our current thinking, stemming from the philosophy of the supremacy of the individual and that of market forces is visibly making our corporations leaner and more efficient but that for those that fall out of the system – the 'devil take the hindmost'.

Charles Handy observes: 'The market is a mechanism for sorting the efficient from the inefficient, it is not a substitute for responsibility.'[1]

Also, as we saw in Chapter 2, innovative potential is not realized within organizations.

Our journey through change issues for organizations and economies has not answered the question for the individual except in terms of the change adopted and accepted by current generations in playing their part in the various partnerships discussed. One can assume that lessons, good and bad, from experience, are transmitted to the next generation. What appears to be lacking is an enduring philosophy of the place of the individual in the future partnership.

How much of a 'leg' can the individual play? Is it just expendable – a 'just-in-time' leg to be dismantled and cast in the heap by technology, outsourcing, social dumping or low wage competition? This leg may then support or be supported by the community leg. Or is the 'leg' the knowledge worker who effectively 'owns' a proportion of the corporation's intellectual capital who makes the stool wobble by voluntary detachment, possibly taking the team to seek the highest price in a volatile market that says 'if you want loyalty – get a dog'. Is that the way to create an agile organization with sustainable development?

Or is it a 'virtual leg' that supports a number of stools in a portfolio role, choosing how work and leisure time is spent, maybe supporting the community leg?

Then there are those who never manage to become connected – who don't manage to become part of any employment leg.

The picture of employment in the industrialized world looks very different today from just 20 years ago and will look different again in a decade. Changing patterns are moving ever faster and new generations will need to cope with very different challenges.

THE NEW LABOUR MARKETS

Twenty years ago the labour market was much simpler. There were those in permanent full-time careers-for-life type jobs and those on the fringe – some temporaries, the unemployed, the unemployable.

Today the pessimist observer sees a society dominated by exclusion, by deprivation. Will Hutton (1995), quoted in Chapter 7, has coined the thirty, thirty, forty society.

First 30 per cent	Disadvantaged; unemployed, married to unemployed, economically inactive.
Second 30 per cent	Marginalized and insecure part-timers, paid half or less than the average wage, fixed term contracts of less than two years service.
Third 40 per cent	Privileged: full-time employees with security.

But what are the facts? Everybody who studies labour market trends seems to exaggerate to make their point. Will Hutton uses fairly elastic definitions to conclude that 60 per cent of the working population is either disadvantaged or marginalized. William Bridges in *Job Shift* writes about the concept of 'jobs' disappearing and being replaced by peripatetic 'work' with no continuity or security. Charles Handy refers to the 'portfolio' worker and companies based on the $\frac{1}{2}$:2:3 principle. Half as many people, paid twice as much, giving three times the old productivity. Everybody talks of the new jobs being created as following US experience – poorly paid part-time employment. Even new successful employment patterns are under attack.

Gunther Kruse and Christine Berry writing in the April 1997 edition of *Management Today* christens the UK as a 'Nation of Sweatshop Keepers'. The accusation is familiar – that inward investment attracts low skill, low value added jobs. The argument is not that the UK is able to attract work and employment from Germany, where labour costs can be three times those in the UK, but that in the writers' estimation Germany is offloading low value added, low skill jobs, and thus retaining high value added, high skill employment (see Figure 9.1). They say that unless the UK makes a step change improvement in vocational training and gains investment in innovation and development of knowledge-based companies, we will find that reliance on low cost manufacturing is a fool's paradise. It is similar to Will Hutton's polemic.

The portfolio career concept can be attractive to the early retired knowledge worker with plenty of contacts and a fallback early pension but for most there are problems as the Royal Institute of International Affairs (1996) report highlights:

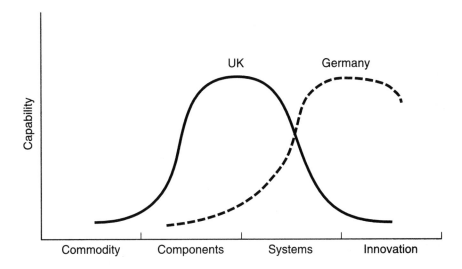

Fig. 9.1 *Industrial value progression: lagging behind the Germans*

- How is such a person to be represented to potential employers? Most promotional circulars are binned.
- The transaction costs of the portfolio worker can be high. IT systems for marketing and focusing on requirements could help.
- We gain much by working in teams. The portfolio worker is inevitably isolated. The trend in any event is towards dedicated suppliers rather than mobile talent.

Richard Donkin, writing in the *Financial Times*, 4 March 1998, comments:

Stuart Hampson, chairman of the John Lewis Partnership, speaking recently at the Royal Society for the Arts Forum for Ethics in the Workplace, accused what he called the 'peripatetic tendency' – consultants and academics who move from job to job – of talking up portfolio working because for them, it was the norm.

John Lewis, which makes long-term commitments to employees by making them partners in its trust ownership structure, retained as many as 100 more staff than required when sales turnover calculations were thrown awry by the last recession.

That, he said, was preferable to a short-term outlook. 'I don't see how an efficient army of engaged citizens can be raised on a short-term basis. Individual talent may be high, but commitment will never be the same as for someone who has spent time coming to know a company and its values, who identifies their personal future with the company's future. To me the portfolio workforce seems like a quick path to muddle and even internal civil war,' he said.

These are strong words with broad implications for internal development and recruitment strategies.

How new are these current labour market trends anyway? The common perception is that there has been a massive growth in recent times in part-time work. However, a report from the Centre for Economic Performance at the London School of Economics, published in 1997, concludes that: 'When compared with the immediate past and the experience of previous decades the UK labour market in the last decade or so has not seen employment shifts which are dramatically out of line with historical experience.'

In hard data terms this is supported as follows:

	1979	1996
Part-time as % of total jobs	16.1%	22.1%
Full-time as % of total jobs	76.7%	65.2%
Self-employed	6.5%	10.2%

Source: Centre for Economic Performance, LSE

With the latter figure, although growth has slowed since 1990, the overall trend is not apparent elsewhere in Europe where there has been less deregulation of the labour market than in the UK.

In the USA, by contrast, the labour market has become so tight that even those once marginalized are now employable.

There is no precise definition of full employment but there is little doubt that the USA has the tightest labour market in the industrial world. The unemployment rate has dropped to 5.2 per cent nationwide, and is below 4 per cent in nearly half of all metropolitan regions. The level of labour force participation is more than 77.5 per cent compared with 69 per cent in Germany, 59 per cent in Italy and 74 per cent in Britain. Finally, the growth rate of the US labour force is projected to fall to between 1 and 1.5 per cent in the next few years from between 2.5 and 3 per cent in the 1970s.

The USA has long had an outstanding performance in job creation compared with Europe. Since 1980 it has created more than 32m jobs in a labour force which is now 134m, while Europe has produced only 14m new jobs in a labour force of 192m. Since 1989 two-thirds of America's job growth has been concentrated in private-sector managerial and office support occupations. Nearly all Europe's job growth has been in the public sector.

Businesses are being forced to recruit workers from the most disadvantaged groups and incur the cost of training them.

The unemployment rate is above 10 per cent for blacks and 8 per cent for Hispanics, compared with 4.6 per cent for whites. Tight labour markets could do more to correct problems with structural unemployment and racial inequality than any phenomena since the economic boom of the Vietnam war era. Tight labour markets will also improve the job prospects of the two million so-called welfare mothers, who now have to seek employment because of 1996 federal welfare reforms.[2]

The explanations for the contrast between the USA and Europe in terms of job creation repay some in-depth research.

Civilian employment increased by more than 50 per cent in the USA between 1970 and 1996, from just under 80m to almost 130m. Employment in Europe barely changed over the same period, rising from just under 140m to less than 150m.

Demographic trends provide part of the explanation for the difference in employment growth. The working age population of the USA rose by more than 11 per cent between 1985 and 1995, compared to an increase of less than 7 per cent in Germany, France and the UK combined (see Figure 9.2).[3]

Alan Krueger and Jorn-Steffen Pischke, economists at Princeton and the Massachusetts Institute of Technology respectively, estimate that 60 per cent of this extra US employment growth is explained by rapid population growth (Krueger and Pischke, 1997).

But why is the USA better at getting extra people into work? The standard explanation is that wages are downwardly inflexible in Europe because of relatively high minimum wages, powerful unions and welfare systems. Technological advances and developing world competition have reduced the demand for less skilled workers in industrial countries, producing growing income inequality in the USA and higher unemployment in Europe.

This would imply that in Europe any increase in joblessness or weakening in employment growth, should be concentrated among less skilled workers, but Krueger and Pischke cite several studies which suggest this is not the case. They also provide their own evidence that falls

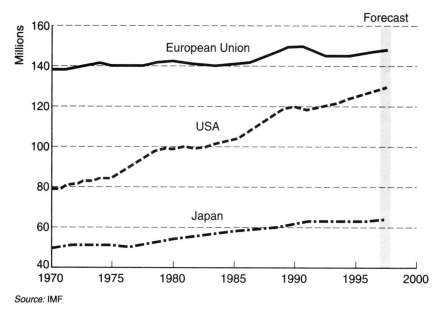

Source: IMF

Fig. 9.2 *The USA creates more jobs than Europe*

in employment in Germany were not concentrated among low paid – and presumably low skilled – workers in the 1980s.

Population growth in the USA means extra spending power as well a bigger supply of labour. It also adds to the economy's pool of 'entrepreneurial talent'. If these entrepreneurs start businesses, they will take on employees and thereby help to ensure that demand for labour increases alongside supply.

Europe's inability to increase employment in line with population may therefore be explained in part by restrictions or impediments to new business start-ups. *Hence Krueger and Pischke's conclusions are that inflexible labour markets and lack of encouragement of entrepreneurs are at least partly the cause of persistent high unemployment in Europe.*

There has been resistance to labour market changes on the adage, *full-time employment good, part-time and self-employment bad.* It is often forgotten that these growing forms of employment do suit individual circumstances.

Andrew Dilnot (1995), Director of the Institute for Fiscal Studies, in his lecture to the Royal Society of Arts in London on 16 October 1995, entitled 'Is the Labour Market working?' stated:

The growth in part-time work is often seen to be unwelcome but only 13% of part-time workers say they are working part-time because they could not find a full-time job, while 87% do so out of choice, many of them because they have other responsibilities. Looked at from the perspective of mothers, the growth in the availability of part-time paid work has much to recommend it.

Many self-employed people find enormous satisfaction from being responsible only to themselves and would not return voluntarily to being employees. But for others, there is little choice and self-employment is simply a less secure, less well-paid substitute for what they would see as a 'proper' job.

Self-employment certainly brings with it some insecurity but insecurity is widely perceived to have grown for full-time employees too.

Employers' enthusiasm for more flexible forms of employment tends to vary with the state of the labour market. In 1995 and 1996 much was being made of the growth of temporary work in manufacturing (Table 9.1). Two years later, in a tighter labour market for skills, the shift can be seen to reverse.

A study of 'Employers' use of flexible labour' by the Policy Studies Institute published in 1997[4] showed that after 1997 companies are beginning to reconsider their employment strategy because of the tighter jobs market.

Table 9.1 *Employees in temporary work 1900–95.*

	1990	**1995**	**Change 90–95**
Manufacturing Temporary Total	120 000 (2.4%[1]) 5.12m	201 000 (4.4%[1]) 4.53m	+81 000 (+67.5%[1]) −590 000 (−11.5%)
Other sectors[2] Temporary Total	1.04m (6%) 17.27m	1.31m (7.6%) 17.14m	+ 270 000 (+26%) −130 000 (−0.8%)
Whole economy Temporary Total	1.16m (5.2%) 22.39m	1.51m (7%) 21.67m	+350 000 (+30.2%) −720 000 (−3.2%)

Notes: 1. % figures in first two columns show proportion of temporary workers in total employment sector. In final column % figures refer to the change between 1990 and 1995.
  2. Relates to other sectors of economy, mainly services.
Annual figures are taken from the GB Labour Force Survey, Spring 1990 and 1995, with adjustments for statistical changes.

Source: Central Statistical Office (*Financial Times*, 1 February 1996)

Labour shortages apply particularly to manufacturing companies that have slimmed their workforce and rely on temporary staff to deal with peak production periods. 'Manufacturing companies have laid off a lot of staff, but are now finding that when they need temporary employees to cope with increased demand, those employees are no longer there, and those who are available may not have the required skills.'

On the other hand the same report concludes that the use of variable hours has dramatically increased.

More than half of all employees work variable hours every week. Bernard Casey, Hilary Metcalf and Neil Millward found that the number of people working a flexible week has more than doubled since the 1980s and that much of this work is in the form of paid or unpaid overtime, rather than flexible employment contracts.

The authors cautiously conclude that an increase in flexible working is not inevitable. They point out that much of the recent shift to short-term and other flexible packages has been driven by the recession and the excessive labour supply, rather than by strategic planning.

Again it appears a situation that may alter with tightening of the labour market. *Hence labour market flexibility tends to be a function of perceived short-term needs rather than progressive deregulation.*

THE FLEXIBILITY PARADOX

The dilemmas in the labour market throughout Europe have been explored by Professor Chris Brewster and colleagues at Cranfield School of Management in the UK (Brewster, 1996).

Starting with the classic economic framework, the proposition is examined that the rapid growth in flexible working patterns over recent years is a product of:

- labour market 'pull' and
- economic 'push'.

Labour market pull

Flexible working patterns provide employment opportunities for people who would otherwise find it difficult to work on standard contracts. Flexibility allows employers to draw on sections of the labour market otherwise unavailable and to retain valued staff who might leave without such options as homeworking or a part-time contract.

Economic push

Organizations have also been forced to examine and change employment practices in the face of increased competition, particularly internationally; volatile markets; fluctuations in demand; and technological change. With associated changes in the organization of production, employers have sought both to reduce unit labour and to vary supply to meet immediate needs.

For managers, flexibility facilitates a focus on necessary work rather than existing jobs, allowing (in fact requiring) managers to set clear performance targets and monitoring standards. Employees on non-standard contracts also tend to be more productive, less prone to absenteeism and less expensive (for example, many part-timers fall below national insurance thresholds).

Yet flexible labour markets have generated controversy, associated by some observers with the creation of an underclass of vulnerable workers by uncaring and irresponsible employers. For others, the flexible work-force represents an overdue shift from the rigidities of standard employment towards forms which may be more 'family friendly' and otherwise responsive to employees' needs, including a more flexible balance between work and leisure.

The implications of flexible working for employers, individuals and the state are notably different. Figure 9.3 indicates the relationships involved.

Organizations need flexible labour, particularly flexible time and contracts, to ensure the most economic use of human resources. But the major benefit of flexibility for organizations lies in the transfer of cost and risk from the organization to individuals and to the state, or to society as a whole – this is a fact of life.

For *individuals*, flexible working patterns can provide additional opportunities to work, enable family incomes to be supplemented and allow work to be fitted in with family responsibilities. However, the transfer of costs means that flexible work is often poorly paid. It is the individual and the family who bear the cost of not working on standard hours and contractual arrangements.

For *society* in general the costs have been transferred directly, because the state will supplement low earnings and provide support for the unemployed. The costs have also been transferred indirectly in that requirements for training, health and safety and the provision of other benefits will be borne by the state. The transfer of risk means that during periods of unemployment, between fixed-term contracts, for example, the state will be expected to provide support.

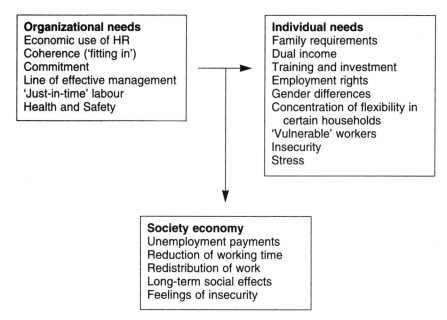

Organizational needs
Economic use of HR
Coherence ('fitting in')
Commitment
Line of effective management
'Just-in-time' labour
Health and Safety

Individual needs
Family requirements
Dual income
Training and investment
Employment rights
Gender differences
Concentration of flexibility in
    certain households
'Vulnerable' workers
Insecurity
Stress

Society economy
Unemployment payments
Reduction of working time
Redistribution of work
Long-term social effects
Feelings of insecurity

Fig. 9.3

All EU countries report a steady increase in flexible working, particularly for temporary fixed-term and part-time workers.

It is easy to assume, coming from yesterday's perspective, that these 'new' flexibilities are necessarily bad news for the individual.

Professor David Guest of Birkbeck College, London has conducted three consecutive surveys in the UK on Employee Motivation and the Psychological Contract for the Institute of Personnel and Development. The 1997 survey differentiated those on fixed-term or temporary contracts from traditional 'permanent' ongoing contracts. The findings are surprising (IPD, 1997).

Thirteen per cent of those in the sample were employed on either fixed-term or temporary contracts. They were more highly motivated and more satisfied with their jobs than staff on permanent contracts. At the same time they do not claim to be any more insecure and do not report lower commitment, less organizational citizenship behaviour or more pressure at work. Of course, much may depend on whether their employment contract is one that they have chosen, but the findings suggest that we should be cautious in assuming that those on non-permanent contracts are necessarily disadvantaged.

However, David Guest postulates that there is a discernible difference between those who chose to take such a newer form of contract and those who gravitated from the 'permanent full-time' employment probably with little choice. The former are likely to be much more positive about their situation.

All of which suggests that flexible forms of employment are here to stay.

THE SELF-EMPLOYMENT MINDSET

Labour market analysis has concentrated so far on statistical change and the paradoxes outlined above.

A new study entitled 'Tomorrow's People' by Professor Amin Rajan and Penny van Eupen (1997) based on data from 350 organizations in the UK's financial, professional and business services sector points out that *by concentrating on new forms of working, the public debate on the flexible labour market has ignored an important requirement from the workforce of today and tomorrow: namely, mindset flexibility. This the authors describe as the 'self-employment mindset'.*

Rajan and Eupen explain:

> At an individual level, it is about coming to terms with three harsh facts of life about the employer–employee relationship in the sector covered here.
>
> First, the culture of jobs-for-life has ended; yet many jobs still remain secure because *security is now based on performance not paternalism.*
>
> Second, to retain their jobs, staff have to:
>
> – treat their employers as *'customers'* of their labour services
> – provide these services when and where they are needed
> – see themselves as *'self-employed'* persons keen to retain their customer's business
> – be rewarded in accordance with their individual contribution
> – acquire progressive skills that improve employability inside and outside their current organizations.
>
> Third, although their employers will provide training towards acquiring progressive skills, *substantive responsibility for development will rest with the individual.*

This self-employment mindset has to occur whether or not the context is 'permanent' full-time jobs, fixed-term contracts or temporary and part-time arrangements.

The report traces the origins back to a response to the changing organizational form – making the point that it is irreversible (see Figure 9.4).

On the 'demand' side a number of commercial imperatives have emerged.

- Peaks for certain financial services and aspects of customer services occur in hitherto 'unsocial' hours: namely evenings and weekends. Meeting such peaks through overtime is cost-ineffective because the customer pays the same price irrespective of the time of day when the service is delivered. The same argument applies to utilities with call centres on extended hours and the retail sector where some stores are now open 24 hours a day.
- New entrants have come to financial services competition, such as retail and utilities with large customer bases. Labour costs are between 50 per cent and 85 per cent of operating costs, hence the new mindset and behaviours that go with it are seen as vital for survival.
- Service and knowledge sectors previously not open to competition are now making corporate cultures more entrepreneurial. For employees it means changing from loyal servant to committed worker.

Does this mean more jobs?

The bad news is that in the service sectors overall in Europe, taking the trend from the UK, it means that the previous expansion in the service sector, which compensated for the relentless decline in manufacturing in the past two decades, has more or less halted. New jobs will represent a

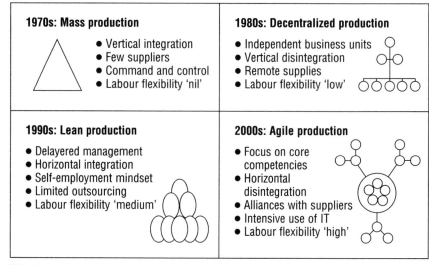

Fig. 9.4 *Changing organizational forms: 1970–2000*

redistribution of the old. The report concludes from its extensive database that the majority of the service sector has reached 'industrial maturity'.

Jobless growth

In hard numbers:

- In the late 1980s, an average annual growth of 1.5 per cent in GDP in Britain was enough to fuel job creation in these industries taken together.
- In the first half of the 1990s, the threshold was 2.0 per cent.
- In the second half, it has edged towards 2.5 per cent.

In the past decade, the service sector was the main creator of new jobs in Britain; now, no more.

The only elements likely to grow are in the new 'knowledge management' industries that have not reached maturity or 'commoditization'. Specifically they are identified in the financial and related sectors in London as:

Securities and Fund Management
Software Services

and specialist institutions including management consultancy.

The new roles will be those of 'knowledge workers' including treasury/investment specialists, business specialists, IT specialists, accountants and lawyers. There will be of course 'the replacement' jobs as some service sector roles move up to become knowledge workers.

Thus, new jobs will go to those with four attributes which are deemed conducive to self-employment behaviours: *higher education, intellectual skills, entrepreneurial flair* and *fee-earning capacity*. The losers will be those involved in day-to-day routine operations.

Differences in the skills mix of prospective winners and losers will severely limit the scope for redeployment. Another limiting factor is the location of call centres, providing routine services. For reasons of cost savings, they are increasingly located in the provinces, away from where the majority of clerical losses will be occurring.

In any event, the forecasts imply worsening shortages of knowledge workers, both in London and nationally (see Figure 9.5). This is because most employers prefer experienced recruits rather than 'raw' recruits. In the finance sector, shortages have been evident since 1995, in view of the reluctance to train internally.

CONCLUSIONS FOR EMPLOYMENT CREATION IN THE
INDUSTRIALIZED WEST

The report (*Tomorrow's People*) taken with the earlier labour market
analyses makes depressing reading for those contemplating prospective
policy on job creation. We have seen that Europe has been hampered in job
creation by an inflexible market in labour and inadequate growth in
population and therefore critical mass, compared with the USA. Flexibility
in labour markets has increased in Europe but meantime the threshold for
job creation in relation to GDP growth has risen. The ratchet factor means
that growth, where it can occur, is in the very area of scarcity – specialist
knowledge workers – worlds away from the capabilities of those that
Western governments are striving to get to *enter* the labour market. The
jobs at the lower end of the employment spectrum will have to come from
replacement of other forms of less flexible employment. With increasing
worldwide commoditization of production and over-capacity the scope for
inward investment into Europe, for example of the scale seen in the 1980s
and 1990s creating large-scale direct employment with spin-offs from
suppliers and service support, will continue to diminish (see Figure 9.6) .

New strategies will be needed by governments in the industrialized
world to develop the 'knowledge workers' – those contributing the higher
value added contribution. At the same time a different mindset is needed
– the '*self-employment mindset*' where entrepreneurial attitudes will be
required by all. Currently, as *Tomorrow's People* puts it, 'this is everyone's concern but nobody's responsibility'.

The danger for the employer or client is that this concentration of
intellectual capital will be able to defect that more easily – chasing the
highest price or latest technology.

Here we must revert to the supply chain analogy and the concept of
Voice or Exit that we explored in Chapter 5. Knowledge workers need to
be kept on board. Microsoft and its competitors understand this only too
well. But as Amin Rajan recognizes, job security is here now by virtue of
performance, not paternalism. *It is the performance of the employer as
much of the employed that will count towards a successful relationship.*

Notes
1. Handy: 1994: 15.
2. *Financial Times*, 14 April 1997.
3. *Financial Times*, 13 October 1997.
4. Casey *et al.*, 1997.

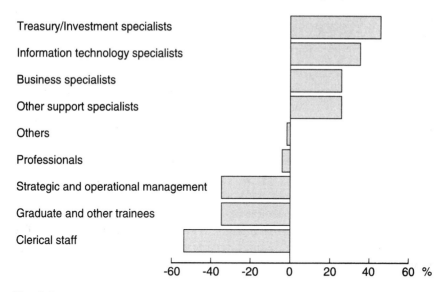

Fig. 9.5 *Occupational mix–change nationally: 1997–2000*

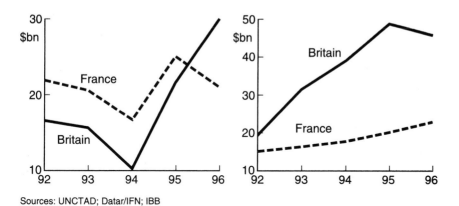

Sources: UNCTAD; Datar/IFN; IBB

Fig. 9.6 *Left-hand chart: foreign direct investment inflows; right-hand chart: jobs created*

Source: Farewell Golden Goose, *The Economist*, December 1997

10 Where is the Individual in this Brave New World of Flexibility?

Flexibility has been, on balance, a success for employers. It has helped to meet demand peaks more productively while covering for holidays and sick leave. For employees, it has accommodated their personal circumstances and improved their access to skills and jobs. In particular, it has accommodated the personal preferences of employees with caring responsibilities; young people wishing to get on the job ladder; and adults faced with the prospect of unemployment.

However, it has often been viewed by employees as a device to replace long-serving colleagues by less expensive labour. It has amounted to a visible shift from one or more of the following:

- Male employees to female employees
- Experienced recruits to raw recruits
- Full-time to part-time work
- Permanent to contract work

Beyond that, flexible workers themselves feel a sense of isolation and remoteness, resulting in high turnover. Their managers are reported as lacking the requisite skills and inclination to manage them or their career advancement, for that matter.[1]

WHAT HAVE BEEN THE PROBLEMS IN PRACTICE?

Amin Rajan and Penny van Eupen have analysed three main areas:

- To those who have, it shall be given. It appears to widen differentials between the knowledge workers who have pay *and* employability and those who have neither.
- Can I get past 'Go'? Learning is left to individuals with neither the ability nor the will to engage in self-development. People need coaching and mentoring in a supportive environment in order to grow.
- Over-emphasis on entrepreneurial behaviour can lead to excessive individualism in specialist areas. This undermines teamworking, coaching and information sharing.

The positive drivers are pay and employer brand; the negative is fear of redundancy.

THE BIG R – FOR THOSE IN 'PERMANENT' JOBS

Is job security via paternalism replaced by job security through performance? What are employees' views on potential redundancy?

International Survey Research (ISR), helps companies across Europe with employee opinion surveys and is able to collate and compare results and trends. European countries vary as to which factor is deemed as most important but Employment Security has universally taken the biggest fall in satisfaction terms right across Europe (see Figure 10.1).

When the tracking is looked at in the UK alone for employment security, the best one can say is that the decline is slowing (see Figure 10.2).

Rather like the earlier conclusions on flexibility, the new forms only actually affect a minority of the working population. Returning to the

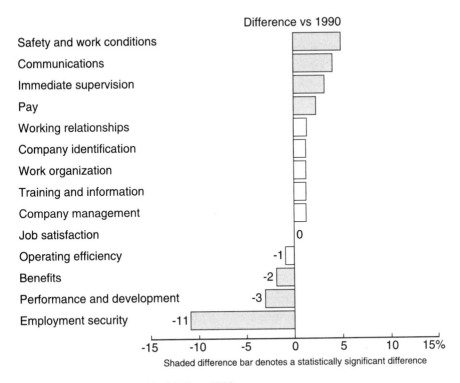

Fig. 10.1 *Category profile 1997 vs 1990*
Source: ISR European survey

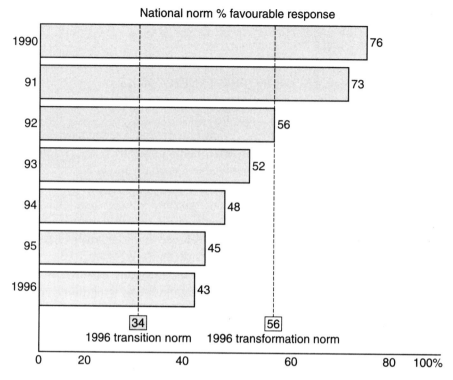

National norm % favourable response

Fig. 10.2 *Satisfaction with employment security – UK*
Source: ISR European survey

1997 report for the IPD by Professor David Guest,[2] not everyone has had direct experience of redundancy or expects to be made redundant:

- **A quarter of the workforce have experienced redundancy.** Twenty-five per cent of those currently in employment have experienced some form of redundancy at some point in their working lives. Nevertheless, 69 per cent say the decision to leave their last job was their own and 58 per cent have not changed employer in the past five years.
- **There is little expectation of future redundancy.** Fifty-six per cent expect to stay with the same employer for the next five years. Only 12 per cent believe it is 'very' or 'fairly' likely that they will be made redundant in the next couple of years.
- **Job security is high and rising.** Eighty-six per cent feel 'very' or 'fairly' secure in their jobs. Forty-two per cent are more secure than a year ago but 22 per cent are less secure.

This is not to gainsay of course the effect of the talk of job insecurity on those seemingly unaffected by it. However, the conclusions of David Guest and colleagues are that the psychological contract is generally positive and, if anything, more positive than in 1996. Their analysis is that the improvement is due to the increasing existence of an involvement climate and greater use of progressive human resource practices which influence the state of the psychological contract. This includes, of course, emphasis on performance management which would support Amin Rajan's conclusion that job security can be related to performance.

Similar improvement is evidenced in the USA.[3] There are signs in the USA that people are beginning to come to terms with the fears associated with cost-cutting. Some time ago it was popular to talk of the 'survivor syndrome' – a feeling of guilt among employees who avoided the chop.

Evidence collected by Towers Perrin, management consultants and actuaries, however, points to a marked rise in job satisfaction between 1995 and 1997. Of 2500 people working for US companies with more than 500 employees, almost three-quarters said they were satisfied with their jobs compared with 58 per cent in 1995.

Employees now have much better awareness of their contribution to their companies' success, said the report. Nearly all of those questioned agreed that it was their responsibility to remain employable by continually learning new skills.

As on the other side of the Atlantic, managers do not get the credit for the improvement.

The bad news for managements is that workforces do not give their managers any credit for this. 'Employee views of management effectiveness appear to be wavering', says the report.

The research found that employees had become less convinced that their managers were helping them to develop and were now more doubtful about the extent to which management considered their interests in decisions affecting them.

THE HUNT FOR A WORKING HYPOTHESIS

As welcome as these improvements are for those in work, there has been an increasing clamour to redefine the way we work.

We have already established that the labour market has changed shape, never to revert.

The RSA (see Chapter 7 on the work of the Centre for Tomorrow's Company) has launched in parallel the 'Redefining Work' project.

To stimulate debate, the society has published a discussion paper, *Key Views on the Future of Work*, which neatly summarizes some of the main arguments on the subject.[4]

It points out that a predominantly male UK labour force has been replaced by one in which nearly half are women.

The dominance of manufacturing has been broken by the service industries which now employ almost half of all workers. The geography of employment has shifted from the north towards the south and east and nearly every workplace is computerized.

Demographic changes mean that fewer young people are entering work under the age of 18. And a quarter of the population of working age is now economically inactive – rising to half for men aged between 55 and 65.

Full-time work, once the norm, is supplemented by increasing numbers of employees on part-time, temporary or fixed contracts. Self-employment is also on the increase with one in eight now working for themselves.

The author of the RSA paper, Valerie Bayliss, finds there is insufficient debate and consensus in a working hypothesis to provide a way forward.

The RSA seems reasonably assured that all these factors amount to a problem – though Bayliss admits there is considerable debate over the nature of the problem.

Bayliss concludes that the chief distinction in the debate is between 'those who believe that the forces operating to reduce jobs are irresistible and those who believe those forces can be controlled'.

She adds: 'There is a near-universal belief that it is a matter of political will how far the available work, and the resulting income, is shared or concentrated among populations.'

Given the history of changing work patterns, it may be pertinent that Bayliss remarks upon the lack of discussion over new work. 'It is remarkable how little credence, or even debating space is given to the notion that technology will, of itself, generate jobs of a kind we cannot yet foresee.'

Indeed the opposite conclusion is given by Jeremy Rifkin in *The End of Work* who forecasts that the march of technology will create an almost workless world. Similar arguments were put by Alvin Toffler in *Future Shock* in 1970! William Bridges on the other hand argues in *Job Shift* (1995) that it is not so much work that is disappearing but the employment package we recognize as a job.

In her search for potential solutions Valerie Bayliss turns to Stanley

Aronowitz and William DiFazio's work, *The Jobless Future; Sci-Tech and the Dogma of Work.*

This work outlines the need for a society where everyone receives a guaranteed income but no able citizen is free from the obligation to work. Such a society, says the paper, would be supported by a more redistributive taxation system and labour market regulation[5] – the former is fine but the latter would be anathema to any known or potential government on either side of the Atlantic.

The only consistent message Valerie Bayliss notes is that all observers agree that acquisition of skills is the issue. Back to knowledge workers and the self-employment mindset.

Perhaps we are again falling into the trap of Western single solution panacea-type thinking? As Charles Handy reminds us in quoting Schumacher[6] '[Some people] always tend to clamour for a final solution, as if in life there could ever be a final solution other than death. For constructive work, the principal task is always to restoration of some kind of balance.'

So we return to another theme in this book – that of process providing solutions, of an existentialist approach where the individual (or individuals) through self-discovery finds a third way, not immediately apparent. Charles Handy also refers to Trinitarian or third angle thinking[7] – always looking for solutions which can reconcile or illuminate the opposites. (See also Alistair Mant, *Leaders We Deserve*, for more comment on third angle thinking.) In so many areas of relationships today, thank goodness, partnership is seen as the potential way forward, not adversarial relationships. Sometimes it needs to be started by the innocent, seemingly naive question that takes your breath away.

Twenty years ago I had a mentor who did just that. I had recently been promoted to manage Personnel and Industrial Relations for the Wimpey construction group and was finding my feet. My mentor was Ralph Cowan, a Managing Director of Wimpey. We were then building, with other contractors, the massive oil terminal at Sullom Voe in the Shetland Islands and had quite sensibly agreed with the trade unions that to minimize problems, with so many construction workers on a small island, wages, apart from 'beer money', would be paid directly into bank accounts even though the law at the time entitled all to receive their wages 'in coin of the realm'.

Problems arose when some construction workers queued for half an hour for their 'beer money' at the cashier's office. It was seen as a long time by them and their shop stewards and a claim was lodged for 'half an hour's waiting time at cashier's office'. Following rebuttal of this claim, one of their number put in an individual application to the Procurator Fiscal in Scotland for payment of his wages, in full, in coin of the realm as was his inalienable right, quite apart from any agreement between management and unions. To remove the issue from the Sullom Voe site, this individual was sent home to the mainland on full pay while discussions continued.

Readers familiar with the industrial relations scene in the 1970s will recognize the cameo immediately. How to get oneself in a corner with no way out. Capitulation was too horrible to contemplate: the transportation and containment of large amounts of cash on a small, remote Scottish island where relationships with the local population were already fragile; the contractors' reputation with the client, BP, one of the largest of the 'Seven Sisters' of oil production worldwide.

I can picture the scene now around the Board table in Hammersmith, London, 500 miles from the hub of the problem. When I had apprised the Board of the situation Ralph Cowan, my mentor and boss, said to me, 'Has anybody gone to talk to the man?' (he at home on full pay). We all sat in stunned silence at such naivety. Of course not – he had been put up to this by his peers and the shop stewards; no way would he make a decision on his own; in any event he was only a pawn – he had no sway or influence.

'Has anybody gone to talk to the man?' came the question again. All shifted uncomfortably in their chairs. Natural justice showed that Ralph had a point. Our mindset would not allow the question in. Ralph was the boss and had a razor sharp mind. We had no better suggestion. With little confidence of a successful outcome, silver-tongued Arnold Nurick, my Industrial Relations Manager for Engineering, was dispatched to the Highlands.

The message came back. Once the consequences of his actions were explained to our construction worker, he conceded it was not sensible to continue his actions with the Procurator Fiscal. He went back to work and peace reigned. I have never forgotten that example of Trinitarian thinking. I have also never forgotten that so many seemingly intractable questions can be resolved by face-to-face honest dealing with reality.

So what is the Trinitarian solution to job creation? Probably that there is no holy grail, no panacea other than equipping our children with the right mix of skills and attitudes to take advantage and to contribute to the growth opportunities that occur in economies at various stages of their cycles. This takes us back to a theme which started in Chapter 1. (See the diagram 'A mission for sustainability' in the Introduction, or Figure 10.5.)

HOW CAN THE INDIVIDUAL GAIN MORE CONTROL OVER PERSONAL DESTINY?

The first port of call must be education. It's appropriate to focus on that first hoop on the three-legged stool; it's also significant that the new UK Labour Government's three priorities are stated as Education, Education and Education.

The Royal Institute of International Affairs (RIIA) argues that the UK education system is one which:

- increasingly fails to meet the needs of an industrial society by delivering a few people with high-order skills and a mass of people with very basic ones or none at all.
- produces poorly educated people who are incapable of using modern methods of manufacture, leading to low productivity, poor profits and weak investment. With intensive training of willing employees 'Kaizen' approaches are possible. Renewal and innovation via 'Hoshin' approaches are still worlds away.
- reflects the national division across class lines with two practical effects. First, that industry has been seen as a battle ground rather than a means of mutual enrichment. Second, that politicians saw problems in terms of outcomes of such conflict not structural issues to be solved.[8]

The product in terms of attitudinal groups is illustrated in Figure 10.3.

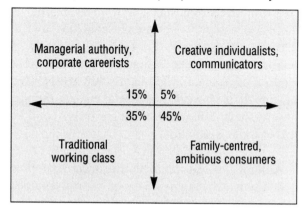

Fig. 10.3 *Primary attitudinal groups – a product of education?*

Three conclusions can be drawn:-

- The great majority, 80 per cent of the population, look to tacit rules, to traditional patterns.
- A very small fraction of the population are involved in shaping the future; however, 75 per cent of this small fraction are fiercely loyal to the values and ways of thinking acquired in formative years.
- As is self-evident, the least capable are also the least capable of adapting to change, and they are also the least prepared to do so.

So why are the results so far adrift from the needs of an industrial society? I believe there are two fundamental roots which have caused dysfunction. First, that as recognized in Chapter 1, European education originates from the original Greek which is fundamentally unsuited to the needs for growth and innovation in a modern industrial society and second, we still have not made the transition from church-led to state-led to business-led education to dovetail to the needs of life-long learning.

The products of the first are a system that values the academic, measurable, 'explicit' knowledge route to 'discovery' of existing knowledge with enormous effort applied to convert 'tacit' practical knowledge into quasi-academic qualifications. This of course contrasts with Japan where the 'tacit' and 'explicit' are seen as elements of learning towards unending development.

Second, education and learning are seen as separate and not as a continuum where the majority of learning happens in business.

If we overlay these with the changing patterns of employment and the 'self-employed mindset' – the reality of the world of work we have discussed earlier – we quickly conclude that the recipe is potentially disastrous.

The 'cognitive elite' coined by Dr Oliver Sparrow of The Chatham House Forum are all right in this new world – but then they were always on top. It is those at the lower end of the spectrum who experience hopelessness. Education no longer offers confidence, plainly unsuited as it is to today's situation.

Attitudes to self-improvement may, at the lowest end of the scale of attainment, be highly distorted by peer opinion. We have noted a strong tendency, however, for two additional attitudes to manifest themselves. At the high end of the scale, professionals' employment not only wins them economic liberties but also provides many of them with intrinsically rewarding jobs. At the low end of the scale, people with limited skills have to dedicate a large amount of time to earning modest amounts of money, in not necessarily interesting jobs. The marginal gain that this money brings may not be satisfying, when compared to the enjoyment of other, non-remunerative pursuits. Indeed, the figure suggests the shift that might be attained in a life dedicated to economic self-improvement. Fantasies within this group are likely to consist of escaping the system, achieving success 'at a bound'.[9]

Oliver Sparrow calls this the 'twang' effect – aspiration for and faith in the lottery rather than progress through education and development. (The Transformation Journey at Anglian Water was able to produce the 'twang' effect for certain individuals – see Chapter 4.)

For the increasing proportion of the new flexible labour market training and development is down to themselves – with probably little confidence of early return.

For the employer the new 'just-in-time' workforce may be productive and economical but it will not naturally innovate or contribute to organizational renewal.

Returning to the second root, who is influencing education? The Church commenced the process and, although today not enormously influential in our schools, is resurrected as a key player whenever the issue of moral values rears its head. The State took over in the debate of the separation of Church and State and teaching became a public service rather than service to God. Despite the transition, there is still the divide between those who see education as a repository and training ground for our moral and intellectual values and those who emphasize the practical reasons for education such as supplying a labour force prepared for enterprise and economic health. The former put social and academic ends before the goals of learning.

We are conscious that learning is the key to future viability. To quote Jack Welch, Chairman and Chief Executive Officer of GE in the USA, *'When the rate of change outside is greater than the rate of change inside the end is in sight.'*

Or to recall the theorem of a much underrated British management guru, Professor Reg Revans

$$L \geq C$$

(rate of learning has to be equal to or greater than the rate of change.)

The rate of learning has to increase today like never before – this is as true for the Education sector as for industry.

The American researchers Stan Davis and Jim Botkin in *The Monster under the Bed* point out the transition for individuals in the USA in the past 30 years:

- The organization man of the 1950s sacrificed flexibility for security.
- The individual entrepreneur of the 1980s was flexible but far from secure.
- In the 1990s flexibility resides in both the individual (knowledge lies within) and in the organization in terms of value added and cost.

Davis and Botkin define the role of business as an educator:

Business's primary purpose is to meet market needs with its production and distribution of goods and services. But as it increasingly produces and distributes knowledge in carrying out this function, it must also accept the social responsibility incumbent on an educator. Business should be acknowledged for its part in extending learning to life long learning.[10]

I am not suggesting that it is the job of business to run education but there needs to be a more engaged partnership so that education is a true foundation for life-long learning. There are fundamental lessons of rejuvenation to be learnt that do not necessarily require injections of money. For instance, a declining education system can learn much from business that has had to come out of decline and reinvigorate and redefine itself while continuing to work smarter.

Business is increasingly displacing school as the locus of learning due to the tide of information technology. This is not just about computer literacy which is only the access point.

Just as we recognized that intellectual capital in companies can today become more valuable than balance sheet type assets, the power of accelerated learning through IT has impact for firms and individuals alike. The first impact of IT was to cut costs and automate tasks; the second to give networking – redefining the way people worked; the third, for example, to reverse the supply chain by retailers dictating to manufacturers; and the fourth by adding knowledge to information-intensive activities. 'Without intending it or realizing it, by using information technology, by humanizing it and advancing it to knowledge-smart products, business is coming to displace school as the locus of learning.'[11]

Davis and Botkin's argument is that both the business world and the home are clear about the drivers – technology and consumer led respectively (see Figure 10.4).

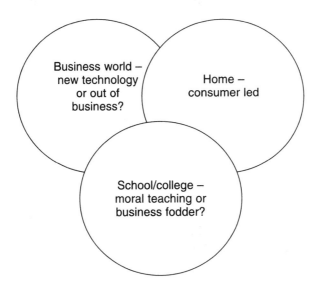

Fig. 10.4

As we saw, there has always been a sharp divide between the ethos of education as a training ground for moral and intellectual values and the ethos of education for enterprise and economic wealth.

Japan has remarkably escaped the see-saw or switch-back of fashion on education veering as education does in the West between these alternative extremes.

Their education is strikingly old-fashioned, learning by rote; morals are infused at home and by strong peer group and group think. School and university experience is very uncreative. Creativity is encouraged in the workplace but then generally in teams, avoiding the extremes of Western individuality. The education ethos of *development* rather than *discovery* means a sense of newness and creation of different worlds.

Davis and Botkin do not hand the baton to business schools.

Employee education is currently better served by business than by business schools. Business schools like the education system in general are locked in the old paradigm. When customer education, the next great learning segment, is added, we have to realize that business is already a very significant educator and is on its way to becoming the major force in education.[12]

The real challenge for business schools in future is not going to be between those who vie to produce the best MBAs but whether they can collaborate with in-company learning, such as what we have termed the 'University of Water' at Anglian Water where we are encouraging a learning business to encapsulate and recognize learning by all employees and associates towards individual and corporate growth. (See Chapter 4.)

Davis and Botkin conclude that the real problem is that the nature of learning in organizations is not understood. Learning, they argue, is a *consumer* good whereas teaching is a *producer* good. The former is received, the latter given. Few businesses set out to be teaching organizations – why?

Bringing the two roots that cause dysfunction together, that is:

- Western education and Greek ethos
- lack of business-led education

we see that one dysfunctional root draws from the other. If the ingrained perception of education is 'discovery' not 'development', then there is little enthusiasm in business for 'teaching'. Indeed it sounds arrogant in a business setting. Managers find the concepts of teaching, mentoring and coaching difficult since they appear in some ways to be analogous to the outmoded 'control and constrain' philosophy. Add to this the flux-like state of employment with the 'self-employment' mindset, and the necessary long-term framework may not be there for 'development' type learning in the workplace.

It is even worse for those not in employment. *If a business setting is a prerequisite for learning then those excluded can get excluded for life.*

We cannot hope or even perhaps desire to replicate the Japanese happy accident which gives them the 'development' business-led learning ethos. In any event their own transition with deregulation of the domestic economy is bringing them closer to the Western model with potentially greater gaps between rich and poor, higher unemployment and more flexible labour markets with the Western emphasis on the individual.

We are dealing with a worldwide problem that is a shared experience whatever the country or culture. Looked at from this perspective the problem is huge. The ILO in 1996 announced that their surveys showed that one-third of all workers in the world were currently unemployed or under-employed.[13] Unemployment among countries in the Organization for Economic Co-operation and Development is running at about 30m people which, because of different national reporting procedures, probably equates to 60m people who are economically inactive. This is a function, as we have seen, of lack of adequate education and opportunity.

In economic terms education pays off handsomely. Oliver Sparrow (RIIA, 1997) points out that: 'Returns over 8–10 per cent are usually seen as attractive in normal commercial transactions. Education is therefore, a spectacularly attractive investment for those who have access to it.'; 'Social returns to the state from investment in education in different parts of the world across different sectors of schooling showed none below 8 per cent and some, in sub-Saharan Africa, as high as 25 per cent. Returns to the individual on personal investment in education were even greater – as high as 41 per cent for primary education in sub-Saharan Africa.' Education and opportunity equal development. Development is a mindset issue which, we know from success, can be inculcated with the right ingredients – what is the recipe?

This is where the model of the three-legged stool returns to useful effect. The individual can be in control of change and personal destiny to some extent but needs society and business to develop, to reach fulfilment.

Where is this 'stool' most effective? The conclusion reached in Chapter 8 is the right one. The economic region is the focus. The three 'C's coined by Rosabeth Moss Kanter

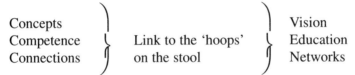

apply to individuals as much as they do to firms and economic regions. The lubricant to bring the three 'C's together is Voice which we saw in Chapter 5 applies equally to the people relationship dimension as it more obviously does within the supply chain, or the value-chain as Michael Porter would describe it. (See Figure 10.5; now we can move from the matrix form to the integrated elements of the three-legged stool.)

Using the region as locus for education is not new, of course. It used to be seen as a recipe for parochialism. With easy and fast worldwide communication today it doesn't need to be. It is *the* way to get business-led education. Input at a national or international level is generally over-diluted and about governance. The models of even local or regional business involvement in education have been centred around governance, not ethos or mindset. The great and good have sat on university councils, school and college governing bodies with an inevitable focus of inputs around efficiency and commerciality. Useful but not formative.

Regions need to redefine the *concepts* for themselves; they can't do this without adequate *connections*, that is, getting the right people involved

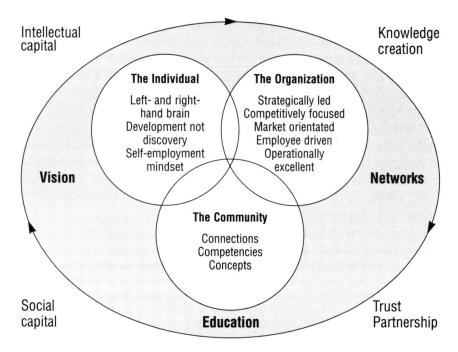

Fig. 10.5 *Products of the three-legged stool. Mission accomplished – sustainability*

with the right terms of reference. What do the regions want to achieve? Are they to be in control of their destiny? Does sufficient community spirit (social capital) exist? What is the ethos which will produce holistic concepts and connections? Assets and *competencies* are an advantage but can be a product of the other 'C's.

Examples abound. Apart from the instances of South Carolina and the North East of England used in Chapter 8, Charles Handy refers to Matthew d'Ancana's study of Swindon in the South of England that has suffered decline and now renaissance.

It is fashionable both to speak in favour of 'community', 'partnership' and 'responsible citizenship' as the link pieces of an individualist society, and at the same time to lament the demise of our traditional communities. Matthew d'Ancona's study of Swindon, one of Britain's old industrial towns turned into a new-style hub for the technological and information businesses of today, should give us hope.

Swindon is not a place to lift the heart at first sight. It has, d'Ancona says, no focus, no cathedral, no university, no beauty. Its citizens are mainly technological sophisticates but they have suffered from labour mobility, de-industrialization and delayering in the organizations. Nevertheless, he left Swindon an optimist. 'The town's capacity for civic regeneration has proved considerable. Its citizens ... have quietly achieved successful race relations; they participate in an ever-widening range of voluntary groups; their churches are diversifying the services they offer, and their schools are expanding their role as civic institutions. In ways mundane and intriguing, the people of Swindon are learning to live with the hectic forces of modernity which one of them described as 'the vagabond way'. In their unhistoric acts there are lessons for us all.'[14]

A contrast with Swindon is Cambridge, also in the south but with very different origins and growth patterns. In terms of education, possibly without challenge, it is by the elite for the elite.

In terms of concept – an issue of conflict. A medieval city with enormous tradition uncomfortably surrounded by high technology science parks.

The 'silicon fen' phenomenon has created 650 science and technology-based companies employing 23 000 people in the Cambridge area – 30 000 in Cambridgeshire as a whole. There is potential for more, but the price could be high.

Cambridge's Cassandra is Peter Dawe, an information technology entrepreneur. He hit a nerve when he wrote to the *Cambridge Evening News* in February 1997 to argue that a 'full' sign should be hung over the city.

Roads were choked, he wrote. Shops were so packed they would have to issue tickets to get in. Schools were overflowing and hospitals turning away patients. With few homes for sale and fewer for rent, Cambridge had the highest proportion of people sleeping rough in the country. There was no development land inside the city and no road space for more to commute from outside. 'We should refuse any further development of Cambridge or the surrounding area', he urged.

'Unless there is an integrated policy we will end up in a muddle', says Walter Herriot, Managing Director of St John's Innovation Centre, where 15 of the 60 fledgling companies are desperate for more space. He wants to see expansion within a ten-mile radius to create up to 15 000 high technology jobs over 20 years.[15]

Cambridge started with competencies (assets), some connections but little integrated community and has yet to get the concept right.

So far so good. Education needs to embrace 'development', not 'discovery'. Education needs to be business led. The best crucible for this is the economic region with a focus on development using the three 'C's, hopefully in the right order.

Business-led education will be about market focus, not product. Davis and Botkin make the point that the educational product reflects the governance of the institution. 'When church education was the dominant form, schools reflected church approaches to organization. Clergy were teachers, pupils were arranged in neat rows like church pews ... in today's government-run schools teachers are civil servants and schools look and are run like government bureaucracies.'[16]

The Davis and Botkin vision is of complete integration with business and business methods. Education outside the classroom, mediated by technology, not instructors. Just-in-time learning as popular as just-in-time manufacturing: 'The educating act will reside increasingly in the active learner rather than in the teacher-manager'; 'As learners turn to technology for expertise about content, teachers will focus their expertise more around process and relationships.'[17]

Educationalists will quickly assert that the teaching world has already caught up with this vision, and in many cases this is true. However, much of the progress is by education mimicking the industrial sector in terms of technique, not in terms of having dialogue with it over curricula or ethos. The fault is shared. Industry needs to see it must invest time in this aspect of Voice in yet another supply chain relationship. Also, that it is the crucible for life-long learning which combined with the self-employment mindset gives a three-cornered responsibility to the individual, the educator and to business for *competency* growth through self-development.

WHAT DO YOUNG PEOPLE THINK THEMSELVES?

It is great to postulate about the issue of the individual in today's society in flux but for change to happen the recipients need to be convinced. The Industrial Society, under the Chairmanship of Sir Bob Reid, published the results of The 2020 Vision programme in October 1997. The Industrial Society surveyed nearly 10 000 young people in the UK between 12 and 25 from a wide range of backgrounds, including disadvantaged young people and those with disabilities and special needs, over a two-year period 1995 to 1997. The object was to give young people a role in influencing work, learning and social issues into the next century.

Key findings from this innovative and extensive survey relative to learning skills, work and social issues were:[18]

Learning

- Eight-six per cent of 16–25-year-olds agree that 'nobody can make you learn, you have to want to', and 63 per cent felt school did not prepare them for life in the real world.
- Forty-six per cent of 11–16-year-olds think a 'good' school depends on teachers who help students understand, 38 per cent think sympathetic, friendly teachers are important, and 29 per cent felt small classes helped.
- Thirty-nine per cent of 11–16-year-olds said they had problems at school due to disruptive pupils, and 34 per cent said they were bored.
- Ninety per cent of 16–25-year-olds feel you carry on learning after you leave school.

'I think it's very difficult to teach someone how to learn.'

Skills

- Eight-two per cent of 16–25-year-olds thought practical vocational training should start at school.
- Sixty-eight per cent of 12–25-year-olds thought reading and writing were the key skills, and 54 per cent felt being able to get on well with people was important.
- Thirty-two per cent of 12–25-year-olds thought expressing yourself clearly when talking was an important skill.
- Fifty per cent of 12–25-year-olds said that if they were unemployed and wanting work they would get more qualifications, and 35 per cent said they'd get specialist training.

'Communication is the most important skill ... to be able to speak to people, listen to people, take advice from people.'

Work

- Eighty-one per cent of 12–25-year-olds have had some experience of paid work.
- Sixty-one per cent of 16–25-year-olds said the most important thing they look for in a job is good pay; good working conditions are their second choice (54 per cent).
- Sixty-seven per cent of 16–25-year-olds said getting on well with colleagues made a job enjoyable.

- Fifty-three per cent of 12–25-year-olds believed they were likely to be in permanent employment with the same employer or consecutive employers; 40 per cent said there would be increased automation, and 28 per cent thought there would be higher unemployment.

'I was working full time as a trainee ... it was an awful job ... the wages were awful, but I still went and did it.'

Social issues

- Only one-fifth (22 per cent of 11–16-year-olds and 20 per cent of 16–25-year-olds) said they felt part of their local community.
- Around a half (51 per cent of 16–25-year-olds and 49 per cent of 11–16-year-olds) said their priority for action was against violent crime. Over two-fifths of 16–25-year-olds said unemployment and homelessness were priorities (45 per cent and 42 per cent respectively).
- Fifty-eight per cent of 16–25-year-olds said the government's spending priority should be the NHS, and 47 per cent said education.
- Ninety per cent of 12–25-year-olds said the government should raise more money from lotteries, and 61 per cent said high earners should be taxed more.

'I feel politicians are so out of touch with reality.'

Young people in this survey clearly recognize the importance of interpersonal skills in relationships and at work. They value learning and want to learn skills for work and life.

Although young people show a degree of individual optimism, we found an alarming collective pessimism. There is a significant gap between what young people want – for themselves and others – and what they expect will happen.

Young people are not looking to everyone else to provide answers and take action. Our research – particularly the face-to-face contact – shows clearly that young people are realistic about the challenges we face, and they are prepared to take responsibility for themselves and for making things happen.

Particular recommendations relevant here are:

Give us opportunities to develop relevant skills
   e.g. promote excellence among teachers
      curriculum relevant to life and work
      work experience that prepares.

Give us the chance to work and learn
   e.g. every school/college leaver has work or learning opportunity to
      go on to
      advice on work and learning
      opportunities to invest in learning at work.

The message could not be clearer. Young people will require well-honed coping skills to survive in the next century.

HOW CAN THE INDIVIDUAL COPE WITH AMBIGUITY AND UNCERTAINTY?

'Changing the mindset is not a matter of introducing performance-related pay; nor direct exhortation. It is about learning to cope with a lot of ambiguity and uncertainty.'[19]

Amin Rajan and Penny van Eupen in *Tomorrow's People* conclude that 'new ways of thinking are more important than new forms of working' in the business of tomorrow.

We have seen that jobs for life have gone but that flexible employment patterns are not necessarily worse than 'permanent' employment. Jobs are now translated into work on a project-to-project basis according to William Bridges (1995).

Tomorrow's People concludes that the key skills for the new 'self-employment' mindset are in three iterative stages:

   Foundation
   Intermediate, and
   Advanced

or Left- and right-hand brain, Development not Discovery and Self-employment mindset (see Figure 10.5).

(a) Foundation capabilities

These relate to two sets of attributes developed in an individual's formative years:

- *Educational basics:* covering broad-based education and training, with strong emphasis on reading, writing, numeracy and IT
- *Personal attributes:* covering traits such as honesty, resilience, reliability, openness and oral communication

Is this happening?

Most employers perceive their young recruits to be ill-equipped in many of the personal traits identified above (confirmed by the views of young people themselves). Many universities and colleges now have courses in subjects such as communication and presentation skills. But their main thrust is perceived to be theoretical. In turn, these perceptions make it difficult to develop the next level of capabilities at the workplace.

(b) Intermediate capabilities

These aim to maximize effectiveness in the early phase of the individual's career. They relate to:

- *Technical skills:* covering skills that are specific to a job.
- *Personal attributes:* covering practical skills that maximize individual performance. They include communication, reasoning, motivation, judgement, initiative and self-management.
- *Business awareness:* covering the ability to understand the structure, operations, products, processes, and the general business environment of the employer in particular and the industry in general.

Currently, an overwhelming proportion of training effort in financial, professional and business services is targeted at developing technical skills. The others are mostly developed through informal learning by doing.

(c) Advanced capabilities

These usually apply to individuals who are at the midpoint in their career. They cover attributes which aim to maximize overall corporate performance:

- Leadership
- Teamworking
- Strategic thinking

- Entrepreneurial flair
- Customer orientation
- Quality awareness
- Resource management

The programmes for developing these attributes are few and far between. Where they exist, the emphasis is on classroom learning and/or learning by doing. In most cases, programmes tend to be ad hoc, organized largely in response to untoward events. They are rarely embedded properly in human resource management systems.

Amin Rajan's formula is remarkably similar to the 'stick of rock' concept we developed in Rolls-Royce IPG in 1995 (Figure 4.6). There the emphasis was on developing the personal characteristics (running through the stick of rock) in parallel to the functional, managerial and experiential elements of career development.

The *Tomorrow's People* report makes a number of points about the progression from (a) to (c) above:

- It is an evolutionary process; it cannot be fast forwarded.
- Some skills are more innate than acquired.
- Classroom-type training only applies to some skills.
- Capability level differs with occupational circumstance.

How to get there?

Capabilities vary between jobs, as do the avenues for development; the four avenues for the new mindset are described as follows (see Figure 10.6):

- *Taught learning*, relying on in-house and external courses, some of which are customized to accommodate the occupational needs of the individual
- *Distance learning*, relying on technology and self-help in accessing a systematic body of knowledge and understanding
- *Mentored learning*, relying on personal encounters with more experienced colleagues capable of providing just-in-time tips on work-related problems and a sounding board for continuous personal development
- *Experiential learning*, relying on routes as varied as lateral transfers, stretch assignments, benchmarking and community involvement in order to broaden and deepen the individual's experience base

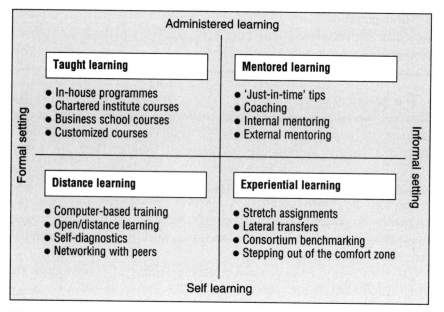

Fig. 10.6 *Suggested avenues for developing the self-employment mindset*

Taught learning and Distance learning. 'What' learning is obtainable, often outside the workplace, but the 'how' learning is becoming more difficult to obtain.

Tomorrow's People find that:

> The extensive rationalization in the first half of this decade has taken a heavy toll on mentors and coaches. In any event, mentoring and coaching have not acquired the significance they deserve because change programmes have substantially undermined the trust that is necessary between mentor and protégé.

Furthermore, in delayered downsized structures, most senior staff are working inordinately long hours, leaving them little time for developing their subordinates. In the City in particular, *entrepreneurial behaviour is breeding excessive individualism that is detrimental to coaching, teamworking and information sharing.*

Finally, the growing segmentation of the workforce between knowledge workers and others, is heavily restricting the scope for lateral transfers and stretch assignments for a vast majority of staff in clerical and administrative grades.

These factors, common in other industries apart from financial services, throw the individual back onto taught and distance learning.

Distance learning is expected to be achieved in the individual's own time and the reality is that a large majority of staff have neither the ability nor the motivation to engage in self-development.

Unless the employer practises being a 'learning business' then employability becomes a Catch 22 concept and the self-employment mindset doesn't evolve:

> Employability is fraught with a major contradiction from the point of view of employees. In order to cope with the initial insecurity that goes with the promise, individuals need to have personal attributes like reliability, drive, energy, resilience, understanding, logic, creativity and judgement.
>
> Yet these are the very attributes that employability is meant to provide over time. Those who have them already are clearly thriving – as evidenced by widening pay differentials. Those who don't are the unwitting victims of new market forces. This is the Achilles' heel of employability.
>
> In OECD countries, individuals are educated and trained to think and act in a linear, cause and effect manner. They are not equipped by the system to cope with the ambiguity and unpredictability of the evolving workplace. Much the same point applies to the extra-curricular activities they engage in while undergoing education and training.
>
> For most individuals, the burden of adjusting to the new mindset is heavy. To compound the problem, there are often no proper counselling systems for staff faced with redundancies or career change.

The ambiguity and uncertainty is even more acute for those out of work who do not even have taught learning and the 'learning by doing' routes of those in work.

Business needs to be sensitive to these issues, otherwise long-term viability is endangered, and far from the learning business being a trendy option it should become *de rigueur* with necessary counselling and support. Business, in partnership with government and educators, needs to extend the hand of support and encouragement to those out of work to fit them for opportunities, which in turn will feed back into the economy.

The evidence from the work of David Guest and colleagues is that today's workforce is coming to terms with ambiguity and uncertainty, but only after a long transition which we know can be shortened, to everyone's benefit, by helping individuals through to a new mindset – the self-employment mindset. *The new entrants to this workplace have to be more self-reliant from the start. This heightens the need for education to be influenced by business and for business to take on the role of educator at work.*

What is the self-employment mindset? How can the individual start?

William Bridges has produced a sequel to *Job Shift* entitled *Creating You and Co* (1997) to help the individual, employed or unemployed to focus on the 'best way to capitalize on a ripe opportunity'. He calls this in acronym form the individual's 'DATA':

D = Desire. Show that you desire the task more than other people who are interested in it.
A = Abilities. Do you have what it will take to get the work done, to accomplish the task, to solve the problem? (NB. Job history is probably irrelevant.)
T = Temperament. 'I look for candidates who have a warm side to their personality. I just hired a man whose ratio of social skills to technical skills is about 70 to 30.' (Samuel Melters, CEO Melters Industries). (An interesting parallel with Emotional Intelligence as described by Daniel Goleman)
A = Assets – characteristics, experiences, areas of expertise giving an advantage over rivals – often very specific to the work to be done.

These are all inherent characteristics. The individual also needs to have antennae into the changing employment and opportunity world. I argue that what is true for businesses in terms of 'double-loop learning' is also true for individuals in coping with ambiguity and uncertainty. Figure 6.1, p. 163, designed for the learning board is equally applicable to the individual who wishes to survive. The connections into the possible worlds of work and development are as important as the assets or DATA (William Bridges). *Networking is now valued as an art form not a waste of time, as hitherto.*

Valuing differing forms of occupation

It is easy to conclude from our past that the ideal model for employment is a fulfilling well-paid role in business. This we must leave behind and embrace a much greater diversity.

I don't just mean the flexible forms of employment we've talked of earlier, or self-employment or 'portfolio' working, all of which now form a legitimate part of the labour market.

Money tends to become an overwhelming measure and eclipses value. Recognition is too often given to those with power, authority and wealth when it would be better diverted to unsung heroes who support society in big and little ways. In this age of increasing gaps between haves and have nots, when the able accelerate while the weak flounder, society (and business) should elevate those who support the weak and aid their development. The fall-out from our industries will increase, not decrease, and individuals will need to change careers maybe up to ten times in a working lifetime to survive. The proportion open to times of instability will increase. Hence instead of chasing rainbows by elevating the latest lucrative form of employment, let us honour teachers, mentors, counsellors, carers, social and charity workers, the not for profit sector and volunteering, without which the fabric of society will not give industry the licence to operate.

THE SEARCH FOR MEANING – A VISION

I started this book with a quote from *The Empty Raincoat* by Charles Handy: 'The market is a mechanism for sorting the efficient from the inefficient, it is not a substitute for responsibility.'

I would like to end with a few thoughts from his later book, *The Hungry Spirit*. He quotes Francis Kinsman's *Millennium, Towards Tomorrow's Society* who borrowed three psychological types developed by the Stanford Research Institute to describe the world as he saw it:

Sustenance driven
Outer directed
Inner directed

- **Sustenance driven**
  The prime objective of sustenance-driven people is security, both financial and social. Although some of them are poor and/or unemployed, others are comfortably off but want to cling on to what they have. Such people are clannish, set in their ways and resistant to change. They are, says Kinsman 'the left-over philosophical products of the agricultural era – the top, middle and bottom of the feudal heap'.

- **Outer directed**

  Outer-directed people are high achievers. They are searching for esteem and status, as the outward symbols of their success in life. They want, therefore, to have the best, or at least the right things in life. They are usually intelligent, well educated and ambitious. They are materialistic, except in those circles where it is smart not to be materialistic. They are the driving force behind economically successful societies.

- **Inner directed**

  The driving force of these people is to give expression to their talents and beliefs. This does not imply that they are withdrawn or aloof, or even unambitious, but they tend to be less materialistic than the other two groups, more concerned with ethics and the way society is run. Their values are based on personal growth, self-fulfilment, sensibility and the quality of their and other people's lives. To return to a now familiar contrast, the emphasis is on 'being' rather than 'doing'. The others call them 'wimps', says Kinsman, yet some others find them dangerous. 'How can we identify these people – and stamp them out?' asked one authoritarian manager.

These categories are based on Maslow's hierarchy of needs. Maslow insisted that the individual is never completely one or the other but a mix which changes at different times throughout life. Charles Handy sees himself as having graduated through the stages to being anchored in the inner-directed group. I too, if not there, am well on the way. Handy makes the relevance of this clear with what he says next: 'If we want control over our own destinies, which, I am arguing, is the only choice we have, then we would be foolish to make our wishes subject to the fashions of others, which is what drives both of the first two dimensions. We would be well advised to shift as quickly as we can to a view of life which is predominantly Inner Directed.'

The key to control over destiny is just that – a process of self-discovery – to enable individuals to 'give expression to their talents and beliefs' 'based on personal growth, self fulfilment, sensibility and the quality of their and other peoples lives'. To this I would add, to be in touch with their spirituality.[20]

This is a function of learning opportunity and support. This makes all the difference between capitalizing on change or being the victim of change. People are more adaptable than we give them credit for. Properly integrated with work and society, linked by good education, networks and a clear vision, individuals will produce a thriving, vibrant society which in turn fulfils their own need.

'Without a vision the people perish.'

Notes

1. Rajan and van Eupen, 1997: 11.
2. IPD, 1997: (vi).
3. The 1997 Towers Perrin Workplace Index.
4. *Financial Times* 16 April 1997.
5. Ibid.
6. Handy, 1994: 19.
7. Ibid.: 90.
8. RIIA, 1996: 41.
9. RIIA, 1997.
10. Davis and Botkin, 1994: 160.
11. Ibid.: 66.
12. Ibid.: 108.
13. Handy, 1997: 139.
14. Ibid.: 147.
15. *Financial Times*, 7 November 1997.
16. Davis and Botkin, 1994: 124.
17. Ibid.: 126.
18. The Industrial Society, 1997: 6, 7, 8.
19. Rajan and van Eupen, 1997: 75.
20. The UK Government Dept. of Education and Employment definition: 'The valuing of the non-material aspects of life, and intimations of an enduring reality'.

Appendix A: Fieldbook for Practitioners

1. BECOMING WORLD CLASS

My first volume *Becoming World Class*, published in 1994, focused on the challenge for Western companies in trying to cope with the competition from Japanese companies.

The context for this was set out in Chapter 1 of *Becoming World Class*.

> Understanding what the Japanese are up to may seem to be obvious to many British managers. A nation that in the space of forty years has accelerated from an image of poor-quality, copy-cat products and cheap labour to the premier manufacturing nation of the world, can now claim to be producing goods of the highest quality, which it designs and develops itself. In Western terms, surely the Japanese cannot be playing according to the rules – it must be because of unfair practices, trade barriers, inscrutability, robots or exploitation of labour, we argue. We refuse to accept that this is real, above-board competition. In fact, we have pretended for decades that this was a passing threat, largely irrelevant to our situation, blithely averting our eyes as large sectors of industry disappeared, starting with motor cycles and ships, and ending with practically everything else that is made.
>
> Now we have been forced to rediscover that we have talent – human resources – under our noses, and not just brilliant inventors and Nobel prize winners.
>
> Strangely, some new reasons for confidence in British talent are starting to come from Japanese firms in the UK. For a variety of reasons, Japanese inward investment in the UK has accelerated in recent years and the approach they use to 'people management' has given the opportunity to British management and labour to demonstrate that poor quality and labour relations are not necessarily synonymous with the UK.

To aid the practitioner I intend what follows as a diagnostic for readers to self assess where they and their companies are on the journey to world class and then into the spectrum of this book Beyond World Class.

The theme of *Becoming World Class* was the stuff of operational excellence:

	Scale Worst ... Best									
	1	2	3	4	5	6	7	8	9	10
Quality										
1 Does your company embrace the principles of Total Quality (TQ)? (Best)										
2 Is the link between QA (Quality Assurance) and TQ understood and encouraged? (BWC, p. 6) (Best)										
3 Do employees practise 'Kaizen' (small steps of continuous improvement)? (Best)										
4 Is the complementary link between step change (innovation) and incremental change (Kaizen) understood and encouraged? (Best)										
5 Are failures thoroughly investigated (5 why's) and learnt from?										
Cost										
6 Are cost-cutting schemes just about reducing staff numbers? (Worst)										
7 Are all staff encouraged to produce ideas to reduce costs? (Best)										
8 Do they know what to aim for? (Best)										
9 Are customer/supplier relations about adversarial bargaining? (Worst)										
10 Does a supply chain operate where you work together to reduce base cost, not margins? (Best)										

	Scale Worst									Best
	1	2	3	4	5	6	7	8	9	10
Delivery										
11 Is there a culture of delivery on time/keeping to promises?										
12 Do employees shoulder the corporate responsibility on delivery promises?										
13 Do employees get support in achieving delivery targets?										
14 Are the targets for individuals, teams and the company stretching? (Best)										
Ethos or culture – comparing with Japan										
15 To what extent does Matsushita's comment apply to the ethos of your company? 'We will win and you will lose. You cannot do anything about it because your failure is an internal disease. You firmly believe that sound management means executives on one side and workers on the other; on one side, men who think and on the other, men who can only work. For you, management is the art of smoothly transferring the executives' ideas into the workers' hands.'										
16 Is there a team-based culture? (Best)										
17 Is faith exclusively placed in individuals (Worst)										
18 Does a silo mentality exist? (Worst)										

	Scale Worst → Best									
	1	2	3	4	5	6	7	8	9	10
19 Do feelings of insecurity affect performance in your company?										
20 Do employees get proper feedback on performance? (via appraisals)										
21 Are employee-bargaining arrangements adversarial? (Worst)										
22 Does a single table/single union ethos exist? (Best)										
23 What is the characteristic over terms and conditions? Single status (Best) or many hierarchical differentials (Worst)										
24 Is the ethos one of flexibility (Best) or of entitlement? (Worst)										
25 Does life long learning and continuous development predominate? (Best)										
26 Are ideas from all welcomed and used? (Best)										
27 Can employees influence direction and policy?										
28 Do team leaders have real responsibility?										
29 Is the ethos: I have two jobs – one to do my job the other to improve my job?										
30 Is change embraced in the organization?										
31 Do you regularly benchmark with world class companies?										

	Scale Worst → Best									
	1	2	3	4	5	6	7	8	9	10
Change										
32 Do you learn from within the supply chain?										
33 Do you practise policy deployment? (cascading vision and values to teams and individuals)										
34 Is there *effective* communication throughout?										
35 Is there wide consultation before key decisions are taken?										
36 Is Equal Opportunity encouraged? Do you manage diversity?										
37 Is 'horizontal' development encouraged?										
38 Are managers people managers or technical experts?										
39 Is faith placed in structural change (Worst) or taking people through a process? (Best)										
40 Is there a mentoring and coaching ethos?										
41 Choice on which way for change • blind faith? (Worst) • ruthless exploitation of the market? • or long-term competitive approach? (Best)										

Becoming World Class – Scoreboard

Total 290 to 410 = World Class leaders
160 to 289 = Getting there
41 to 159 = Laggers!

POSTSCRIPT TO BECOMING WORLD CLASS

'Think quality. Never be satisfied. Strive constantly to improve your product. Inspire everyone from chairman to newest employee to seek ways to do everything better. Cut the product rejection rate. Be proud of what you help to make and of how it will benefit people.

Be competitive. Match or exceed every improvement made by competitors. Keep prices in line. Give 100 per cent service. Think not of protectionism but of ways to outperform competitors. Aim to make your product, your packaging, your promotion, the best in the business.

And a corollary: *Treasure your employees*. Of course, these goals call for an efficient dedicated workforce. So treat workers fairly. Give all employees equal consideration. As nearly as possible, provide lifetime employment, or at least, fire no one before exhausting every other possibility. Let everyone share in the company's good times with regular bonuses. In a word, treat all employees like the conscientious, loyal, intelligent, and hardworking people you want them to be. And that's what they will surely be.'

Japanese Style Management by Keitaro Hasegawa (p. 156): 32

2. BEYOND WORLD CLASS – SELF-ASSESSMENT

The theme of *Becoming World Class* was the stuff of Operational Excellence. *Beyond World Class* talks of sustainability – ensuring that the

    individual
    organization and
    society

gain synergy and momentum for mutual self-development.

	Scale Worst									Best
	1	2	3	4	5	6	7	8	9	10
1: The Learning Society – Individuals and Teams										
1 If Quality, Cost and Delivery are entry points what differential does your firm have in the market place?										
2 How good is your firm at organization knowledge creation?										
3 Hoshin – What about contribution of ideas to strategy and step change?										
2: The Learning Business										
4 How good are individuals at sharing knowledge? (Tacit to Tacit)										
5 How good are groups and teams at sharing knowledge and finding new ways? (Tacit to Explicit)										
6 Does the organization pool and use team and individual knowledge? (Explicit to Tacit)										
7 Do middle managers play a proactive role in change?										
8 Have project teams a formative role in organizational transformation?										

	Scale									
	Worst									Best
	1	2	3	4	5	6	7	8	9	10
3: Change Management										
9 How effective is the current style of change in your organization?										
10 Where is momentum for change coming from? • top down only (worst) • bottom up (mediocre) • the middle (better) • all levels (best)										
11 Can your middle managers be described as 'knowledge engineers' and champions of change?										
4: Change in Practice										
12 Do you use the logic of transition management to enable and smooth the change process? (see e.g. William Bridges)										
13 Do structure change and process change complement each other? (Lewin Model)										
14 Are goals in change programmes clear?										
15 Is there sufficient autonomy for motivation and self learning?										
16 How good is communication – approach 'surfeit' of information?										
17 How effective is the benchmarking process?										

	Scale									
	Worst									Best
	1	2	3	4	5	6	7	8	9	10
5: Change Tools and Techniques										
18 Too many confusing initiatives or co-ordinated focus for change?										
19 Does the organization understand the link between Learning and Change?										
20 Have you teams or groups of individuals?										
21 What is performance like from teams?										
22 What is the contribution from psychometrics?										
23 Does Emotional Intelligence feature in the language? (yes – Best!)										
24 How much of the people potential is used?										
25 What characterizes relation-ships within and with suppliers? Voice (Best) or Exit (Worst)										
26 Can you talk in terms of trust?										
6: Role of Leadership and Strategy										
27 Does the Board work as a team?										
28 How well are the 'Directoral Dilemmas' balanced?										

	Scale Worst → Best									
	1	2	3	4	5	6	7	8	9	10
29 Is it a Learning Board? Are 'conformance' and 'performance' separated and balanced?										
30 Are methods of selection for Board membership world class?										
31 Is leadership vested in one person?										
32 Can your leadership be described as visionary?										
33 Is the workforce flexible and motivated?										
34 Is there a culture of innovation?										
35 Where is the organization on the world class scale? • strategically led • competitively focused • market orientated • employee driven or • focused on operational excellence?										
36 Is strategic planning confined to a few specialists and the leader? (Worst)										
37 Or is scenario planning cascaded through the organization? (policy deployment)										
38 Does passion for the business exist?										
39 Is boundarylessness a characteristic?										
40 Are you still in the quality revolution or now into strategy evolution?										

	Scale Worst 1-10 Best									
	1	2	3	4	5	6	7	8	9	10
7: Organization and Society										
41 Are stakeholder interests balanced in the company?										
42 What characterizes the stakeholder relationship? • an insurance policy (Worst) • a licence to operate • or a dynamic which gives synergy to the organizations operations? (Best)										
43 Does double loop learning represent your decision making process?										
44 What does the corporate dashboard look like? • Confused signals? (Worst) • Pure bottom line short term financials? • Balanced scorecard? • EFQM or similar? • or Triple Bottom Line for sustainability? (Best)										
45 How does the ethos of your company/organization rate against the examples of, say, Johnson & Johnson and Toyota? (pp. 221, 222)										
8: Economic Revival and Regional Development										
46 Sustainability Rate your organization, your wider community and typical individuals against Rosabeth Moss Kanter's (a) Concepts (b) Competence (c) Connections? (see pp. 236, 241)										

	Scale									
	Worst									Best
	1	2	3	4	5	6	7	8	9	10
9: New Patterns of Employment and Unemployment										
47 'If you want loyalty get a dog.' Does this characterize attitudes in your organization?										
48 Are we creating high value added jobs or low skill low value added?										
49 Are 'portfolio' workers an increasing element of jobs market? Or a marginalized declining section in your experience?										
50 Does the labour flexibility mindset suit your organization form? (see p. 258) i.e. decentralized production – low flexibility Lean production – medium flexibility Agile production – high flexibility										
10: Where is the Individual in this Brave New World of Flexibility?										
51 How do you rate the state of the psychological contract in your organization? What is the feeling on job security?										

	Scale Worst → Best									
	1	2	3	4	5	6	7	8	9	10
52 Education. How well does the education system equip people for: • The world of work? • Left-hand brain? • Development not Discovery? • The self-employed mindset? • Life long learning? • Adaptation to change? • Leveraging knowledge? • Sharing knowledge with others?										
53 Learning in business. Do employees see themselves as active learners? Or expect to be taught?										
54 Do managers see themselves as educators – via coaching and mentoring?										
55 How well does your organization use: • Mentored Learning • Distance Learning, and • Experiential Learning?										
56 Where do you place yourself? • Sustenance Driven? • Outer Directed? • Inner Directed? (see p. 287)										

(see p. 287)

Beyond World Class – Scoreboard

Total 390 to 560 = Sustainable World Class leaders
        220 to 389 = Getting there
          56 to 219 = Laggers!

Appendix B: Guiding Principles – People Strategy

Rolls-Royce IPG will realize its business vision and achieve commercial success through people by the progressive application of key people principles across the entire organization.

Personal Development

Every employee will be given the opportunity to own and develop the skills and competencies, critical to Rolls-Royce IPG, to realize their full potential.

Communications

Communication will be exceptionally open and effective; communication will be at and between level, in every direction, and include every individual and team.

Continuous Improvement

Every employee will be involved in a quality improvement process and encouraged to learn from every experience.

Recognition and Reward

Efforts which result in increased business, achieving quality and reducing costs will be recognized, and rewarded through visibly consistent, fair and flexible remuneration arrangements in line with overall business performance.

Involvement and Consultation

All employees will be involved and consulted on aspects of the business relevant to both their own and the Company's activities.

Leadership and Relationships

The leadership style will be open, challenging and focused on success through people. Quality relationships will be created through open communications and an emphasis on teamwork, networking and partnerships.

In summary we will create an environment in which people can enjoy their work and experience personal satisfaction, motivating them to succeed for the business.

Personal Development

Guiding principle
Every employee will be given the
opportunity to own and develop the skills
and competencies, critical to Rolls-Royce
IPG, to realize their full potential.

Objective
A partnership between the Company and
its employees recognizing that improved
performance and future business success
depends on unlocking the full capabilities
of people and helping empower them at
every level through education and training.

Standards Statement
- All employees should participate in a
  discussion about their individual or
  team performance with the recipients of
  their output services at least annually.

- There will be access to competencies for
  all roles where these exist.

- Training education and development
  necessary to enhance current individual
  and team performance will be given to
  meet the business needs.

- The concept of a personal development
  plan will be introduced. The production
  and implementation of this is a shared
  responsibility between the employee
  and their supervisor/manager.

- There will be an openness of
  opportunity for jobs whilst recognizing
  the requirement for senior management
  to manage personal development and
  succession.

- Sufficient provision will be built into
  budgets to resource these standards.

- Processes will be developed to deliver
  these standards and maintained against
  best benchmarked practices.

Benefits Statement
- Feedback to individual, improved
  motivation and identification with the
  success of the business. Improved
  communication.

- Improved performance, clear training
  requirements, attainment of
  competencies.

- Commitment to continuous
  improvement, growth of an individual
  and improvement in team-working.
  Acceptance of broader roles and
  responsibilities.

- Development of partnership with the
  business. Visible development and
  challenge.

- Movement of people through the
  business. Visible development and
  challenge.

- Visible commitment to personal
  development.

- Leading to IIP and/or European Quality
  Awards. Recognition as 'good'
  employer, continuously improving
  standards.

Communications

Guiding Principle
Communication will be exceptionally open and effective; communication will be at and between level, in every direction, and include every individual and team.

Objective
High productivity and acceptance of continual change are best achieved where effective communications are established between management and employees can see the 'big picture' and management understand the views of employees.

Standards Statement
- The Trading Company Communications Strategy should address (but not necessarily involve) all aspects; face-to-face, written, visual and new technology etc.

- There must be regular face-to-face briefing to all employees.

- Everyone involved in briefing must be trained (and as this is usually two-way this effectively means everyone).

- There must be an element of two-way communication to ensure upward feedback.

- All upward feedback and questions must be addressed and answered.

- All relevant information should be communicated wherever possible although commercially sensitive information should be orally briefed.

Benefits Statement
- This will ensure that the strategy is comprehensive and appropriate medium is applied to particular issues.

- Only face-to-face briefing with the local supervisor ensures that meaningful communication has taken place and the individual understands the needs and interest of his/her team.

- An initial input is needed if all personnel are to know and understand the system and briefers are trained in briefing skills. Increased understanding of the process will yield commitment to maintain it as a meaningful exercise.

- This tells management what concerns and interests of the workforce are. The feedback issues will indicate whether messages are getting through and level of understanding.

- Answering questions ensures future participation by employees and signals commitment of management to the communications process.

- Prevents internal communication documents being circulated to external organizations whilst giving employees need-to-know information.

Communications *(cont'd)*

Standards Statement

- The Trading Company Communication Strategy must take account of the role(s) of senior management and a need for particular involvement in the communications process.

- Employees should be involved in identifying how communications should be developed and improved.

- Regular audits of effectiveness must be undertaken involving all employees.

- A regular management review of the effectiveness of the communications strategy in supporting the organization aims.

Benefits Statement

- Ensues support of these two key groups.

- Ensures better commitment by those involved, greater sense of commitment and less 'policing' of the system once established.

- Ensure meaningful communications are taking place and being developed in line with business employee needs.

- To ensure communication processes are developed so they continually meet the changing requirement of the business.

Continuous Improvement

Guiding Principle
Every employee will be involved in a quality improvement process and encouraged to learn from every experience.

Objective
To create a 'culture' where the need to change and improve is accepted by all employees and their contribution to continuous improvement is recognized and supported by management.

Standards Statement
- All our employees will be encouraged and trained to practise continuous improvement as a way of life, regularly assessing and, wherever possible, improving our business.

- We will constantly seek to use the accumulated experience of all employees to minimize the cost of running the business.

- We will continually strive to make the Company more competitive.

- Customer satisfaction will be at the forefront of our thinking and actions.

Benefits Statement
- The achievement of the highest quality products and services.

- The encouragement of innovation and new ideas from employees.

- A more successful and competitive business.

Recognition and Reward

Guiding Principle
Efforts which result in increased business, achieving quality and reducing costs will be recognized, and rewarded through visibly consistent, fair and flexible remuneration arrangements in line with overall business performance.

Objective
To encourage overall business performance the development and achievement of personal competencies, the devolution of accountability, team-working, the achievement of business objectives, personal development and world class quality and business performance standards.

Standards Statement
- Recognition and reward for demonstrated achievement of personal competencies.

- Recognition for successful team results against set objectives.

- Recognition of individual's contribution by identification of status (e.g. 'badge or rank').

- Recognition of individual's willingness to take initiative and responsibility in producing effective results.

- Reward for achieving standards of world class performance.

- Visible consistent and fair treatment of people of similar status/performance.

- Recognition of service with the company.

Benefits Statement
- Quality of performance and employee motivation.

- Achievement of business results and development of teamworking and common purpose.

- Identification of key contributors in a flat structure.

- Commitment to a continuous improvement culture and personal development.

- Encouragement of world class performance to achieve business objectives.

- High morale and motivation through a 'felt-fair' climate.

- Creation of esteem and reward for loyalty.

Involvement and Consultation

Guiding Principle
All employees will be involved and consulted on aspects of the business relevant to both their own and the Company's activities.

Objective
Develop and introduce processes, systems and procedures which allow for genuine two-way dialogue and consultation.

Standards Statement
• Provide a means for employees and their representatives, managers and directors to meet regularly to inform and discuss commercial, financial, organizational and contract related issues specific to the business.

• Provide as much information as possible relating to the business in an open and comprehensive manner, recognizing that occasional limitations will be necessary when dealing with market sensitive information, etc.

• Provide a means of involving directors, managers and employees and safety representatives in the process of achieving the highest possible standards relating to health, safety and environmental matters.

• Provide a means of involving management and employees in determining policies aimed at the potential development of each individual.

Benefits Statement
• The creation of an environment that encourages teamwork and open communication.

• The commitment of all employees towards the success and profitability of the business.

• Employees having an opportunity of influencing and being involved in decisions which affect their interests.

• Participation enabling all employees to understand customer needs and expectations thus enhancing the Company's prospects and those who work in it.

• Full utilization of employees' skills, knowledge and experience to maximize business performance.

Leadership and Relationship

Guiding Principle
The leadership style will be open, challenging and focused on success through people. Quality relationships will be created through open communications and an emphasis on teamwork, networking and partnerships.

Objective
The objective is to develop leaders at all levels who: optimize team performance, achieve and surpass business objectives, maximize employee satisfaction through personal contribution and develop individual potential to the full to meet future business needs/opportunities.

Standards Statement
- Leaders should share understanding of the requirements and the broader business situation with the team continuously – explains 'what and why' not 'what and how'.

- Leaders must recognize the different strengths in their team to participate and contribute in particular recognizing individual skills and abilities.

- Leaders must encourage all members of the team to participate and contribute in particular recognizing individual skills and abilities.

- Leaders must create opportunities and encourage individuals to develop their abilities and potential.

- Leaders must inspire the team by personal enthusiasm and example.

- Leaders need also to share the bigger picture with the team as well as specific team requirements and objectives.

- Leaders must recognize the need to vary their approach according to different business circumstances and changing team compositions.

Benefits Statement
- Ensures focus on priorities – Team chooses how to achieve requirement and thereby are committed to making it work.

- To make the performance of the team be 'more than the sum of the parts' requires the leader to ensure all members of the team feel they are contributing.

- Listening shows respect for the individual's abilities and in turn earns respect for the leader.

- Personal development adds further to individual motivation and at the same time equips the business for future opportunities.

- It's easier for employees to identify with and make extra efforts for an inspiring leader.

- Prevents inward focus, destructive competitiveness between teams and insularity from company objectives.

- Managing high team performance needs to take account of changing circumstances. As teams develop, leaders need to modify their 'management' to maintain high performance.

Appendix C: Gateshead Hospitals NHS Trust 1993

GROUP/SELF PERCEIVED ROLES

In groups we each developed a list of key elements of our roles in the Trust 'team'. The outcomes are detailed below:

Non-executives

'A'

Using business and personal background and experience to assist Executive Directors
Monitor and evaluate Executive Director performances
Represent public and external ideas
Act as a resource
Use these to manage the Trust by
- setting and achieving vision and strategy
- managing substantial public funds
- delivering health care

'B'

Contribute to strategic decision making by bringing professional and personal experience from a locally based public sector organization to question, challenge, confirm and support decisions of the Trust Board

'C'

To ensure there are objectives for good patient care within financial limits by identifying problems and finding solutions by
- liaison with GP fundholders, patients, non-fundholding GPs and Consultants
- advising on matters of specialist knowledge – e.g. workings of general practice, patient expectations and perceptions

- watching brief on performance of executives in achieving objectives
- assisting where possible in gaining contracts for referrals, etc.

'D' Provide strategic direction to move Gateshead Hospitals from a closed environment to a competitive open market situation by bringing
- marketing skills
- general business experience
- watching brief on the performance of the hospital within the community

'E' Assisting the team to think through strategic issues including vision and strategic objectives
Challenging the team about assumptions, decisions, etc.
Supporting the team once decisions have been reached
Monitoring performance against agreed measures and targets
Requirements – listening, learning, understanding, bringing external perspective
(The above is a classic blend of conformance and performance issues – see Chapter 6, p. 162).

Clinical Directors

'A' Provide a supportive role giving advice and implementation
Gathering information from users
Identifying developments
Identifying necessary resources

'B' Coordinating and acting as focus for the separate constituents of the directorate to produce the efficient integrated function of those constituents
To provide the Board with information and advice regarding the directorate and its functional role
To contribute to strategic planning at directorate and hospital-wide levels

'C'   Contribute information regarding the time and
                                   scale of technical and service developments in
                                   response to anticipated clinical needs
                                   Anticipate the marketing strategies of relevant
                                   outside organizations
                                   Provide a speciality overview and teach across the
                                   District, and regionally and nationally
                                   Provide a safe environment, be involved in quality
                                   assurance programmes and be a scientific resource
                                   Provide support to the hospital, the community
                                   and the interaction between them
                                   Moderate and control unrealistic ambitions on the
                                   personal, practical and technical level, leading to
                                   appropriate service delivery

Executive/Trust Directors

Chief Executive   Facilitate discussion and views from everyone,
                                   drawing out indvidual expertise
                                   Offer observation and views on vision and priority,
                                   facilitating convergence
                                   Lead in developing implementable strategy
                                   Lead formal approval and implementation
                                   Lead monitoring and review

*Deputy Chief   Shape and coordinate the business planning
Executive   process and information gathering/presentation
                                   processes
                                   Specific tasks include providing information and
                                   direction to the Board on contracting and
                                   marketing and on information strategy
                                   To deputize for the Chief Executive
                                   *NB: a role that subsequently disappeared to be
                                     shared out within the team

Finance Director   Provide financial advice
                                   Assist the Board to
                                   • safeguard resources
                                   • maintain financial stability
                                   • ensure value for money
                                   • comply with the financial regime

HR Director	Take a corporate role in defining and agreeing the overall strategic direction of the Trust Provide specialist Human Resource Management advice to the decision making process – considering in particular the 'people' implications of strategic directions for change
Medical Director	Provide the clinical position Share experience of hospital procedures and professional attitudes Communicate with the Board/team with guidance on the way forward in developing and maintaining quality and services in line with the needs of the patient, the overall community and the hospitals Be a moderator of expression of extreme views of professional groups
Nursing Director	Provide advice, knowledge and information in relation to • basis and post-basic training • change management • needs of patients and staff • developing a continuously improving service • professional development of staff
Estates Director	Provide expertise to ensure the effective management of the estate by ensuring • a safe environment (compliance with all legislation) • a quality environment for patients and staff • utilization and functional suitability
Services Director	Ensure that the Board is provided with efficient, cost-effective management and advice on its operational services in the provision of quality patient care, for example • strategic decision making • implementation of new legislation

Appendix D: Anglian Water Transformation Journey

THE JOURNEY – A CASE STUDY

Business benefits

Journey Group known as The Circus

A group of Customer Services staff joined together to play their part in creating the Learning Organization from within ... they examined their own skills, developed them and encouraged others to embark upon their own Journeys ...

This Journey Group ...

- were motivated to examine their own learning needs and those of their team;
- continued their own individual development whilst improving their team-playing skills;
- acted as ambassadors of the Journey within Anglian Water;
- helped the Company to develop the concept and practical application of the University of Water;
- accepted that for the Company to succeed and grow, it needs to single-mindedly address the needs of the customer and are actively playing their part in that process.

Journey Group known as Lindum Collonium

A disparate group of people came together to embark upon a Journey ... what they had in common was an office in the same building ... they reported to the same person ... and they performed much the same job as each other ... what they achieved is another story ...

This Journey Group ...

- learnt about their own strengths and weaknesses and those of their fellow team members; this has enabled them to make best use of skills in the workplace;

316

- developed a working relationship with Lincoln University and are now able to make use of those contacts for developing opportunities abroad;
- learnt how to use everyday skills to teach others and put together a module for an MBA course in Systems Management for Lincoln University. This will be an income generator for the business and could be utilized by the University of Water;
- undertook marketing training which helped them to understand the needs of their customers better;
- stimulated contracts with the MOD and UK developers and are exploring the potential for business abroad;
- received a delegation from Hong Kong this year with a view to working on joint projects.

Journey Group known as SS–R

The Journey Group called SS–R are a team of people driven by a common desire to make a difference ... they have elected to try to address environmental issues in a practical and business-oriented way ... what they need now is a commitment one way or another from Anglian Water ...

This Journey Group ...

- split into small teams to investigate initial ideas. They used creative thinking as a means of developing an outward focus;
- then came together and forged a team determined to make something happen, something which could benefit both the Company and the environment;
- learnt how to research projects in a thorough manner, contacting experts in the relevant fields and creating a network of contacts that the Company could use in the future;
- created a new procedural guide which can be used by colleagues throughout the business with immediate effect and creates a quality controlled documentation and project check list;
- in a pragmatic, Western manner, costed their ideas in order to prove the potential benefits for the business;
- prepared to work to move the project from planning stage to fulfilment in the future, expanding the boundaries of their current roles within Anglian Water;
- learnt skills which will stand them in good stead for developing creative business strategies for Anglian Water, whether or not their ideas come to fruition.

Journey Group known as 'Into Business'

Eight scientists formed a Journey Group hoping that it would help them focus on building the commercial side of the business. They almost fell at the first hurdle, but ended up with a relaunch of Scientific Services and a strategy and vision for future development.

This Journey Group ...

- developed an understanding of each other's roles, particularly that of the Commercial Scientist;
- examined their core knowledge and skills base and developed a strategy for the business from that;
- researched the views of others working within Water Quality;
- investigated various options for centralizing laboratories, a management buy-out, etc.;
- published a 'Yellow Pages' of points of contact for external scientific enquiries;
- helped others within their Process develop a marketing-led brochure;
- presented their vision of the future to the Process Director.

Journey Group known as 'Yellow Brick Road'

This group of Travellers formed the Yellow Brick Road in search of a new future for Anglian Water ... they examined the status quo and believed that they could improve things for themselves, their colleagues and the Company ... they are about to explore new worlds.

This Journey Group ...

- began by learning more about the dynamics of their own team, they worked through challenges and problems together and came out the stronger for it;
- improved their business knowledge and increased their personal skills, particularly in strategic planning, creative thinking and bottom line management;
- have put a business case to the organization for a new way of running the engineering Process within or independent of the Company;
- actively worked at improving their commercial skills in order to be able to share them with colleagues;
- acknowledged that for the business to move on, new ideas must be examined and tested and they have instigated the biggest of those tests.

Journey Group known as 'The Crack'

Twenty-two Travellers formed a Journey Group, they began as one team, split into two and then joined once more to realize the benefits of teamwork ...

This Journey Group ...

- learnt how to work together and stick together through thick and thin;
- learnt to enjoy each other's company and utilize new found friendships in their day-to-day work;
- developed contacts with Christ's Hospital School, Lincoln, and Lincoln University, which has potential benefits throughout the business;
- offered practical support to Anglian Water International and now provide a source of expertise that can be tapped into from throughout the world;
- have cut through much of the red tape previously experienced within the business and have, in so doing, increased the efficiency of their Process.

Bibliography

Argyris, C. (1993) *Knowledge in Action*, San Francisco: Jossey-Bass.

Ashby, W.R. (1956) *An Introduction to Cybernetics*, London: Chapman & Hall.

Bandler, R. and Grinder, J. (1979) *Frogs into Princes*, Real People Press.

Barger, N. and Kirby, L. (1995) *The Challenge of Change in Organisations*, CA: Davies Black Publishing.

Barnett, C. (1995) *The Lost Victory*, Macmillan.

Barnevik, P. (1997) *The European Way to Excellence*, DG III, European Commission.

Barrell, R. and Pain, N. (1997) *Foreign Direct Investment, Technological Change and Economic Growth within Europe*, NIESR.

Belbin, M. (1997) *Team Roles at Work*, Butterworth-Heinemann.

Binney, G. and Williams, C. (1995) *Leaning into the Future*, Nicholas Brealey.

Blair, M. (1995) *Ownership and Control: Rethinking corporate governance for the 21st Century*, Washington Brookings Institute.

Brewster, C. (1996) *Working Time and Contract Flexibility in Europe*, Cranfield University.

Bridges, W. (1991) *Managing Transitions*, Nicholas Brealey.

Bridges, W. (1995) *Job Shift*, Nicholas Brealey.

Bridges, W. (1997) *Creating You and Co.*, Addison-Wesley Longman.

Burns, T. and Stalker, G.M. (1961) *The Management of Innovation*, Tavistock.

Business Process Resource Centre (Warwick University) and Department of Trade and Industry (DTI) (1997) *Managing Change: Key to Competitiveness*,

Carlzon, J. (1989) *Moments of Truth*, Harper Perennial.

Casey, B., Metcalf, H. and Millwall, N. (1997) *Employers' Use of Flexible Labour*, Policy Studies Institute.

Clutterbuck and Crainer (1990) *Makers of Management. Men and Women who changed the business world*, London, Mercury.

Colenso, M. (1988) Managing in the 21st century, *Professional Manager*, January.

Collins, J. and Porras, J. (1995) *Built to Last*, Random House.

Commission on Public Policy and British Business (1997) *Promoting Prosperity*, London: Vintage.

Coopers & Lybrand report (1974).

Darnell and Evans (1995) *The Northern Regional Economy*, Mansell London

Davis, S. and Botkin, J. (1994) *The Monster under the Bed*, New York: Simon & Schuster.

Department of Health (1998a) *Cmnd. 555*, London: HMSO.

Department of Health (1989b) *Working for Patients*, London: HMSO.

Department of Health (1989c) *The New Health Service: Chairmen & Members*, HMSO.

Department of Health and Social Security (1983) NHS Management Inquiry DA (83/38), HMSO.

DiFazio, W. (1995) *The Jobless Future; Sci-Tech and the Dogma of Work*, University of Minnesota Press.

Dilnot, A. (1995) Is the labour market working? Lecture at the Institute of Fiscal Studies, 16 October 1995.

Dove, R. (1993) Goodwill and the spirit of market capitalism, *British Journal of Sociology*, 34, 459–982.

Drucker, P. (1994) The age of social transformation, *The Atlantic Monthly*, November.

Eccles, T. (1994) *Succeeding with Change*, McGraw-Hill.

Foundation for Manufacturing and Industry (1997), *The Middle Market. How they perform*, Coopers & Lybrand.

Fox, A. (1973) *Beyond Contract: Work, Power & Trust Relations*, London: Faber and Faber.

Fukuyama, F. (1992) *The End of History and the Last Man*, Free Press, Macmillan Inc.

Fukuyama, F. (1995) *Trust: the Social Virtues and Creation of Prosperity*, London: Hamish Hamilton.

Garratt, B. (1996) *The Fish Rots from the Head*, HarperCollins.

Garvin, D. (1991) *Harvard Business Review*, November–December.

Gatley, S. (1997) *The Journey Goes On ...*, EML.

de Geus, A. (1997) *The Living Company*, Nicholas Brealey.

Ghoshal, S. and Bartlett, C. (1994) Beyond strategy to purpose, *Harvard Business Review*, December.

Ghoshal, S. and Bartlett, C. (1995) Changing the role of top management: Beyond structure to processes, *Harvard Business Review*, February.

Goldsmith, W. and Clutterbuck, D. (1997) *Winning Streak Mk II*, London: Orion Business Books.

Goleman, D. (1996) *Emotional Intelligence*, Bloomsbury.

Goyder, M. (1998) *Living Tomorrow's Company*, Gower.

Griffiths (1994) *Social Services Committe Findings*, HMSO.

Grunebaum, L.H. (1970) *Philosophy for Modern Man*, New York: Horizon Press.

Hamel, G. and Prahalad, C.K. (1994) *Competing for the Future*, Boston: Harvard Business School Press.

Hammer, M. and Champy, J. (1993) *Re-engineering the Corporation*, Nicholas Brealey.

Hampden-Turner, C. (1990) *Charting the Corporate Mind*, Oxford: Blackwell.

Handy, C. (1994) *The Empty Raincoat*, London: Hutchinson.

Handy, C. (1997) *The Hungry Spirit*, London: Hutchinson.

Harrison, S. (1988) *Managing the National Health Services – Shifting the Frontier*, London, Avebury.

Harrison, S. (1994) *NHS Management in the 1980s: Policy-making on the Hoof*, London: Avebury.

Helper, S. (1997) *Complementarity and Cost Reduction – Evidence from the Auto Supply Industry*, Working Paper 6033, National Bureau of Economic Research.

Helper, S. and Sako, M. (1995) Supplier relations in Japan & US: are they converging? *Sloan Management Review*.

Hirschman, A. (1970) Exit, Voice and Loyalty, *Cambridge News*, Harvard.

Hutton, W. (1995) *The State We're In*, Jonathan Cape.

IPD (1995) 'Getting teams off the ground'. People Management. IPD, May.

IPD (1997a) *Impact of People Management Practices on Business Performance*, Institute of Personnel and Development.

IPD (1997b) *Employee Motivation and the Psychological Contract*, Institute of Personnel and Development.

Industrial Society (1997) *Speaking Up, Speaking Out. The 2020 Vision Programme.*

Jones, Womack, and Roos, (1990) *The Machine that Changed the World*, Rawson Assoc.

Kaplan, R.S. and Norton, D.P. (1992) The balanced business scorecard, *Harvard Business Review*, January–February.

Katzenbach, J. and Smith, D. (1994) *The Wisdom of Teams: Creating the High Performance Organisation*, McGraw-Hill.

Kay, J. (1995) *Foundations of Corporate Success, How Business Strategies add Value*, Oxford: Oxford University Press.

Klein, R. (1989) *The Politics of the NHS*, London: Longman.

Kolb, D. (1974) *Organisation Psychology – a book of readings*, Prentice Hall, New Jersey.

Kreuger, A. and Pischke, J. (1997) *Observations and Conjectures on the US Employment Miracle*, Working Paper 6146, National Bureau of Economic Research, Cambridge, MA, August.

Lessem, R. (1991) *Total Quality Learning*, Blackwell.

Lessem, R. and Palsule, S.P. (1997) *Managing in Four Worlds*, Blackwell.

Mant, A. (1983) *Leaders We Deserve*, Martin Robertson.

Mintzberg, H. (1988) *The Rise and Fall of Strategic Planning*, Hemel Hempstead: Prentice-Hall.

Morgan, G. (1986) *Images of Organisation*, London: Sage Publications.

Morton, C. (1994) *Becoming World Class*, Macmillan

Moss Kanter, R. (1995) *World Class*, Simon & Schuster.

Myers Briggs, I. (1993) *Introduction to Type*, 5th edn, Palo Alto, CA:

NHSME (1989) HMSO.

NHSME (1990) HMSO.

Nonaka, I. and Takeuchi, H. (1995) *The Knowledge Creating Company*, Oxford University Press.

Ohmae, K. (1995) Putting global logic first, *Harvard Business Review*, January.

Ohmae, K. (1996) *The End of the Nation State*, HarperCollins.

Oram, M. and Wellins, R. (1995) *Re-engineering's Missing Ingredient*, Institute of Personnel and Development.

Pedler, M, Burgoyne, J and Boydell, T. (1997) *The Learning Company*, McGraw-Hill.

Plender, J. (1997) *A Stake in the Future*, Nicholas Brealey.

Porter, M. (1990) *The Competitive Advantage of Nations*, Macmillan.

Porter, M. (1996) What is strategy? *Harvard Business Review*, Nov./Dec.

Rajan, A. and van Eupen, P. (1996) *Leading People*, Create & CILNTEC.

Rajan, A. and van Eupen, P. (1997) *Tomorrow's People*. Study for Focus. Create.

Ramsden, P. and Zacharias, J. (1993) *Action Profiling*, Gower.

Rayner (1994) *NHS Management Inquiry Report*, HMSO.

Reder, A. (1995) *75 Best Business Practices for Socially Responsible Companies*, New York: GP Putnaum.

Reichheld, F.F. (1993) Loyalty-based management, Bain & Company, *Harvard Business Review*, No. 93210, March, 64–73.

Rigby, R. (1996) Business needs strikers, *Management Today*, February.

RIIA (1996) *Unsettled Times*, Chatham House Report, Royal Institute of International Affairs.

RIIA (1997) *Navigating Uncharted Waters*, Chatham House Forum, Royal Institute of International Affairs.

Romnel, G. *et al.* (1997) *Quality Pays*, London: Macmillan.

RSA (1995) *Tomorrow's Company*, Report, Royal Society of Arts.

Sabel, C.F. (1991) 'Learning by Monitoring: the institutions of economic development', in *The Handbook of Economic Sociology*, edited by N.J. Smelser and R. Swedberg, NJ: Princeton University Press.

Sako, M. (1996) *Effects of Supplier Relations and Worker Involvement on Corporate Performance*, Westall.

Sako, M. (1997a) Synergy between direct and representative forms of employee voice. Evidence from the European car components industry, *HRM Journal*.

Sako, M. (1997b) 'Does trust improve business performance?', in *Trust Within and Between Organisations*, edited by C. Lane and R. Beckmann, Oxford University Press, Chapter 4.

Sako, M. Lamming, R. and Helper, S. (1995) Supplier relations in the UK car industry: good news–bad news, *Europe Journal of Purchasing and Supply Management*.

Senge, P. (1990) *The Fifth Discipline*, Nicholas Brealey.

Senge, P. *et al.* (1996) *The Fifth Discipline Field Book*, Nicholas Brealey.

Sternberg, R. and Williams, W. (1988) Group intelligence: Why some groups are better than others, *Intelligence*.

Tichy, N. and Sherman, S. (1992), *Control Your Destiny or Someone Else Will*, HarperCollins.

Tricker, R.I. (1980) *Corporate Governance*, London: Gower Press.

West, M. and Lawthom, R. (1994) *Still Far to Go*, Institute of Work Psychology, University of Sheffield.

Wheeler, D. and Sillanpää, M. (1997) *The Stakeholder Corporation*, Pitman.

Wickens, P. (1995), *The Ascendant Organisation*, Macmillan.

Index